An introduction to applying social work theories and methods

Second edition

Barbra Teater, PhD

Open University Press

Open University Press
McGraw-Hill Education
McGraw-Hill House
Shoppenhangers Road
Maidenhead
Berkshire
England
SL6 2QL

email: enquiries@openup.co.uk
world wide web: www.openup.co.uk

and Two Penn Plaza, New York, NY 10121-2289, USA

First published 2010
First published in this second edition 2014

A catalogue record of this book is available from the British Library

ISBN-13: 978-0-33-524763-9 (pb)
ISBN-10: 0-33-524763-6 (pb)
eISBN: 978-0-33-524764-6

Library of Congress Cataloging-in-Publication Data
CIP data applied for

Typesetting and e-book compilations by
RefineCatch Limited, Bungay, Suffolk

Fictitious names of companies, products, people, characters and/or data that may be used herein (in case studies or in examples) are not intended to represent any real individual, company, product or event.

Printed by Bell & Bain Ltd, Glasgow

An introduction to applying social work theories and methods

Praise for this book

"This new edition of Barbra Teater's already valued text offers an accessible route into understanding social work theory. It supports learning to apply theories in practice as well as critical reflection on theory. The chapters on group work and community work add very useful new dimensions to the book, which will be appreciated by readers looking to understand social work theory across a wide range of service user groups and different settings. This is an excellent resource for students, also providing a knowledge base to accompany and support them into practice."

Penelope Welbourne, Associate Professor of Social Work, Plymouth University, UK

"The first edition of this book has been on my reading lists for undergraduate and post graduate students since its publication and has been appreciated as a plainly written, well organized, and comprehensive introductory source. The strengths of this text lie in the detailed and plausible case examples, bulleted strengths and limitations, and consistent references to contemporary and seminal research. I can highly recommend the second edition which includes updated sources and case material, including a focus on dementia, and the addition of chapters on Community Work and Groupwork, which are particularly pertinent to social work in this age of austerity and demographic change."

Mandy Hagan, Senior Lecturer, Manchester Metropolitan University, UK

To Todd

Contents

Boxes

Figures

Tables

1 Introduction to theories and methods

Introduction

Theory is an essential ingredient in practice that guides the way in which social workers view and approach individuals, groups, communities and society. Theory helps to predict, explain and assess situations and behaviours, and provide a rationale for how the social worker should react and intervene with clients who have particular histories, problems or goals. Methods are the specific techniques and approaches that social workers utilize in their work with clients to accomplish tasks and reach specific goals. Theories often inform social workers of the type of method that is most appropriate for use with a client. Social workers are tasked with approaching, assessing and providing interventions, or methods, with clients based on psychological, sociological and social work theories.

Every social worker practises from a theoretical framework, whether they recognize it or not (Coulshed and Orme, 2012). Some social workers may not necessarily acknowledge or understand their theoretical framework, but rather practise from assumptions and beliefs that are guided by their personal or professional experiences and not necessarily from established and researched theories. In such situations, the social worker could be putting clients at risk of harm by practising from assumptions and the social worker's values versus established theories and the values set by the social work profession. Social workers have an ethical and professional responsibility to have knowledge of established and researched theories that are grounded in social work values and to draw continually upon these theories in social work practice. This chapter provides an overview of a theory and a method by providing definitions and explanations of the role and use of theories and methods in social work practice. It then turns to an overview of psychosocial theory, which historically and currently provides a foundation for many social work theories and methods, and several processes to consider when initiating a social worker–client relationship. The chapter concludes with an explanation of anti-oppressive practice and an overview of the layout of this book.

What is the difference between a theory and a method?

The concepts 'theory' and 'method' are both independent and interrelated. As independent concepts, a theory is a hypothesis, an idea or prediction about what can or might happen in certain situations given certain circumstances. A method is what the social worker actually does when working with a client. In simple terms, a theory is what you *think* about a specific situation and what you *speculate* might occur based on that situation, and a method is what you *do* given your thoughts or speculations about a situation. A theory helps to predict or describe a particular phenomenon and a method specifies what to do when faced with that particular phenomenon. Table 1.1 provides a list of synonyms for theory and method, which can assist in understanding the difference between the two concepts. The term 'method' is often used interchangeably with 'approach', 'intervention' or 'practice'. These terms all denote action, which is synonymous with method, in regard to something the social worker does or implements.

As interrelated concepts, a theory often informs social workers as to the type of method they should use with clients in certain situations. A theory assists social workers in understanding various situations, difficulties, behaviours and experiences, and a method instructs the social worker in what to do in response to the identified phenomenon (see Figure 1.1). For example, the stages of change theory (often depicted as a five-stage model) specifies that individuals proceed through distinct stages when making a change and they often cycle through the stages several times before the change is maintained. Therefore, when working with clients to make a change, social workers should use the stages of change theory to assess the current stage of the client as this will determine the type of method, or technique, that is used with the client. If the client is in a contemplation stage, where she or he is ambivalent about making a change, the social worker would know to utilize techniques, such as the decisional-balance or scaling in an attempt to resolve the ambivalence in favour of change. In this situation, the social worker utilizes the stages of change (*theory*) to assess where the client currently sits in regard to change and then, based on this assessment, implements specific techniques and interventions (*method*) to reach the goal of change. Therefore, as interrelated concepts, theories inform practice.

Table 1.1   Synonyms of theory and method

Theory	Method
Hypothesis	Means
Premise	Way
Presumption	Process
Conjecture	System
Speculation	Scheme
Assumption	Technique
Guess	Mode

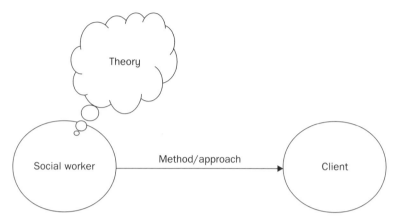

Figure 1.1   Theory informs practice.

In addition to the terms *theory* and *method,* social workers may also come across the terms *perspective, model, approach, intervention* and *practice.* As stated earlier, method is used interchangeably with approach, intervention or practice. A perspective is slightly different to a theory as it does not necessarily predict or describe a phenomenon, but more often describes a framework or a way of viewing and understanding particular situations. A model is usually a theory or method depicted logically and/or graphically and is concerned with what and how something happens. As you will see when reading this book, more than one of these terms can be used to describe the topics of each chapter. For example, social constructivism is often viewed and described as a theory as it attempts to explain or describe a particular phenomenon, but it can also be referred to as a perspective when influencing the way in which social workers view or understand certain experiences. Social workers can also incorporate aspects of social constructivism into their interventions, such as taking a position of curiosity, which can then make social constructivism a method. Other topics are clearer in their identification, such as motivational interviewing, which is a method informed by the person-centred theory and the stage of change theory (often depicted as a visual model) or crisis intervention, which is a method informed by crisis theory. Table 1.2 provides a list of commonly used terms and their definitions.

Table 1.2   Commonly used terms

Term	Definition
Theory	Describes, explains or predicts certain phenomenon
Method	Specifies what to do when faced with certain phenomenon
Perspective	A way of viewing or understanding certain experiences; based on words and principles
Model	A theory or method depicted logically or graphically

The function of social work theory

Why should social workers utilize theory in practice? Theories assist social workers in understanding, explaining or making sense of situations or behaviours and provide insight into what might have occurred in the past or might occur in the future. For example, a social worker working with a child who was placed in foster care as a baby and subsequently moved to numerous foster homes, might explain the child's 'disruptive' behaviour in foster homes as a result of an inability to create a secure connection to a parent or caretaker as an infant, which is based on Bowlby's (1979; 1988) attachment theory. Another example includes the use of systems theory or the ecological perspective, which holds that individuals and their environments are separate systems that are interconnected and interdependent and a change or movement in one of these systems results in a change or movement in the others. Therefore, when social workers utilize systems theory or the ecological perspective, they conduct an assessment of the individual and her or his environment in order to determine which system requires an intervention. As the examples illustrate, theories inform social work practice by providing a foundation or basis from which to understand clients and their situations and what might happen when certain methods or approaches are applied.

Social workers have a professional and ethical responsibility to observe, assess, interact and intervene with clients and their environments in a way that is based on theories and methods shown to be credible and in alignment with social work values. This is in contrast to social workers observing, assessing, interacting and intervening based on intuition, what feels right, their gut feelings or the social worker's assumptions, which could put the client at risk of harm. This does not mean that 'practice wisdom' does not exist, but rather acknowledges that practice wisdom is actually based on previous experiences where theories and methods have been successfully or unsuccessfully utilized and, therefore, inform future thinking when faced with similar situations. Practice wisdom does not indicate a lack of applying theories or methods, but rather a quick, more accurate response to situations based on prior experiences and similar situations when theories and methods have been applied.

Theories and methods that are utilized in social work practice are to be reliable and effective, which is usually established through quantitative and qualitative research. Social workers should critically assess, evaluate and reflect on their own practice and implementation of theories and methods in social work situations in order to determine what works, what does not work, or what needs to be modified, adjusted or maintained for future situations. This process enables the social worker to utilize theories and implement methods that are found to be the most appropriate and effective for the current client and situation. As Payne et al. (2009, p. 3) state, 'reflecting critically entails reviewing different perspectives and options before deciding on "best practice"'.

Critically reflective practice requires social workers to be both reflective and critical about social work practice. Social workers can begin to participate in this process by asking themselves the following questions after a social work encounter (Adams, 2009, p. 234):

- What happened?
- How did it compare with previous experience?
- How did I do?
- How well did I do?
- What could I have done better?
- What could I have done differently?

The first three questions above involve the social worker reflecting on the situation and what happened, and the last three questions involve the social worker critically reflecting on the experience, what was learned and what will be adjusted or modified in future practice.

Exercise box 1.1   Incorporating theories and methods in practice

In pairs or small groups answer the following questions based on your personal or practice experience:

1   What is one method that you have utilized in practice?
2   What was the theory that informed this method?
3   Explain your rationale for utilizing this theory and method.
4   Was this the appropriate theory and method to utilize in this situation? Explain your answer.

Theories and methods: options for practice

How do social workers begin to establish what theories or methods to utilize in practice? Becoming knowledgeable and effective as social workers begins with a familiarity with and an understanding of the common, well-established theories and methods used in social work practice. Once this knowledge is established, the social worker can then assess a situation and determine which theory, method or combination of theories or methods are most appropriate for the client, the situation and the social worker. Often, social workers favour particular theories or frameworks as they are in alignment with the ethos of the social worker or the agency/organization in which they work. For example, a drug and alcohol treatment centre may suggest the use of motivational interviewing in order to challenge the addictive behaviours of clients, while an eating disorder clinic may suggest the use of cognitive behavioural therapy in order to change the eating routines of clients. Both of these approaches have been established as effective when attempting to change behaviours. The key is ensuring that what the social worker utilizes is appropriate for the client and situation, and that the theory or method is working. If the theory or method is not working, the social worker must *not* try harder, but must change the theory or method to fit the needs of the client.

Social workers have a range of options when incorporating theories and methods in practice. Social workers can utilize a single theory or method, or they may choose to take an eclectic approach. An eclectic approach involves the social worker selecting different theories and methods and combining all or various aspects of them in practice. For example, some social workers and agencies specialize in the implementation of one method, such as solution-focused practice, motivational interviewing or cognitive behavioural therapy, yet other social workers and agencies incorporate numerous theories and methods depending on the client, situation and end goals. For example, the social worker may begin with aspects of the person-centred approach while simultaneously working through the task-centred approach, and end with aspects of cognitive behavioural therapy in order to achieve one or more of the established goals. The choice of theories and methods must depend on what is most appropriate for the clients and their situations as well as the knowledge of the social workers. Again, if the theory or method is not working, the social worker must not try harder or assume the client is resistant, but rather must reassess the client and situation and adjust the theories and methods to best fit the client and the established goals of the work together.

Theory and methods in social work practice: an overview of psychosocial theory

Theories and methods have an established place within social work practice. At the foundation of current social work theory and practice is psychosocial theory. Modern social work theorists have emphasized the importance of contextualizing the person in relation to their social environment (Robinson and Kaplan, 2011), and the social work profession has viewed the person as interrelated and interdependent with their environment. Not only are individuals' development and social situation in part a product of their environment, but individuals are able to influence and change their environment (Kondrat, 2002). Psychosocial theory provides the context in which other theories and methods should be understood by social workers, particularly as it provides the foundation for modern social work theories.

Psychosocial theory, which originated from psychoanalytic and psychodynamic casework, has had a significant impact on social work. Psychosocial theory served as the most articulated theory available in the beginning stages of social work and continues to impact social work today (Robinson and Kaplan, 2011). Psychosocial theory originated in social work through the work of Frank Hankins (1931) from Smith College and Mary Richmond, author of *Social Diagnosis* (1917) and *What Is Social Casework?* (1922), both of whom stressed an understanding of individuals based on their psychological and sociological aspects. Mary Richmond and Florence Hollis (1958; 1972) have been viewed as the pioneers of the psychosocial approach as they discussed the necessity to consider individuals and their environments simultaneously. Hollis drew upon psychoanalytic concepts from Freud to explain the individual aspects to casework and drew upon the assumptions of systems theory to explain the environmental aspects (Robinson and Kaplan, 2011). The integration of psychosocial theory with social work practice meant that, 'people are to be understood as products of the interaction among their biogenetic endowment, the effects of significant rela- tionships, the impact of life experiences, and their participation in societal, cultural, and current events' (Turner, 1978, p. 2). Much of social work practice is based on the psychosocial concepts from the work of psychoanalytic and psychosocial theorists (Robinson and Kaplan, 2011). In particular is the acknowledgement that social workers should consider persons and their environments simultaneously.

Psychosocial theory can provide a foundation for social workers in practice. This theory stresses an acknowledgement and assessment of the individual and her or his psychological processes, the interpersonal or the relationships of the individual, and the environment in which the individual lives and obtains or seeks to obtain needed resources. The basic ideas of psychosocial theory can be seen in other social work theories and methods, such as systems theory, the ecological perspective, feminist theory, empowerment-based work, anti-oppressive work, the strengths-based approach, task-centred social work, crisis intervention and cognitive behavioural therapy. Therefore, a basic understanding of this theory and its concepts are necessary before exploring specific theories and methods as covered within this book.

In taking a general psychosocial approach to social work practice, we highlight the necessity to establish and focus on the relationship between social worker and client, and acknowledge some of the basic concepts of psychodynamic and psychosocial work that could hinder the relationship and work between the client and social worker.

The social worker–client relationship

The social worker–client relationship is a crucial factor in the effectiveness of social work interventions and is an aspect of social work that cannot be ignored. In order to be a competent social worker, one must have knowledge and understanding of a variety of social work theories and methods, understand how to apply the theories and methods to various clients and social work situations, and acknowledge the importance of the social worker–client relationship.

Ruch et al. (2010) argue for social workers to give considerable attention to the building and sustaining of the social worker–client relationship and propose a model of relationship-based social work that is grounded in the following key points: '(1) human behaviours and the professional relationship are an integral component of any profes- sional relationship; (2) human behaviour is complex and multi-faceted. People are not simply rational beings but have affective (both conscious and unconscious) dimen- sions that enrich but simultaneously complicate human relationships; (3) the internal and external worlds of individuals are inseparable, so integrated (psychosocial), as opposed to one-dimensional, responses to social problems are crucial for social work practice; (4) each social work encounter is unique, and attention must be paid to the specific circumstances of each individual; (5) a collaborative relationship is the means through which interventions are channelled, and this requires a particular emphasis to be placed on the "use of self"; and (6) the respect for individuals embedded in relationship-based practice involves practising in inclusive and empowering ways' (p. 21).

The beginning of a positive social worker–client relationship often includes three of the initial therapeutic conditions as specified by Carl Rogers (1957), which consist of: (1) a genuine social worker who demonstrates a warmth and concern for the client; (2) an empathic social worker who attempts to understand the clients' experiences and perceptions; and (3) a social worker who holds an unconditional positive regard, or non-judgemental attitude, towards the client. As discussed in Chapter 7, these three conditions enable the client to feel comfortable, acceptable and more capable of making necessary change.

To foster a positive relationship with clients, social workers should be familiar with psychoanalytic concepts of transference and countertransference initially defined by Freud. These concepts acknowledge the influence of the unconscious on personality, behaviour and functioning and therefore the ability to develop a positive relationship (Turner, 2009). The unconscious is viewed as influencing both the client and the social worker and, therefore, social workers should be cognizant to the effects of the unconscious on their or their clients' ability to develop a positive relationship. Each of these terms is described in detail below.

Transference is 'the idea that in our current relationships and interactions we may unconsciously "transfer" feelings into the here and now which actually belong in our previous relationships' (Ruch, 2010, p. 34). Transference occurs when past experiences of the client are revived, which initiates feelings, thoughts and behaviours that are then transferred to the social worker either exactly as they were experienced in the past or in a revised form. These transferred feelings, thoughts and behaviours can be both positive and negative (Ruch, 2010). For example, if a client who historically has been taken care of and treated as if she could not accomplish anything on her own may look to the social worker as a helpful figure who will care for the client and do the necessary work for her. An alternative example could consist of a client who had repeatedly been hurt and manipulated by those who were supposed to help her and therefore is speculative of whether the social worker is attempting to manipulate or hurt her as well. The client may respond to the social worker in a guarded and suspicious way as if she is waiting for the social worker to hurt or manipulate her. As these examples illustrate, the client–social worker relationship may be challenged and result in the social worker feeling pressured to act out the role as transferred by the client or may act out the role unconsciously. In these situations, social workers may begin to feel as if they are attempting to help a client who is resistant, hostile, demanding or unappreciative (Preston-Shoot and Agass, 1990), or the client may begin to idealize or become overly attached to the social worker (Kenny and Kenny, 2000).

Countertransference is defined as 'the worker's capacity to pick up those different types of unconscious communication from the client and to understand their meaning. The worker may be induced not only to experience a particular feeling-state but also to act out a particular role' (Preston-Shoot and Agass, 1990, p. 42). In this situation, the client is influencing the unconscious of the social worker, which elicits feelings, thoughts and behaviours that the social worker then transfers to the client. For example, the social worker may take on a role of parent or caretaker for the client instead of that of a social worker who collaboratively works with the client. Another example could include a social worker taking a punitive or authoritarian role with a client who is not ready to make a behavioural change. The social worker's unconscious is influenced by her or his personal experiences, histories and even past experiences from the work with other clients. Countertransference and its impacts can be explored and minimized through self-examination, reflection and skilled supervision (Kenny and Kenny, 2000; Preston-Shoot and Agass, 1990; Ruch, 2010). Social workers need to be aware of their emotions, the impact of their past experiences and histories on their thoughts, feelings and behaviours and any current concerns that could impact the social worker–client relationship (Robinson and Kaplan, 2011).

Attachment theory

The social worker–client relationship can also be influenced by the relationships and quality of attachments of the client's past. Bowlby's (1979; 1988) theory of attachment can assist social workers in understanding and making sense of clients' behaviour and abilities or inabilities to develop relationships both within the social work context and within the interpersonal and environmental systems. In developing the attachment theory, Bowlby stressed the importance of past relationships in determining how individuals will develop emotionally and socially, and form relationships with others in the future. Bowlby was particularly concerned with the interactions and attachments that individuals had with their parents, caretakers, or other family or non-family members. Attachment 'specifically refers to an emotional bond experienced by a relatively more vulnerable person in relation to a relatively stronger one' (Page, 2011, p. 32). He theorized that the ability or inability of a child to attach to the parent, caretaker or significant other, the level of consistency of the parent, caretaker or significant other to meet the emotional needs of a child, and the ability or inability of the child to feel safe and secure with the parent, caretaker or significant other predicted how the child would develop emotionally and socially and view or react to others in future relationships. If a child was made to feel safe and secure and was given appropriate attention and affection, then the child would develop future relationships and interact with others in a way that mirrored this positive relationship. These individuals would develop a more positive psychological and emotional base. Alternatively, a child who did not receive attention, affection or feel safe and secure was more likely to develop emotional and/or social problems and have a distorted or inaccurate view of others in future relationships and interactions. These individuals would develop a more negative psychological and emotional base. Therefore, the basic premise of Bowlby's attachment theory is that past experiences with relationships and interactions affect psychological, emotional and social development and functioning, which further impacts new relationships and interactions.

Mary Ainsworth furthered Bowlby's attachment theory through the experiment of the Strange Situation (Ainsworth et al., 1978) where she examined the reactions of infants when separated and reunited with their mothers. Based on this experiment she developed three attachment categories (secure, insecure-ambivalent and avoidant) and through subsequent studies a fourth category (disorganized) was added (Main and Solomon, 1990). The four types of attachment between child and parent, caretaker or significant other can help to explain an individual's behaviour in interacting with others. The four types of attachment, as summarized by Howe (2009, pp. 141–3), are described below:

1   *Secure attachments.* Parents or caretakers are consistently loving, responsive and sensitive to the child's thoughts, feelings and needs. The child and parent interact with mutual interest and care for one another and the child feels safe and secure with the parent or caretaker. The parents or caretakers' behaviours are predictable to the child. 'I love you and will protect and provide for you, but there are some rules to follow and consequences for actions.'

2   *Insecure, ambivalent attachments.* Parents or caretakers are inconsistent in displaying love, affection or sensitivity to the child's thoughts, feelings and needs, and the parents' or caretakers' behaviours are unpredictable to the child. The child may feel anxiety or distress due to the inconsistency in behaviours and a failure of the parent or caretaker to display affection and attention in a consistent manner. The child may view her- or himself as unworthy of obtaining a comfortable, loving relationship. 'I love you when you behave the way I want you to, but not when you behave in ways which I don't like.'

3   *Insecure, avoidant attachments.* The parent or caretaker responds to the child in a hostile, violent or rigid manner and displays indifference to the child's thoughts, feelings and needs. The inconsistency in the parent or caretaker's behaviour leaves the child to feel alone and unable to deal with feelings. 'You are unworthy of love.'

4   *Disorganized attachments.* The parent or caretaker is not consistent in their behaviours as evidenced by displaying hostile, violent or rigid behaviours on some occasions and more compassionate, loving, affectionate behaviours at others. The child is receiving mixed messages from the parent or caretaker. 'I will protect you and keep you safe, and I will frighten and hurt you.' This confusion leads the child to feel anxious and unable to explain feelings.

The attachment theory is helpful to social workers in assessing the social worker–client relationship and understanding how past experiences of the client can impact on the behaviours and ability or inability of the client to form a positive relationship. Attachment theory is compatible with the concepts of transference and countertransference, and these psychosocial theories are often used in conjunction to assess the social worker–client relationship as well as other social relationships. Robinson and Kaplan (2011) stress the importance of psychosocial theories in social work practice, particularly as it assesses the interrelationship and interconnectedness of the person in the environment and explains the development and quality of relationships by considering the impact of both the social worker and client's conscious and unconscious thoughts and feelings on behaviours.

Integrating anti-oppressive practice with theories and methods

Social workers are in the business of facilitating change, which not only includes change among individuals, families, groups and communities, but change within each of the systems' environments that is oppressing or prohibiting them from positive growth and development. Social workers seek to challenge inequality and disadvantage, promote social justice and advocate for resources and opportunities for individuals, families, groups and communities (Burke, 2013; Burke and Harrison, 2009). In accomplishing these tasks, social workers should work in an anti-oppressive way with individuals, families, groups, communities and society.

Anti-oppressive practice focuses on the use and abuse of power on and by various systems within society. Anti-oppressive practice is viewed as a stance or perspective that should be integrated in social work practice alongside other theories and methods (Robbins, 2011). Individuals, community establishments and societal structures can oppress other individuals, groups and/or communities through overt or covert acts of racism, classism, sexism, ableism or ageism. Anti-oppressive practice involves acknowledging that oppression can arise from an unequal distribution of power and resources at social and political levels (Burke, 2013; Robbins, 2011). Such oppressive practices disadvantage some in favour of advantaging others and can lead to restraints on an individual, family, group or community's ability to grow, develop and reach their full potential.

Anti-oppressive practice is empowering in nature as it seeks to provide a working environment that is egalitarian, where clients identify their needs and collaborate with social workers to identify their strengths and resources to overcome barriers and obstacles within the environments. Anti-oppressive practice requires an acknowledgement that social workers may need to intervene at multiple levels (personal, interpersonal, structural and cultural) (Robbins, 2011) in order to combat oppression and enable clients to access resources to grow and develop. The end result will be that the clients are empowered and able to combat oppression, access resources and opportunities, and meet needs.

Thompson (2012) developed an approach to analysing anti-discriminatory and anti-oppressive practice by building on the works of Dalrymple and Burke (1995). Thompson's approach, referred to as the PCS model, sees anti-discriminatory and anti-oppressive practice as occurring on three levels: personal, cultural and societal. The model is often depicted as a set of three circles each embedded within the other. The personal level (P) involves interpersonal relationships, personal feelings, attitudes and self-conceptions, and interactions between individuals, which would often include social work practice relationships (Payne, 2005). The personal is embedded within the cultural context (C) where the person's culture establishes norms and rules that shape how the individual feels about themselves, others around them and interactions between people and the environment. Both the personal and cultural levels are then embedded within the societal framework (S), which sets the structures, norms, rules and order within society. The PCS model is important to social workers in illustrating that anti-discriminatory and anti-oppressive practice may not only take place on the personal level, where social workers are most likely to intervene, but may also take place on the cultural and societal levels as these levels are each embedded within another. Social workers often working on an individual level are able to challenge discrimination and oppression, but may find it more difficult to change discriminatory and oppressive behaviours of larger groups of people, such as a group with a shared culture or society as a whole that continues to discriminate and oppress. Social workers can begin this process by first examining and reflecting on their personal views, culture and societal norms, rules and structures.

Anti-oppressive practice should permeate different aspects of social work practice, which should include the social worker–client relationship, the employer–employee relationship, the ethos of the social service agency and the social context, all with a driving force of challenging inequalities and disadvantage (Burke, 2013; Burke and Harrison, 2009; Dominelli, 2002). In accomplishing this goal, social workers should participate in self-reflection and become self-aware of how inequalities, disadvantage and injustices impact upon them and/or how they may be privileged by advantages and power. Social workers' values, past experiences and current perceptions shape the way in which they practise and, therefore, acknowledging and reflecting on what the social worker brings to the working relationship can assist in delivering anti-oppressive practice. According to Dominelli (2002, p. 15), social workers are required to consider three key levels when implementing anti-oppressive practice: (1) intellectual – understanding the principles and methods of working in an anti-oppressive way; (2) emotional – ability to deal with oppression and discrimination in a confident way, and the ability to learn from one's mistakes; and (3) practical – ability to implement the principles of anti-oppressive practice.

Summary and overview of the book

This chapter has defined the concepts of theory and method, and has discussed how these two concepts are both independent and interrelated. A theory helps describe, predict or explain human behaviours and social work situations, and a method provides the techniques or steps that the social worker can utilize in working with clients to reach goals. The two concepts are interrelated in the sense that knowledge about theories helps to inform social workers as to the most appropriate method to use based on the situation. In some circumstances there are theories that also specify techniques that can be used, which can then turn the theory into a method. For example, the theory of empowerment holds that individuals who have access to resources and opportunities are able to grow, thrive and develop, and the method of empowerment provides techniques, such as use of language and political advocacy, that can be used in work with the client that moves towards a goal of the individual being empowered. Therefore, in determining the difference between a theory or method, one should assess whether it is something that helps inform, predict, explain or hypothesize a behaviour or situation (theory), or whether it is steps, techniques or actions that the social worker utilizes to foster change (method).

This chapter provided a summary of psychosocial theory, particularly as it informs the development of social worker–client relationships. Although this book does not devote a complete chapter to this theory, a foundational understanding of some of the key concepts, such as transference, countertransference and attachment were deemed necessary to begin the process of relationship development. Further resources on psychosocial theory and relationship-based practice can be found at the end of this chapter.

The aim of the second edition of this book is to provide the reader with a basic, yet solid, understanding of the commonly used social work theories and methods. Two new chapters have been added to include community work and groupwork. Each chapter explores a theory or method in depth by providing the definition, history and origins, basic premises or characteristics with a discussion on any relevant tools or techniques of the method, an illustration of how to utilize or implement the theory or method in practice through a case example, a discussion of the strengths and limitations, the ethical and cultural considerations, how the method fits with anti-oppressive practice, a discussion on the research as to the effectiveness of the theory and/or method, and a final case example to encourage the reader to further explore the application of the theory or method. Each chapter has been updated with a list of further reading on the theory or method to assist readers in their studies of the particular topic.

Further reading

Davies, M. (ed.) (2013) *The Blackwell Companion to Social Work*, 4th edn. Chichester: John Wiley & Sons.
  An overview of social work with different populations in different settings. Provides an overview of 25 theories and methods.
Dominelli, L. (2002) *Anti-oppressive Social Work Theory and Practice*. Basingstoke: Palgrave Macmillan.
  Provides an overview of anti-oppressive practice as a theory and method.
Fook, J. and Gardner, F. (2007) *Practising Critical Reflection: A Resource Handbook*. Maidenhead: Open University Press.
  Provides a detailed discussion on critically reflective practice.
Howe, D. (2008) *The Emotionally Intelligent Social Worker*. Basingstoke: Palgrave Macmillan.
  Discussion of how to understand and manage emotions in social work practice.
Ruch, G., Turney, D. and Ward, A. (2010) *Relationship-based Social Work: Getting to the Heart of Practice*. London: Jessica Kingsley Publishers.
  An overview of relationship-based social work practice and its application in various settings.

References

Adams, R. (2009) Being a critical practitioner, in R. Adams, L. Dominelli and M. Payne (eds), *Critical Practice in Social Work*, 2nd edn. Basingstoke: Palgrave Macmillan.

Ainsworth, M.D.S., Blehar, M.C., Waters, E. and Wall, S. (1978) *Patterns of Attachment: A Psychological Study of the Strange Situation*. Hillsdale, NJ: Erlbaum Associates.

Bowlby, J. (1979) *The Making and Breaking of Affectional Bonds*. London: Tavistock.

Bowlby, J. (1988) *A Secure Base: Clinical Application of Attachment Theory*. London: Routledge.

Burke, B. (2013) Anti-oppressive practice, in M. Davies (ed.), *The Blackwell Companion to Social Work*, 4th edn. Chichester: John Wiley & Sons.

Burke, B. and Harrison, P. (2009) Anti-oppressive approaches, in R. Adams, L. Dominelli and M. Payne (eds), *Critical Practice in Social Work*, 2nd edn. Basingstoke: Palgrave Macmillan.

Coulshed, V. and Orme, J. (2012) *Social Work Practice: An Introduction*, 5th edn. Basingstoke: Palgrave Macmillan.

Dalrymple, J. and Burke, B. (1995) *Anti-oppressive Practice: Social Care and the Law*. Buckingham: Open University Press.

Dominelli, L. (2002) Anti-oppressive practice in context, in R. Adams, L. Dominelli and M. Payne (eds), *Social Work: Themes, Issues and Critical Debates*, 2nd edn. Basingstoke: Palgrave.

Hankins, F. (1931) The contributions of sociology to the practice of social work, *Proceedings of the National Conference of Social Work, 1930*. Chicago, IL: University of Chicago Press.

Hollis, F. (1958) Personality diagnosis in casework, in H. Parad (ed.), *Ego Psychology and Dynamic Casework*. New York: Family Service Association of America.

Hollis, F. (1972) *Casework: A Psychosocial Therapy*, 2nd edn. New York: Random House.

Howe, D. (2009) Psychosocial work: an attachment perspective, in R. Adams, L. Dominelli and M. Payne (eds), *Critical Practice in Social Work*, 2nd edn. Basingstoke: Palgrave Macmillan.

Kenny, L. and Kenny, B. (2000) Psychodynamic theory in social work: a view from practice, in P. Stepney and D. Ford (eds), *Social Work Models, Methods and Theories*. Lyme Regis: Russell House.

Kondrat, M.E. (2002) Actor-centered social work: re-visioning 'person-in-environment' through a critical theory lens, *Social Work*, 47(4): 435–48.

Main, M. and Solomon, J. (1990) Procedures for identifying infants as disorganized/disoriented during the Ainsworth Strange Situation, in M.T. Greenberg, D. Cicchetti and E.M. Cummings (eds), *Attachment in the Preschool Years: Theory, Research, and Intervention*. Chicago, IL: University of Chicago Press.

Page, T. (2011) Attachment theory and social work treatment, in F.J. Turner (ed.), *Social Work Treatment: Interlocking Theoretical Approaches*, 5th edn. Oxford: Oxford University Press.

Payne, M. (2005) *Modern Social Work Theory*, 3rd edn. Basingstoke: Palgrave Macmillan.

Payne, M., Adams, R. and Dominelli, L. (2009) On being critical in social work, in R. Adams, L. Dominelli and M. Payne (eds), *Critical Practice in Social Work*, 2nd edn. Basingstoke: Palgrave Macmillan.

Preston-Shoot, M. and Agass, D. (1990) *Making Sense of Social Work: Psychodyamics, Systems and Practice*. Basingstoke: Macmillan Education.

Richmond, M.E. (1917) *Social Diagnosis*. New York: Russell Sage Foundation.

Richmond, M.E. (1922) *What Is Social Case Work? An Introductory Description*. New York: Russell Sage Foundation.

Robbins, S.P. (2011) Oppression theory and social work treatment, in F.J. Turner (ed.), *Social Work Treatment: Interlocking Theoretical Approaches*, 5th edn. Oxford: Oxford University Press.

Robinson, H. and Kaplan, C. (2011) Psychosocial theory and social work treatment, in F.J. Turner (ed.), *Social Work Treatment: Interlocking Theoretical Approaches*, 5th edn. Oxford: Oxford University Press.

Rogers, C.R. (1957) The necessary and sufficient conditions of therapeutic personality change, *Journal of Counseling Psychology*, 21(2): 95–103.

Ruch, G. (2010) Theoretical frameworks informing relationship-based practice, in G. Ruch, D. Turney and A. Ward (eds), *Relationship-based Social Work: Getting to the Heart of Practice*. London: Jessica Kingsley Publishers.

Ruch, G., Turney, D. and Ward, A. (2010) *Relationship-based Social Work: Getting to the Heart of Practice*. London: Jessica Kingsley Publishers.

Thompson, N. (2012) *Anti-discriminatory Practice*, 5th edn. Basingstoke: Palgrave Macmillan.

Turner, F.J. (1978) *Psychosocial Therapy*. New York: Free Press.

Turner, F.J. (2009) Psychosocial therapy, in A.R. Roberts (ed.), *Social Workers' Desk Reference*, 2nd edn. New York: Oxford University Press.

2 Systems theory and the ecological perspective

Introduction

The profession of social work has consistently been concerned with 'helping people and promoting responsive environments that support human growth, health, and satisfaction in social functioning' (Gitterman and Germain, 2008, p. 51). The acknowledgement of social work to focus on the interaction of person and environment is expressed in the international definition of social work: 'social work intervenes at the point where people interact with their environments' (International Federation of Social Work, 2012). Therefore, one of the basic functions of social work practice is to consider individuals within their environment which is often expressed as 'person-in-environment'. The extent to which the environment is considered varies based on the theoretical framework from which the social worker approaches a situation. Often the environment is minimally considered in the sense that the social worker assesses or asks questions about the individual's social situation or the impact of environmental factors on her or him but continues to target the intervention on the individual, but in other situations the social worker completes a full assessment of the individual's environment and considers various targets within the environment that could be the focus of the intervention. This latter approach to considering persons and their surrounding environment is referred to as systems theory or the ecological perspective. These two related theories provide a framework for assessment in social work situations and assist in the identification of the multiple target areas in which the social worker can intervene. This chapter describes these two related theories and how they can be applied to social work practice.

The origins of systems theory and the ecological perspective

The origins of systems theory is from general systems theory as developed by Ludwig von Bertalanffy who examined the complex parts that together created a functional whole. The ideas of general systems theory went on to influence different physical and social science disciplines, such as engineering, biology, psychology, sociology and management (Forder, 1976). Systems are defined as being either open, where the system is receptive to and influenced by outside stimulus, or closed, where the system is solid or unreceptive to outside stimulus. The purpose for the theory development stems from the desire to explain the complex interplay of various parts of a system and how these different parts interact to purposely create a whole. According to von Bertalanffy, the human being is the most complex system (Andreae, 2011).

Among the first to apply general systems theory to social work were Pincus and Minahan (1973; 1977) and Goldstein (1973; 1977), who used systems theory in their discussion and application of the unitary model, and Specht and Vickery (1977), particularly in the UK, who discussed the application of the systems theory to case-work. These theorists believed that systems were open systems and therefore could provide a framework for social workers in their assessment of individuals, families and communities, and provide various targets of intervention when attempting to facilitate change in a system. For example, in attempting to alleviate problems or issues posed by an individual the social worker may determine that the most effective system to target in an attempt to facilitate change in the family or a social service organization versus individuals themselves.

The application of the general systems theory in social work practice became more prominent in the 1970s and its proposed benefits during this time are best described by Forder (1976) who wrote an article entitled 'Social work and systems theory'. Forder described the general systems theory and then discussed the theory's value for social work practice in relation to four areas: (1) philosophical contribution of presenting man and society; (2) its incorporation into the social work perspective in encouraging social workers to assess a situation through the interaction of different systems; (3) the perspective contributing to social workers' decisions as to which system(s) to target for intervention; and (4) the contribution towards explaining the social work process. Systems theory is still present within social work practice, but has a particularly strong presence within family therapy.

As with systems theory, the ecological perspective emphasizes the interaction and interdependence of individuals and their environment, yet stems more from ecology, which is the study of the interdependence and interaction between organisms and their environment (Gitterman, 2011). The ecological perspective is a form of general systems theory and was brought to the attention of social work predominately by two social work academics, Alex Gitterman and Carel Germain, in the late 1970s and early 1980s. Although systems theory and the ecological perspective tend to hold the same premises and basic assumptions, they each have their unique terminology. The ecological perspective was developed within the social work profession due to a criticism of the non-human language of systems theory, such as 'system', 'equilibrium' and 'homeostasis', and a lack of direction for the social worker after assessment of systems. Because ecology focused on the study of person-in-environment and was based more on biology rather than on physical origins, theorists found the language and approach to be more appropriate for explaining and assessing individuals in their environments and providing a foundation for social work practice (Germain, 1979; Gitterman and Germain, 2008). The ecological perspective has influenced the Life Model of social work practice.

Systems theory explained

Systems theory is best summed up by the phrase, 'the whole of a system is greater than the sum of its individual parts'. The focus of this theory is on the development and transformation of systems and the interaction and relationships between them. In order to understand the theory, one must understand the definition and purpose of a system. A system is defined as a 'a complex of elements or components directly or indirectly related in a causal network, such that each component is related to at least some others in a more or less stable way within a particular period of time' (Buckley, 1967, p. 41). The different parts or elements of a system do not function in isolation but function by depending on and interacting with each other to complete the system as a whole. The whole cannot be complete without the presence and participation of each of the elements.

The definition of a system can be applied to humans, who are comprised of biological, psychological and physiological elements, families, that are comprised of different members as elements (that is, mother, father, sister, brother, daughter) and with different types of relationships as elements (that is, spousal/couple, parent-child, sibling) or a social work class, which is comprised of the teacher and students as elements and the social work curriculum as an element that dictates what is taught in the class. Each of the elements of these systems can be separated from the system and examined in more detail but the system cannot function effectively if any of the elements are removed (Preston-Shoot and Agass, 1990). In order to have the system, each of the elements must be functioning together.

Elements can also be subsystems. All systems, except for the largest, can act as smaller subsystems of a system, and all systems, except for the smallest, are environments for other systems (Forder, 1976). For example, the family system could be comprised of the element and subsystem 'parent-child' and the parent-child, as a system, is comprised of individuals as elements or subsystems which act as systems themselves comprised of subsystems. Therefore, one of the main features of systems theory is the ability to distinguish the main system with which you are working and identifying the various subsystems and/or elements that comprise and make up the main system.

Exercise box 2.1   Common systems in social work

In pairs or small groups make a list of systems commonly present in social work practice and their elements/subsystems.

Before continuing on with the basic assumptions of systems theory, the terminology used in describing this theory needs to be defined. Table 2.1 highlights the main concepts used in systems theory with a brief description of each. You may find it useful to refer back to this table as you read the remainder of this section.

Table 2.1 Concepts and definitions used in systems theory

Concept	Definition
System	A set of elements that are orderly and interrelated to make a functional whole[1]
Subsystem	A subsystem is one part or element of a larger system, but the subsystem can act as a smaller system on its own (that is, an individual as a subsystem of its family, yet the individual is a system on its own)
Open system	Open systems interact with their environment and are affected and influenced by these interactions. The open system is continually reacting and adapting to the influences from the environment. There are two dimensions to a open system: (1) open to the environment (allowing new information to enter the system); and (2) open to itself (allowing new information to circulate within the system).[2] Different systems vary in the degree to which they are open, some being more open than others
Closed system	Closed systems do not interact with their environment and are unaffected and uninfluenced by the environment. Different systems vary in the degree to which they are closed, some being more closed than others (that is, a family may be influenced and affected by their environment, but they are resistant to change and prefer to remain stuck in their static processes)[3]
Boundaries	Each system has a boundary that distinguishes it from other systems. Boundaries may be physical or psychological.[3] The extent to which the boundaries are permeable differs by system as some systems allow information to freely enter or cross their boundary and others do not
Homeostasis	Homeostasis is the process by which a system is regulating and maintaining a constant internal state while responding to messages (input, feedback) from the environment; this process ensures the internal elements are remaining stable
Equilibrium	The system is responding to the messages (input, feedback) from the environment and is able to maintain an internal sense of balance despite conflicting influences
Disequilibrium	The system is off balance and the responses to and from the environment are prohibiting positive growth and change
Steady state	The system is responding to the environment, growth and change are taking place and the system is experiencing positive inner tension. A system in a steady state is continually goal directed and once one goal is achieved the system moves forward towards another goal
Equifinality	There are many different routes to reach the same end or goal. A problem can be viewed in different ways and there is more than one way to reach a solution to the problem[1]

Notes: [1] Kirst-Ashman and Hull (2002); [2] Alexander (1985); [3] Preston-Shoot and Agass (1990).

Systems theory tends to describe systems as open where there is a constant flow of material or information in and out of the system and the system is goal directed. An open system is on the other side of the spectrum from a closed system, which is unresponsive or unaffected by outside stimuli. An open system is goal directed to maintain homeostasis, which maintains the system and allows it to respond to change

(Andreae, 2011; Forder, 1976). The system may also be goal directed to reach a steady state, where growth and development is taking place. A steady state does not mean equilibrium but more the presence of some tension that exists when moving towards a goal. Forder (1976: p. 25) states that 'inner tension is maintained' when the system achieves one goal and then moves towards another goal, which is all part of the positive process of growth and development. There are usually many different routes to reach the same goal, which is termed 'equifinality'. Therefore, two similar systems may be responding to outside stimuli differently yet are both reacting in an effort to reach the same goal. Systems theory is focused on systems, their behaviours, their interaction with other systems and their ability to reach a steady state where they are positively growing and developing.

When applying this theory to social work, the basic aim of utilizing systems theory is for assessing and for determining the target system or subsystem for intervention or to bring about positive change. The assessment is in regard to identifying the main system, the system's subsystems and the other systems that are positively and/or negatively affecting the system, but particularly assessing the interaction between all of these systems. Based on this assessment, the social worker is able to best determine which system or subsystem requires intervention to bring about the necessary change. For example, when working with a child who presents with behavioural problems at school a social worker may determine that the child is the target for intervention and will utilize a cognitive behavioural approach in an attempt to change the negative behaviours. Alternatively, the social worker may fully assess the child as a system, examining the physical, biological and physiological subsystems of the child as well as the systems that interact with the child, such as family, school and community. After a full assessment the social worker discovers that the parents are in the middle of a divorce and a custody battle over the child, and many mornings before the child goes to school he witnesses an argument between his parents. The social worker then decides to focus the intervention on the parents and attempts to change their patterns of interaction versus focusing on the child. Thus, a full systems assessment has enabled the social worker to determine the best system in which to intervene.

Pincus and Minahan (1973; 1977) have identified four systems for social workers to consider when determining intervention strategies.

1   Change agent system – the system that is facilitating the change, for example the social worker, the agency, the legislations and policies that influence the resources and work.
2   Client system – the individual, family, community or other groups with whom the change agent system is working.
3   Target system – the system identified as most appropriate to receive the intervention (that is, the parents as the target system versus the child).
4   Action system – other systems that assist or work collaboratively with the change agent system to help facilitate change.

When considering each of these systems, the social worker may discover that several of these systems are often the same. For example, the client system and the target system may be the same (that is, a child is the client system and the intervention is conducted with that child to bring about change), or the change agent system and the target system are the same (that is, as a change agent system a social worker from a social service agency is working with a client system, and the social worker needs to assist in changing policies of the social service agency in order to bring about necessary change). The important aspect to remember is that utilizing a systems approach requires social workers to fully assess a system and enables them to be creative in their intervention strategies.

Basic assumptions

Before discussing how to apply systems theory to social work practice the basic assumptions are reviewed and summarized as follows:

1   *The whole system is greater than the sum of its parts.* A system should be viewed as consisting of several interlocking elements and/or subsystems that interact together to form a functional purposeful whole. These elements and/ or subsystems each have a purpose and are not randomly constructed together. For example, an individual should be viewed as a whole consisting of biological, physiological and psychological elements that interact together to fulfil a basic purpose of existing and surviving. When considering the individual, these elements should not be viewed in isolation but should be considered together in creating the whole individual.

2   *The parts of a system are interconnected and interdependent.* A change or movement in one part of the system will cause a change or movement in other parts of the system. For example, in considering a couple relationship as a system, the actions and behaviours of one subsystem, person A, should be viewed in relation to the actions and behaviours of the other subsystem, person B. A's behaviour towards B will influence B's behaviour towards A, and A's response to B's behaviour will influence B's response to A's behaviour. Figure 2.1 demonstrates how the subsystems of the couple system interact and influence each other. Therefore, when examining a system one must look at the ways in which the parts of the system interact and interconnect to make the whole. As with this example, the behaviour and actions of A cannot be explained without considering the behaviours and actions of B.

3   *A system is either directly or indirectly affected by other systems.* Not only do the different elements and subsystems of a system interact and affect each other, but systems interact and affect other systems. For example, individuals, as a system, are either directly or indirectly affected by their families, friends, employers, teachers, communities and society. Some of the influence can be direct, such as a mother implementing consequences for a child in order to decrease the child's negative behaviour (Payne, 1991). Other influences can be

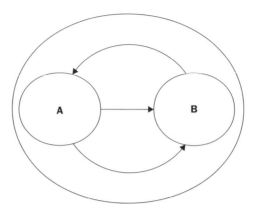

Figure 2.1   Illustration of the interconnection and interdependence of systems.

indirect, such as a decrease in funding for social service agencies, which limits the amount of services a client can receive. Therefore, in addition to understanding and assessing the interaction and influence of elements and subsystems of a system, outside systems that directly or indirectly affect a system should be considered.

4   *All systems have boundaries.* Each system has a boundary that distinguishes it from other systems although there may be overlapping boundaries in some situations. For example, the family system has subsystems that overlap, such as a parent-child subsystem, and sibling subsystem. Although each system has boundaries, they are permeable at different points. This depends on the extent to which a system is open or closed. An open system is more permeable and more receptive to change and development. A closed system is less permeable and is resistant to outside influences and prefers to remain static.

5   *All systems need to maintain homeostasis and a state of equilibrium.* This is achieved by the system maintaining an internal balance despite conflicting influences. When in a state of equilibrium, the system is able to grow and develop in an effort to reach goals. Systems can sometimes experience an imbalance or experience blocks in attempting to reach their goals and this is what social workers are most likely to observe when clients present to social service agencies. The goal is to return the system to a state of equilibrium.

Based on these assumptions, systems theory can be argued to place the emphasis on the interactions, interrelatedness, interdependence and transactions between various systems (Payne, 1991). Systems theory would not recommend a medical model that places the focus of intervention on one aspect of an individual, but rather would recommend a full assessment of the individual as a system and interactions of this system with other systems in the environment. Therefore, the intervention is not necessarily focused on the presenting problem or the client system, but after a complete multi-system assessment may focus on another system that will alleviate the problem and create needed change.

Implementing systems theory

Systems theory is primarily used in social work practice for assessment. This theory provides a framework for the social worker in assessing the client system and how that system is influenced and affected by other systems in the environment. Based on this thorough multi-system assessment, the social worker will then determine the most appropriate system in which to intervene. Systems theory enables social workers to widen their view of the client problem and the many other systems that could be contributing to the problem, thus allowing social workers to determine where the intervention should best be focused (that is, on the individual, the family, community, social service agency or society). The theory also holds that the social worker and client system may reach the same goal through several different avenues.

In order to facilitate change in a system, one must assess how the system is currently operating. Systems theory hypothesizes that a system's operations are influenced by the continual exchange of information from and interactions with the environment (Andreae, 2011). A system receives information (inputs), processes the information (throughputs) and then feeds back (feedback) to the environment how the system had received and processed the information and how well or unwell the system is operating (Andreae, 2011). An example is when a child interrupts a mother when she is talking to a friend. The mother boldly tells the child not to interrupt her when she is talking to someone else (input). The child processes this information from the mother (throughput) and gives her feedback by verbally confirming that he understands (feedback). The child does not interrupt the mother again while she is talking to her friend (output) nor does he interrupt in the future, which provides feedback to the mother that her method of intervention worked.

The combination of a multi-system assessment and the analysis of how systems are currently processing inputs provide a social worker with a basis for understanding the system, the influence of and interaction with other systems and an identification of where to focus the social work intervention. In using this theory the social worker needs to have a fundamental belief that there is a potential for the system to change even when systems have become stuck and begin to become rigid or closed. The social worker's aim in working with a client system is to facilitate change that enables the system to function in a steady state where the system allows the environment and other systems to pass information to the system that encourages positive growth and development.

The ecological perspective explained

The ecological perspective focuses on the person-in-environment and the continual interactions and transactions between persons, families, groups and/or communities

Table 2.2 Concepts and definitions used in the ecological perspective

Concept	Definition
Person: environment fit	Is the actual fit between an individual's or a collective group's needs, rights, goals and capacities and the qualities and operations of their physical and social environments within particular cultural and historical contexts. This fit could be classified as favourable, minimally adequate or unfavourable[1]
Adaptations	Are continuous, change-oriented, cognitive, sensory-perceptual and behavioural processes people use to sustain or raise the level of fit between themselves and their environment[1]
Life stressors	Are generated by critical life issues that people perceive as exceeding their personal and environmental resources for managing them. A stressor represents serious harm or loss and is associated with a sense of being in jeopardy[1]
Stress	Is the internal response to a life stressor and is characterized by troubled emotional or physiological states, or both[1]
Coping measures	Are special behaviours, often novel, that are devised to handle the demands posed by the life stressor. Successful coping depends on various environmental and personal resources[1]
Relatedness	Refers to attachments, friendships, positive kin relationships and a sense of belonging to a supportive social network[1]
Self-esteem	Represents the extent to which one feels competent, respected and worthy[1]
Self-direction	The capacity to take some degree of control over one's life and to accept responsibility for one's decisions and actions while simultaneously respecting the rights and needs of others.[1] Oppression, discrimination and a lack of empowerment will threaten or limit one's self-direction
Habitat	Habitats include dwelling places; physical layouts of urban and rural communities; physical settings of schools, workplaces, hospitals, social agencies, shopping areas and religious structures; and parks and other amenities[1]
Niche	The status occupied by an individual or family in the social structure of a community. The existence of oppressive niches is related to issues of power[1]
Coercive power	Is the withholding of power from vulnerable groups on the basis of a group's personal and cultural characteristics. The result is oppression of vulnerable populations that renders them powerless[1]
Exploitative power	Dominant groups who pollute our air, food, water, soils and oceans, and increase the presence of toxic chemicals and hazardous wastes in dwellings, schools, workplaces and communities[1]
Life course	Conceives biopsychosocial development as consisting of non-uniform, indeterminate pathways of development from birth to old age within diverse environments, cultures and historical eras[1]
Individual time	Refers to the continuity and meaning of individual life experience over the life course[1]
Historical time	Refers to the impact of historical and social change on the developmental pathways of a birth cohort[1]
Social time	Refers to the timing of individual and family transitions and life events as influenced by changing biological, economic, social, demographic and cultural factors[1]

Note: [1] Germain and Gitterman (1995, pp. 817–20); Gitterman (2011)

and their environments. The focus on the ecological perspective is on 'the growth, development and potentialities of human beings and with the properties of their environments that support or fail to support the expression of human potential' (Gitterman and Germain, 2008, p. 8). Social workers who work from an ecological perspective will focus on directing their practice towards improving the interactions and transactions between individuals, families, groups and/or communities and their respective environments in order to promote continual positive growth and development (Germain, 1979).

When examining the fit between person and environment, the social worker must take into account the physical and social aspects of the environment and how culture impacts the interplay between them (Gitterman and Germain, 2008). The physical environment includes the natural world (that is, nature) as well as the built world (that is, construction of the environment made by humans), and the social environment includes the human communication and relations within society. The interactions could be with family and friends, social and community networks, and the societal structures that shape the way in which the environment operates and orders itself, such as through political, legal and economic structures (Teater, 2014). Both the physical and social environments are influenced by the culture, values and norms within the society. As Gitterman and Germain (2008) describe, the culture of society determines the type of physical buildings that are built, which then determines the type of social interactions that can take place within and around them. For example, in the 1960s the social housing construction in Chicago, Illinois, consisted of high-rise buildings away from the main businesses of the Chicago area. This type of construction left families and children with little to nowhere to interact with others in the housing complex or with the communities around them, leading to segregation and concentration of low-income families in one location. The physical buildings limited the amount and type of social interaction of the residents, which was supported by the cultural values and norms of placing low-income, predominately African American families, away from mainstream society. In this sense, the physical and social environments contribute to the development of one's identity, competence and autonomy (Gitterman and Germain, 2008). For example, families in the social housing complex were physically and socially removed from mainstream society, which could have led to doubts in their self-worth, competence and autonomy.

Systems theory and the ecology perspective are very similar in their basic premises and assumptions, but each has their distinct terminology. Before continuing with a description of the ecological perspective, the terminology used in describing this theory needs to be defined. Table 2.2 highlights the main concepts used in ecological perspective with a brief description of each. You may find it useful to refer back to this table as you read the remainder of this section.

The ecological perspective holds four basic principles that are also evident in systems theory (Gitterman, 2011; Gitterman and Germain, 2008), which include the following:

1   *Interdependence of networks.* As with systems theory, persons in their environments are viewed as interrelated and interdependent, thus, the person and environment can only be understood when examining the relationship between the two and their various elements (physical, social, cultural). Within the

ecological perspective, this relationship is often written as person:environment fit and can be further explained as being positive, negative or neutral (Gitterman and Germain, 2008).

2   *Individuals strive for a good person:environment fit.* Individuals strive to maintain a good level of fit between themselves and their environment as they move through the life course. Individuals who experience a good level of person:environment fit that is positive and healthy can be assumed to have a good level of adaptedness. A good level of adaptedness means that individuals view themselves as full of strengths, resources and the capacity to grow and develop while also feeling as if their environment is providing the necessary resources in order to grow and develop. A poor level of adaptedness would involve individuals feeling that the environment does not provide the necessary resources nor do they feel as if they have the strengths, resources and capacity to grow and develop. Individuals may feel negatively towards their environment because the resources are unavailable, inaccessible or non-existent. This leads to feelings of stress, which is often the point at which individuals seek help or become involved with social services (Gitterman, 2011; Teater, 2014).

3   *Cyclical nature of ecological processes.* The ecological perspective requires ecological thinking, which examines the relationship and exchanges between A and B (as explained above within systems theory) while also considering the environmental factors that could influence A and B's interaction and the ways in which they are responding. As Teater (in press) states, 'a social worker might find that the target of intervention is neither A nor B, but rather the family in which A and B belong (social environment) or the physical environment in which they live, which could be the source of stress and strain'.

4   *Non-linear.* The interaction between the individual and the environment is non-linear as stated above under principle number three. The individual responds to the environment and the environment in turn changes and responds to the individual. Often the individual or the environment has to self-regulate or self-organize in order to have a more positive person:environment fit (Gitterman, 2011).

Thus, taking an ecological perspective requires a consideration of the relationship and connection between the individual, family, group and/or community and the political, social and cultural environments and how they influence and shape one another (Gitterman, 2011). For the social worker, this can require intervention in the person, environment or both.

Interventions with the individual can work to increase self-esteem, self-worth, coping skills, autonomy and competence, or attempt to decrease psychic discomfort. Interventions in families and groups can work to enable the members to recognize and change their interactions and patterns of communication. Alternatively, interventions into the environment can work to increase the adaptive fit for individuals, such as attempting to reduce and eliminate discrimination, oppression and prejudices, and increase opportunities for individuals and groups to actively engage with the environment to meet their specific needs (Germain, 1979; Gitterman and Germain, 2008).

The person:environment fit is at the centre of the ecological perspective. When there is a positive person:environment fit, individuals feel a sense of adaptedness, which includes feelings of security and perceptions of themselves and their environment as holding resources necessary to support their human growth and potential. Alternatively, a negative person:environment fit is a result of individuals lacking a sense of security within their environment and experiencing inadequate personal and environment resources which are needed to maintain and feed their growth and development. A negative person:environment fit leads to the individual experiencing stress (Gitterman and Germain, 2008). Stress is defined as the 'outcome of a perceived imbalance between environmental demands and capability to manage it with available internal and external resources' (Gitterman, 2011, p. 281). This level of stress varies by the extent to which the individuals perceive their ability to obtain the necessary resources.

Over the life course, individuals are continually striving to maintain a positive level of fit with their environments (Gitterman, 2011). Yet, as individuals move through the life course, they are likely to encounter stress during particular difficult life transitions (e.g. puberty and adolescence, starting a new job, getting married) and traumatic life events (e.g. medical diagnosis, loss of a loved one), environmental pressures (e.g. lack of resources, such as food, money, housing, healthcare), and dysfunctional interpersonal processes in family, group and community life (e.g. conflicted relationships) (Gitterman, 2011; Teater, 2014). Such experiences may be perceived as a challenge to individuals who have the resources to cope, or they may lead to internal stress, such as physiological and/or emotional consequences when individuals do not have adequate resources to enable them to cope. For example, an individual may feel overwhelmed and stressed with a recent diagnosis of terminal cancer of a family member who contributed to the financial and emotional resources of a family, but the individual may seek help, assistance and resources from extended family members and the community church in order to meet the family's needs, which in turn greatly reduces the level of stress. Alternatively, another individual in the same situation may not have the extended family or community church to assist and alleviate stress and, thus, the individual experiences an amount of stress that she or he perceives as unbearable. Therefore, the first individual may be able to improve her or his level of person:environment fit, while the second individual is experiencing a gradual decline in her or his person:environment fit. Therefore, the ability and extent to which individuals cope with external pressures and factors depends on the availability and adequacy of their environment's resources.

The aim for social workers working from this perspective is to evaluate the level of person:environment fit and then tailor interventions for either the person, environment or both to increase the level of fit. The intervention should reduce stress within the individual, family, group and/or communities, and promote positive growth and development. An extended aim is to assist the individual in dealing with stressors in the future by utilizing the available and adequate resources.

Gitterman and Germain (2008, p. 55) report three different ways in which individuals attempt to create or maintain an adaptive person:environment fit: (1) change oneself in order to meet the environment's perceived expectations or demands, and take advantage of its opportunities; (2) change the environment so that the social and physical environment are more responsive to one's needs and goals; or (3) change the person:environment transactions in order to achieve an improved fit. Although individuals are continually adapting to their environments, this does not mean that they are passive or do not challenge the status quo in favour of a more suitable environment. The ecological perspective seeks to support individuals in creating person:environment fits that promotes diverse, supportive environments and positive human growth and development (Gitterman and Germain, 2008).

Implementing the ecological perspective: the life model

The life model of social work practice was developed within social work by Gitterman and Germain (1976), which was based on the ecological perspective. The life model views the purpose of social work as assisting in the improvement of the level of fit between people and their environments particularly by helping people find and utilize their personal and environmental strengths and resources to assist in alleviating life stressors and/or to intervene in the environment to create better resources to meet the needs of individuals (Gitterman, 2011).

The life model focuses on the life course or the 'unique pathways of development that each human being takes – from conception and birth through old age – in varied environment, and to our infinitely varied life experiences' (Gitterman and Germain, 2008, p. 57). The life model works to the life course, particularly as it is non-uniform and perceives the life course as varying based on diverse environments, cultures and diversity within human specificities, such as race, ethnicity, gender, sexual orientation, socioeconomic status and physical/mental health (Gitterman and Germain, 2008). Working from a life course perspective versus a life stages perspective allows individuals to grow and develop as necessary for their environments, based on their cultures and determined by their historical, individual and social time versus predetermined stages as defined by the predominately dominate culture set in a specific time.

In working from a life course perspective, the life model seeks to help individuals alleviate the life stressors that emerge throughout the life course, such as stressful development transitions, difficult social transitions and traumatic life events. Developmental transitions include moving through the life course and into the different roles of humanity, such as adolescence, adulthood, parenthood and older adulthood. Each of these developmental transitions brings with it some adjustments for the person, which will vary in difficulty for each individual depending on the rules and norms of the dominant culture, subcultures and the availability of resources from the environment. Social transitions will also vary in difficulty for each individual and can include starting a new job, having a child or ending a relationship. Lastly, traumatic life events also can cause difficulty and stress for individuals such as the loss of a loved one, or loss of something that has value and significance to an individual (Gitterman and Germain, 2008).

Life-modelled practice seeks to work with individuals to utilize their strengths and resources in order to create a positive person:environment fit and, thus, alleviate the stressors and achieve positive growth and development. The level of fit can be improved by choosing to: '(1) improve a person's (collectivity's) ability to manage stressor(s) through more effective personal and situational appraisals and behavioural skills; (2) influence the social and physical environments to be more responsive to a person's (collectivity's) needs; and/or (3) improve the quality of person:environment exchanges' (Gitterman, 2011, p. 285).

The model is phasic and is organized into the preparatory, initial, ongoing and ending phases (Gitterman, 2009). The model's preparatory phase involves gathering information and preparing to enter the life of the client. Empathy is a key skill during this stage, which will enable the social worker to hear and attempt to understand the client's story. The initial phase involves assessing the current level of person:environment fit, including personal biopsychosocial features and environmental properties. This assessment includes considering the level of stress as experienced by the person and her or his coping strategies. The problems and goals are to be defined by the client and shared by the social worker in order to collaboratively participate in problem-solving activities, which initiates the ongoing phase. This phase involves interventions that can be tailored to the individual by working to increase self-esteem, self-worth, competence and autonomy or by attempting to change the physical or social environment to create a better person:environment fit. In the ending phase the social worker and client address feelings around termination and develop plans for addressing any future life stressors. Life-modelled practice is an empowerment-based approach and is sensitive to race, ethnicity, gender, sexual orientation, physical and mental states, and other differences between the social worker and the clients, and includes the following principles (Germain and Gitterman, 1995, pp. 821–2):

1   *A collaborative relationship between social worker and client.* The relationship between the social worker and client is viewed as a partnership where both parties bring knowledge that influences the work together.
2   *The client is viewed as the expert not the social worker.* The social worker acknowledges that clients are the experts in their own experiences and the social worker is not to place her or his values and beliefs onto the clients.
3   *Empowerment.* The social worker and client are working to enhance the power of the client. Empowerment could be enhanced by linking the client to informal or formal support systems and/or participating in political activities in order to advocate for services and resources.

Case example: applying systems theory and the ecological perspective to practice

Randeep is a 43-year-old, Indian male who was born in Southern India and moved to England at the age of 19 to attend university. Randeep has been married to Natalie, a 42-year-old white British female, for 22 years and they have both continued to live in

England with their three children. Randeep was made redundant from his place of employment approximately six months ago and has been unable to retain a new job. He has suffered from feelings of depression since his redundancy and states he does not have the energy or strength to search for a new job especially as he feels he was discriminated against in his last place of employment. Natalie has been left responsible for supporting the family through her employment and feels she is not getting any help or support from Randeep. Natalie has threatened Randeep with a separation if he does not begin to deal with his depression and start helping to support the family. You receive a referral for Randeep with the presenting problem of depression.

You are a social worker who works from a systems/ecological perspective to assist in assessing the individual from a holistic perspective in determining which system or network requires intervention. You talk to Randeep to gather more information about his personal, interpersonal and social relationships and interactions in order to fully assess the presenting problem. Randeep describes the discrimination that he received while at his place of employment and how he was the focus of racial jokes despite his outstanding sales performance. Randeep was surprised when he was made redundant over other less productive sales representatives and was told that the other employees 'have more in common with the customers'. Randeep stated he was anxious about obtaining another job as he felt he would be subject to the same type of discrimination. Randeep further explained that he felt like a failure because he lost his job and believes it was due to his ethnicity, and he perceives Natalie to have a difficult time understanding his experiences. Further, Randeep deeply misses his family and most of his friends who still live in India and feels that a lot of his English friends do not fully understand where he comes from. Randeep states that he would just like to feel better and provide for his family again.

Based on the information from Randeep, you are able to determine that there could be several situations or factors that are contributing to Randeep's presenting problem of depression versus focusing solely on him as an individual. For example, Randeep has described how he experienced discrimination at his place of employment and believes he was wrongfully let go because of his ethnicity. This experience has deeply affected Randeep as he was a high performer at work, but due to his ethnicity, the employer believed him to be of less value to the company. These acts of discrimination could have greatly contributed to Randeep's feelings of depression. Because Randeep feels Natalie and his friends do not understand him, he has stopped expressing his thoughts and feelings to them, which in turn has caused Natalie and his friends to lessen the amount and extent of their involvement and interaction with Randeep. This situation could also have contributed to Randeep's feelings of depression.

Systems theory

You are able to determine that Randeep is experiencing racism and discrimination and feelings of frustration from Natalie (inputs) that when processed by Randeep (throughput) contribute to his feelings of low self-worth and depression (outputs). Randeep's feelings of depression are further played out through isolation and a lack of interaction with Natalie, which reinforces her thoughts that Randeep is not attempting to help her (feedback). The various systems in Randeep's life could all be contributing to his feelings of depression (disequilibrium) and interventions to alleviate the depression may extend beyond Randeep.

Interventions in this cyclical process of racism and discrimination against Randeep, his feelings of depression and Natalie's feelings of a lack of support from Randeep could be in one or more of the following systems:

- Individual system (Randeep) – individual counselling, anti-depressant medication and/or alternative therapies prominent in Randeep's culture to decrease depressive feelings and symptoms.
- Couple system (Randeep and Natalie) – couple counselling in order to explore the communication and interaction between Randeep and Natalie and to allow each to express their thoughts and feelings in an attempt to better understand and support one another and participate in joint problem-solving.
- Legal system (in regard to Randeep's prior place of employment) – pursue legal involvement due to the discrimination Randeep experienced and potential unlawful redundancy.
- Employment system – explore with Randeep future places of employment.
- Community system – explore with Randeep support groups or community activities where Randeep can interact with other individuals of the same ethnic background.
- Society system – advocate on behalf of Randeep in order to promote the importance of diversity and fight against discrimination and racism.

You explore with Randeep the various systems (equifinality) by which you could intervene in order to reach his goal of feeling better and providing for his family. He expresses a desire to explore the legal options in regard to his potential unlawful redundancy, and to explore community activities and couple's counselling with Natalie. Therefore, the work that you do with Randeep involves the following: (1) you as the *change agent system* along with the relevant anti-discrimination legislation; (2) the couple system (Randeep and Natalie), legal system and employment system as the *client systems*; (3) the couple system, legal system and employment system as the *target systems*; and (4) the legal system as the *action system* with whom you and Randeep will work in order to reach his goal and achieve homeostasis.

Ecological perspective and life model

From your preparatory and initial work with Randeep, you are able to determine that Randeep is currently experiencing a negative person:environment fit where he is not able to access his internal and external strengths and resources to adequately deal with his life stressors, which is prohibiting him from continual positive growth and development. Randeep's current negative person:environment fit is causing stress within his life leading to feelings of depression, low self-worth and a lack of security, which in turn is negatively affecting his relationship with Natalie. In addition to the racism and discrimination that he experienced at work, you also identify that Randeep has experienced a difficult social transition by being made redundant. Randeep has coped with these life stressors by withdrawing from his family and spending time alone. In order to assist Randeep in alleviating the life stressors present in his life and returning to a positive person:environment fit, you first need to collaborate with Randeep in order to determine the aspects of either himself and/or the environment affecting him that require intervention keeping in mind his individual, social and historical time.

During the ongoing stage, you and Randeep explore his problems and goals. Randeep has expressed a goal of obtaining a job and helping to take care of his family. He has identified that he would like to pursue the legal options around his potentially unlawful redundancy, explore community activities with other individuals from the south of India, and participate in couple counselling with Natalie in order to attempt to restore their relationship. The interventions are penetrating into both Randeep and his environment. Randeep believes that the selected interventions will work towards decreasing his depression and increasing his self-esteem, self-worth, competence and autonomy. Once the interventions have been delivered, you and Randeep move into the ending phase where you both deal with feelings around termination and develop plans for addressing future life stressors.

Exercise box 2.2 Systems theory or ecological perspective?

In pairs or small groups discuss whether you would prefer to incorporate systems theory or the ecological perspective in your social work practice. Give specific reasons for your answer.

Strengths and limitations

There are several strengths and limitations of systems theory and the ecological perspective that are worth exploring before incorporating these theories into practice. The strengths of the theories include the following:

- The theories encompass empowerment-based approaches as they both seek to enhance clients' identity, autonomy, competence and relatedness to their environments. The theories stress a collaborative relationship between the social worker and client and the work together is to enhance the client's power in order to obtain and use informal and formal resources to maintain equilibrium or a positive person:environment fit.
- Both theories allow the social worker to take a holistic approach by fully assessing what might be going on around the client versus just seeing things as an individual problem. This enables the social worker to see diverse points of entry into difficult situations and base the interventions on the client's needs

and not the social worker's preferred methods (Gitterman, 2009; 2011). However, a criticism of such theories is often that they inform social workers of *how* the problem is maintained, but not necessarily *why* the problem was created.

- The theories are anti-oppressive in the sense that they stress trying to eliminate discrimination and oppression that is causing disequilibrium or a negative person:environment fit. However, the language used in systems theory is often considered to be dehumanizing as it often equates the individual to a 'system' being influenced by other systems around them and can ignore the power of human agency.
- The theories are flexible in that they can provide a way of assessing the individual, family, group or community and then the social worker can use other methods to deliver the interventions. For example, a social worker may use systems theory to assess a situation and then incorporate a cognitive behavioural approach and/or political advocacy to fulfil the intervention.

The limitations of the theories include the following:

- Social workers are sometimes forced to work from limited information and therefore are unable to conduct an accurate assessment of all the systems/ variables affecting the client. In such situations, this theory may not inform the social worker of how or where to penetrate a system. For example, less verbal clients may not fully disclose all the systems that are currently contributing to their presenting problems. Therefore, the social worker and client may be addressing symptoms to an underlying problem that is unknown or not disclosed. This limitation could be reduced by maintaining a collaborative relationship with the client where a complete personal, interpersonal and environmental assessment is conducted.
- Social workers may be limited in their work with the client due to time or resources of the agency. For example, a social worker may assess a client's situation from either a systems or ecological perspective and identify several systems that required intervention (that is, policy, family and individual), yet due to the lack of time and resources of the agency, the social worker and client are not able to intervene fully into all the necessary systems. In such situations, the social worker and client will have to make a decision about what interventions are most necessary at the time. In such situations the social worker and client may not be able to fully address the underlying problem (that is, social inequality or abuse of power) and may just be treating the symptoms.
- Social workers may find themselves working with systems that will not allow them to intervene. For example, a social worker and client may identify that a family system requires intervention, yet different members of the family are not willing to participate in the intervention. Social workers and client should collaborate in attempting to permeate the boundary of the system that is reluctant to participate and, if unsuccessful, the social worker and client should

explore other interventions that will move the client towards the end goal. Additionally, involuntary clients may not be receptive to interventions or may not recognize a need for interventions. In such situations, the social worker may need to incorporate aspects of motivational interviewing (see Chapter 8) in order to move the client to a necessary stage of change in order to acknowledge a need for intervention.

- In conducting a holistic, person-in-environment assessment there is a danger that the social worker could over-assess the systems involved in the client's life and completely miss what should be the focus of the work together. Social workers should be mindful of conducting a thorough assessment with the client and continually checking in with the client to ensure the focus of the work together is beneficial to the client and is working towards her or his goal.

Ethical and cultural considerations

Systems theory and the ecological perspective both value the importance that culture and diversity play in the lives of clients. In assessing the person in her or his environment, the social worker and client should explore the values, beliefs and assumptions of the client's subculture and culture and how these fit with the client's own values, beliefs and assumptions. Social workers and clients are to work in collaboration with social workers acknowledging that clients are the experts in their own experiences and, therefore, social workers are not to push their values and beliefs onto clients. In certain situations, a client's culture, or the dominant culture of society, may be contributing to the presenting problem through discrimination and/or oppression, and may require intervention by either the social worker and/or the client in an attempt to create a more positive person:environment fit. Additionally, there may be situations where social workers believe that the values, beliefs and culture of the client may be contributing to the presenting problem, but the client does not agree. In such situations, social workers should value the client's position while also adhering to the values, principles and ethics of social work to ensure that the client is safe from harm.

Systems theory and the ecological perspective and anti-oppressive practice

Systems theory and the ecological perspective/life model would be considered anti-oppressive based theories in social work practice. The theories are empowerment based as they seek to identify the level of fit between individuals and her or his environment and then reduce and/or eliminate any barriers that challenge the ability for individuals to have power and control over their lives. Both theories are sensitive to race, ethnicity, gender, sexual orientation, physical and mental states and other differences between the social worker and client. In acknowledging these differences, the social worker and client should consider the client's culture and subculture that impact upon her or his life and develop interventions that are congruent with the client's values and assumptions and not those of the social worker. In maintaining anti-oppressive practice, the social worker and client should work in collaboration where the client is viewed as the expert of her or his own situation and life experiences. Any interventions should involve joint decision-making between social workers and clients in order to empower clients by enabling them to have control over their life. At the end of the work together, social workers and clients can discuss how the clients will deal with future obstacles and stressors by pulling from the clients' internal and external strengths and resources.

Research on systems and ecological theory

Since systems theory and the ecological perspective are theories, the research tends to be conducted more with the specific methods and approaches that are based on the theories. Such approaches tend to be classified as family systems therapy, which views the family as a unit or system and then works with the family members to bring about change and can include such approaches as Murray Bowen's intergenerational, Salvador Minuchin's structural, Jay Haley's strategic, de Shazer and Burg's solution-focused brief, Virginia Satir's humanistic, and Epston and White's narrative therapies (Sharf, 2012). Research on family systems therapies has found family therapy to be no less effective than other types of therapies (Sharf, 2012).

Systems theory and the ecological perspective have also contributed to the development of the common assessment framework (CAF) often used in social service agencies to assess holistically a child or young person. The CAF is a four-step process that assesses the following three areas: (1) development of child or young person; (2) parents/carers; and (3) family and environment (Department for Education (DfE), 2012). The CAF is voluntary and is a request for services when a practitioner or parent/ caregiver is concerned about either how a child is progressing and developing, or the child or young person's needs are either unclear or outside of the scope of work of the agency (DfE, 2012). A study by Easton et al. (2011) on the effectiveness of the CAF in early intervention found that the use of the CAF has lead to better outcomes for children, such as improved home life, better engagement in education, improved child development, better emotional health and enhanced service engagement. The early engagement, through the use of the CAF, was found to lead to less use of services in the future, thus, was found to be cost effective (Easton et al., 2011). A study by Holmes et al. (2012) on the cost and impact of the CAF found that parents/carers reported that the CAF enabled them to access the support they needed and that professionals had an increased awareness of the services available. Despite this, as noticed above under the limitations to the use of systems theory and the ecological perspective, Holmes et al. (2012) also found that time constraints were cited as a barrier to the professionals' use of the CAF. Such findings report to the ability of a holistic assessment of a person and his/her environment can lead to a more positive person:environment fit.

Summary

Systems theory and the ecological perspective are two theories that aim to see the person in her or his environment, conduct a holistic assessment of the individual, family, group and/or community, and explore all possible areas around the client that may require or benefit from intervention. In utilizing these two theoretical frameworks, the social worker must 'strive for a full understanding of the complex interactions between the client and all levels of the social and physical system as well as the meaning that the client assigns to each of these interactions' (Andreae, 2011, p. 246).

Systems theory holds that the whole of a system is greater than the sum of its parts and stresses the need to assess the interconnection and interdependence of systems and how these interactions are feeding the presenting problem. The goal of systems theory is to intervene in one or more systems to alleviate the presenting problem and return the client to a state of equilibrium. The ecological perspective also explores the interconnection, interdependence and current level of fit of a person and her or his environment. The perspective assumes that each individual should have a positive level of fit that will create a sense of adaptedness, reduce the level of stress and promote positive growth and development of the individual. Interventions, particularly through the use of the life model, seek to explore the life stressors associated with difficult life transitions throughout the life course by intervening into the person, environment or both. The four phases of the life model, preparatory, initial, ongoing and ending, provide a framework for alleviating life stressors and moving the client towards achieving a positive person:environment fit.

Case study

An anonymous referral has come into children and families social services in regard to a mother, Karen (white British, aged 38) who is alleged to be neglecting her daughter, Amie (18 months) during the day, due to drinking alcohol. Karen is married to Keith (white British, aged 43) who is a supervisor at a factory and works the day shift. Karen and Keith live in a rural area, which does not leave many opportunities for Karen to engage with neighbours or her community during the day. Karen is alleged to drink wine from the time Keith goes to work till Keith arrives home. Keith has reported that he often finds Karen asleep when he arrives home and Amie unattended to. Keith has restricted Karen's access to money in an attempt to reduce her alcohol intake but it is suspected that a friend brings her boxes of wine. Keith's mother, Sue (aged 73 and reported to be in poor health), lives about 15 minutes away and often comes to check up on Karen and Amie. When Karen is intoxicated, Sue will stay with Amie until Keith arrives home. Amie is Karen's first and only child and was unplanned. Karen had worked as a 'beauty and make-up' manager for a retail store, but she and Keith decided that she should stay home when the baby arrived. Karen has no previously known problems with alcohol. You receive the referral and are preparing for your visit to Karen.

First, describe how you would utilize the social systems theory in conducting the assessment and identifying possible interventions with Karen. Then, describe how you would utilize the ecological perspective and the life model of social work practice with Karen.

Further reading and web resources

Andreae, D. (2011) General systems theory: contributions to social work theory and practice, in F.J. Turner (ed.), *Social Work Treatment: Interlocking Theoretical Approaches*, 5th edn. New York: Free Press.

Provides an overview to general systems theory and its application to social work practice.

Gitterman, A. (2011) Advances in the life model of social work practice, in F.J. Turner (ed.), *Social Work Treatment: Interlocking Theoretical Approaches*, 5th edn. New York: Free Press.

Provides an overview to the ecological perspective and the life model of social work practice.

Gitterman, A. and Germain, C.B. (2008) *The Life Model of Social Work Practice: Advances in Theory and Practice*, 3rd edn. New York: Columbia University Press.

Explores the ecological perspective and details the life model of social work practice.

Global Alliance for a Deep Ecological Social Work: http://www.ecosocialwork.org

Teater, B. (2014) Social work practice from an ecological perspective, in C.W. LeCroy (ed.), *Case Studies in Social Work Practice*, 3rd edn. Belmont, CA: Brooks Cole.

Provides a succinct overview of the ecological perspective and a detailed application of the perspective to a case example.

References

Alexander, P. (1985) A systems theory conceptualization of incest, *Family Process*, 24(1): 79–88.

Andreae, D. (2011) General systems theory: contributions to social work theory and practice, in F.J. Turner (ed.), *Social Work Treatment: Interlocking Theoretical Approaches*, 5th edn. New York: Free Press.

Buckley, W. (1967) *Sociology and Modern Systems Theory*. New York: Prentice Hall.

Department for Education (DfE) (2012) *The CAF Process*. http://www.education.gov.uk/childrenandyoungpeople/strategy/integratedworking/caf/a0068957/the-caf-process (accessed 11 May 2013).

Easton, C., Gee, G., Durbin, B. and Teeman, D. (2011) *Early Intervention, Using the CAF Process, and its Cost-effectiveness: Findings from LARC3*. Slough: National Foundation for Educational Research.

Forder, A. (1976) Social work and system theory, *British Journal of Social Work*, 6(1): 23–42.

Germain, C.B. (ed.) (1979) *Social Work Practice: People and Environments*. New York: Columbia University Press.

Germain, C.B. and Gitterman, A. (1995) Ecological perspective, in R.L. Edward and J.G. Hopps (eds), *Encyclopedia of Social Work*, 19th edn. Washington, DC: NASW Press.

Gitterman, A. (2009) The life model, in A.R. Roberts (ed.), *The Social Workers' Desk Reference*, 2nd edn. New York: Oxford University Press.

Gitterman, A. (2011) Advances in the life model of social work practice, in F.J. Turner (ed.), *Social Work Treatment: Interlocking Theoretical Approaches*, 5th edn. New York: Free Press.

Gitterman, A. and Germain, C.B. (1976) Social work practice: a life model, *Social Service Review*, 50(4): 601–10.

Gitterman, A. and Germain, C.B. (2008) *The Life Model of Social Work Practice: Advances in Theory and Practice*, 3rd edn. New York: Columbia University Press.

Goldstein, H. (1973) *Social Work Practice: A Unitary Approach*. Columbia, SC: University of South Carolina Press.

Goldstein, H. (1977) Theory development and the unitary approach to social work practice, in H. Specht and A. Vickery (eds), *Integrating Social Work Methods*. London: George Allen and Unwin.

Holmes, L., McDermid, S., Padley, M. and Soper, J. (2012) *Exploration of the Costs and Impact of the Common Assessment Framework*. London: Department for Education.

International Federation of Social Work (2012) *Definition of Social Work*. http://ifsw.org/policies/definition-of-social-work/ (accessed 3 March 2013).

Kirst-Ashman, K.K. and Hull, G.H. (2002) *Understanding Generalist Practice*, 3rd edn. Pacific Grove, CA: Brooks Cole.

Payne, C. (1991) The systems approach, in J. Lishman (ed.), *Handbook of Theory for Practice Teachers in Social Work*. London: Jessica Kingsley.

Pincus, A. and Minahan, A. (1973) *Social Work Practice: Model and Method*. Itasca, IL: Peacock.

Pincus, A. and Minahan, A. (1977) A model for social work practice, in H. Specht and A. Vickery (eds), *Integrating Social Work Methods*. London: George Allen and Unwin.

Preston-Shoot, M. and Agass, D. (1990) *Making Sense of Social Work: Psychodynamics, Systems and Practice*. London: Macmillan Education.

Sharf, R.S. (2012) *Theories of Psychotherapy and Counselling: Concepts and Cases*, 5th edn. Belmont, CA: Brooks Cole.

Specht, H. and Vickery, A. (eds), (1977) *Integrating Social Work Methods*. London: George Allen and Unwin.

Teater, B. (in press) Social work practice from an ecological perspective, in C.W. LeCroy (ed.), *Case Studies in Social Work Practice*, 3rd edn. Belmont, CA: Brooks Cole.

3   The strengths perspective

David C. Kondrat

Introduction

The strengths perspective is a way of working with clients that shifts social workers away from a focus on clients' problems, deficits and labels towards interactions and interventions that focus on clients' strengths, abilities, resources and accomplishments. The strengths perspective is based on the fundamental belief that focusing on individual strengths, versus deficits or limitations, is the true avenue for therapeutic progress (Weick et al., 1989). Strengths-based practice can be defined as:

> [A] way of viewing the positive behaviours of all clients by helping them see that problem areas are secondary to areas of strengths and that out of what they do well can come helping solutions based upon the successful strategies they use daily in their lives to cope with a variety of important life issues, problems, and concerns.
>
> (Glicken, 2004, p. 3)

While not dismissing the pain and problems of clients, the strengths perspective emphasizes both the discovery of client strengths, which alone is cathartic, and the use of these strengths in treatment planning. The strengths perspective is often employed by social workers from assessment through to intervention and can be utilized in combination with other strengths-based approaches, such as the person-centred approach and solution-focused practice. This chapter provides an overview of the strengths perspective, a discussion of the principles of the strengths perspective and an illustration of how to apply the strengths perspective to social work practice.

The origins of the strengths perspective

Aspects of the strengths perspective have existed for many years and in various forms, particularly through such fields as philosophy and religion and through such practice approaches as person centred, empowerment and feminism. The origins of the strengths perspective as a formal theory and method began to emerge in the 1980s when social work practitioners and theorists, such as Dennis Saleebey, criticized the social work profession for focusing on pathologies, deficits and labels often fuelled by the problem-based or medical model. Historically, social work practice operated from a problem-focused approach with the roots of this approach being traced back to the Charitable Organization Society, which articulated a belief that clients suffered from moral weaknesses (Weick et al., 1989). As social workers started to view themselves as professionals and social scientists, the language of moral weakness became one of pathological diagnosis. One of the pioneers of the move away from viewing human problems in terms of moral weakness towards diagnosis was Mary Richmond, who coined the term 'social diagnosis' (Blundo, 2001). Following scientific bases of this new problem-based paradigm, once a diagnosis was made a treatment could be devised to fix the underlying problem, and without a definable diagnosis, treatment could not be provided (Weick et al., 1989).

The strengths perspective was developed by social work academics, such as Dennis Saleebey, Charles Rapp and Ann Weick, as a counter movement to the problem-focused approach to social work practice. The movement towards a strengths-based practice came from two fronts (Weick et al., 1989): (1) the value base of the profession of social work as geared towards respecting the dignity and worth of every human being, regardless of their current situation – focusing on problems, limitations or diagnoses diminishes a person to a problem-saturated label, which is antithetical to the values of social work; and (2) the diagnostically driven system which places the social worker in a position of power over the client: social workers determine what is wrong with the client and then determine how best to fix the client's problems. Strengths-based practice was developed to bring the practice of social work back to its foundation of valuing and collaborating with the client. It moved the profession from focusing on the problems and deficits as defined by the social worker or other helping professional, to identifying and focusing on the strengths, abilities and possibilities of clients through an egalitarian, collaborative relationship (Blundo, 2001). The strengths perspective continues to be explored and researched specifically through the work of the Strengths Institute at the University of Kansas.

The strengths perspective explained

Social workers must first understand the term *strength* in order to implement the strengths perspective. According to Greene and Lee (2002, p. 182) a strength involves 'the capacity to cope with difficulties, to maintain functioning in the face of stress, to bounce back in the face of significant trauma, to use external challenges as a stimulus for growth, and to use social supports as a source of resilience'. A strength can be any personal or environmental attribute that has the potential to stimulate growth and solutions (Saleebey, 2013a), and can be both within the individual and within the community in which an individual lives (Rapp and Goscha, 2011). In terms of individuals, strengths can be aspirations, competencies and confidence, and in terms of communities, strengths can be opportunities, social networks, resources and tangible services.

Table 3.1 Possible areas in which to find strengths

What people know/have learned	Education and workplace
Qualities, traits, virtues	Prior life successes
Talents	Persistence
Personal pride	Passion
Spirituality	Curiosity
Coping skills	Conviction
Cultural and personal stories and lore	Flexibility
Community	Past attempts to solve problems
Support network	Socio-political support/resources
Motivation	Health
Interpersonal relationships	Opportunities
Resiliencies	Hopes

Sources: Cowger and Snively (2002); Glicken (2004); Saleebey (2013a).

According to Saleebey (2013b), strengths can be framed within a triangle with three points: C, P and R. This triangle is referred to as the CPR of strengths and helps social workers identify clients' strengths under each of these three headings. C stands for competence, capacities and courage; P symbolizes promise, possibility, positive expectations and potential; and R signifies resilience, reserves, resources and resourcefulness. Therefore, when identifying clients' strengths, social workers must look beyond the obvious personal strengths and delve into clients' possibilities, competencies and resiliencies. Table 3.1 provides a list of areas or traits which social workers can explore with clients when assessing for strengths.

The assumptions and principles of the strengths perspective

The strengths perspective consists of the following six guiding assumptions (Saleebey, 2013b, pp. 17–20):

- Every individual, group, family and community has strengths.
- Trauma, abuse, illness and struggle may be injurious, but they may also be sources of challenge and opportunity.
- Assume that you do not know the upper limits of the capacity to grow and change and take individual, group and community aspirations seriously.
- We best serve clients by collaborating with them.
- Every environment is full of resources.
- Caring, caretaking and context.

The strengths perspective holds that social workers and clients should work collaboratively to assess for and identify strengths and resources that can be used and capitalized upon to foster client self-determination and control in order to grow and develop (Greene and Lee, 2002). These assumptions are embedded within the discussion that follows and underpin all strengths-based approaches.

The strengths perspective is comprised of a set of principles that guide the social worker in strengths-based helping. These principles represent an overarching philosophy of the strengths perspective and should be used in developing the client–social worker relationship, assessing for strengths and developing interventions that are strengths based. These principles, as described by Kisthardt (2013, pp. 59–65), include:

1   *The initial focus of the helping process is on the strengths, interests, abilities, knowledge and capabilities of each person not on their diagnosis, deficits, symptoms and weaknesses as defined by another* (Kisthardt, 2013, p. 59). Clients are often aware of the problems they are facing when they begin to work with a social worker, but they are often not aware of the positive attributes they possess and bring to the relationship (De Jong and Berg, 2008; Walter and Peller, 1992). Focusing on problems and, particularly, diagnostic labels can have a tremendously negative effect on clients. For example, clients who hold psychiatric labels often suffer from reduced life chances and weaker psychosocial functioning (Link et al., 1989). While helping clients to solve problems is an essential aspect of social work that cannot be ignored (McMillen et al., 2004), strengths-based practice places a premium on exploring and exploiting clients' strengths. Focusing on what clients do well has the effect of increasing hope, including a sense of personal agency (Greene et al., 2006). Exploring and acknowledging what clients do well will help them change their problematic view of themselves to one of capable human beings. Social workers can begin to initiate this process by showing respect and admiration for clients and taking an interest in clients' hope, dreams and aspirations (Kisthardt, 2013).

2   *The helping relationship becomes one of collaboration, mutuality and partnership. Power with another, not power over another* (Kisthardt, 2013, p. 60). One of the primary criticisms of the traditional problem-focused approach is that it places social workers in a position of power over clients. Through this approach, the social worker is an expert with answers to the client's problems. The strengths perspective holds that social workers operating as experts are not fully exploring clients' strengths, resources and assets as the social worker is operating from a pre-defined frame of reference and/or assumptions that do not consider the clients as experts of their own experiences and perceptions or as capable of solving their own problems (Saleebey, 2013b). Kisthardt (2013) argues that operating from a frame of reference is in some respects oppressing the already oppressed clients. By working collaboratively and creating a partnership, social workers and clients are acknowledging that clients have power and are capable of positively impacting their own lives versus having experts solve their problems. Further, developing a mutually collaborative

relationship provides clients with a sense of hope that they can overcome life's problems (Rapp et al., 2005).

3   *All human beings have the inherent capacity to learn, grow, and transform. People have the right to try, the right to succeed, and the right to fail* (Kisthardt, 2013, p. 62). Clients are limited by labels, which can stem from the effects of poverty, physical or neurological disability, structural oppression, stigma, discrimination and/or racism (Kisthardt, 2013). Such labels can limit society's belief in the ability of clients to grow and develop and can equally limit clients' belief in themselves. In describing her experience of having a mental illness, Gallo (1994, p. 408) writes, 'I perceived myself, quite accurately, unfortunately, as having a serious mental illness and therefore as having been relegated to what I called "the social garbage heap"'. This quote demonstrates how labels have a negative impact on the selfhood of persons holding the label. Clearly, Gallo felt that she held a low position in society. By viewing clients as capable of learning, growing and changing, social workers challenge the negative aspects of labels and encourage clients to become more than their label suggests they should become. Helping clients see that they have the inherent capacity to change can break a person free from the bonds of a label or diagnosis and provide them with the opportunity to become something new – a real person.

4   *Helping activities in naturally occurring settings in the community are encouraged* (Kisthardt, 2013, p. 64). Research on persons with serious mental illnesses suggests that client learning in office- or hospital-based settings does not translate into successful community-based mastery of taught skills (Stein and Test, 1980). Rapp and Goscha (2004) argue that an *in vivo* approach to working with clients allows for skills that are learned in treatment to generalize to the community. In addition, providing services in the community leads to greater treatment retention and allows the social worker to make a more accurate assessment of client and community strengths and resources (Rapp and Goscha, 2004). Providing services in the community further de-stigmatizes clients by recognizing that they have a right to exist in the community.

5   *The entire community is viewed as an oasis of potential resources to enlist on behalf of service participants. Naturally occurring resources are considered as a possibility first, before segregated or formally constituted 'mental health' or 'social services'* (Kisthardt, 2013, p. 65). In a problem-based model, services typically occur in formal social service agencies with the 'technology' to treat the maladies of clients. Further, social workers have often viewed the environment as a harsh contributor to client problems. Saleebey (1996, p. 19) argues that all environments, even those that may appear to be poisonous, are filled with resources, as he states, 'No matter how harsh an environment, how it may test the mettle of its inhabitants, it can also be understood as a potentially lush topography of resources and possibilities [. . .] there are individuals, associations, groups, and institutions who have something to give, something that others need: knowledge, succour, an actual resource or talent, or simply time and place'. Looking to the community, and not to the traditional treatment system, for solutions to clients' concerns, further integrates clients back into

their communities and helps them to feel less separated from humanity. It is incumbent on the social worker to help clients seek out these reservoirs of opportunities within the community and think beyond the traditional service setting.

Exercise box 3.1   Thinking of strengths

In pairs or a small group, take turns answering the following questions. Consider how your family, friends, community, culture and history affect your answers.

1   Think of a client population with which you would have trouble working and describe how you would recognize their abilities to grow, learn and change.
2   Identify three strengths within yourself.
3   Identify three strengths within your community.
4   Describe how you would develop a mutual partnership with clients.
5   Debate the relative merits of a problem-focused approach and a strengths-based approach.

The elements of a strengths-based approach

The principles of the strengths perspective provide a context from which social workers can begin to think about practice. Saleebey (2009) identifies four elements of a strength-based approach to practice that may occur sequentially or simultaneously when implementing the strengths perspective. These stages, phases or elements of practice can be used when working with individuals, families and communities. The four elements are:

1   *In the struggle – the harbingers and hints of strengths* (Saleebey, 2009, p. 104). Clients come to see a social worker because of problems, difficulties or stressors they have in their lives, whether defined as a problem by the client or from an external source (that is, courts, child welfare). In such situations, clients are often focused on the problem or stressor and do not recognize that they have strengths. In telling their painful stories, clients often drop hints of past successes, coping skills, hopes and aspirations. While listening to the clients' story of their problems, social workers should always be on the lookout for strengths and, when appropriate, reflect these strengths back to the client. For example, 'It sounds like you have a really strong family support system' or 'You've been really successful in managing your work and parenting responsibilities'. The work on identifying clients' strengths begins at first contact.
2   *Stimulate the discourse and narratives of resilience and strengths* (Saleebey, 2009, p. 104). As the conversation continues, social workers need to help clients move from talking in terms of pathology and problems, towards conversations

of strengths and capacity. This step may be difficult as clients' identification of strengths and resources is buried under years of self-doubt, self-blame or blame from others, or oppression from others and/or society. The social worker should model this behaviour of identifying strengths and resources with clients and affirm the clients' own recognition of their strengths and capacities. This process involves the social worker assessing and identifying strengths, providing statements to clients that reflect their strengths and discussing possibilities with clients that will fit into their daily lives.

3   *Acting in context: the project* (Saleebey, 2009, p. 104). In addition to being able to identify their own strengths, clients must learn the language of strengths and be able to see themselves as full of strengths and capabilities. Clients should identify their hopes and goals and capitalize on their strengths and external resources in moving themselves towards their goals. As this project is to be collaborative, social workers will assume a brokerage or advocacy role where they link the clients to external resources or work with clients to oppose barriers that will move the clients towards their goals.

4   *Move toward normalizing and capitalizing on one's strengths* (Saleebey, 2009, p. 105). As clients move through treatment, their abilities to recognize their own strengths and the strengths in their community, as well as their ability to use these strengths, need to be reinforced and normalized. Clients need to be able to take what they have learned in the work with the social worker and apply it to the rest of their lives.

Two additional aspects of strengths-based practice need to be amplified. The first is the strengths assessment. While many practitioners argue that they practise from the strengths perspective, they merely pay lip service to the approach where 'often, the strengths assessment is consigned to a few lines at the end of the evaluation or planning form' (Saleebey, 1996, p. 303). According to Cowger (1994, p. 264), the assessment of client strengths is fundamental to the strengths perspective as he argues: 'If assessment focuses on deficits, it is likely that deficits will remain the focus of both the worker and the client during the remaining contacts. Concentrating on deficits or strengths can lead to self-fulfilling prophecies'. By assessing strengths, social workers and clients are setting the groundwork for finding solutions. Every client, including persons who are homeless and/or impoverished, has strengths. The purpose of the strengths assessment is not to deny the reality of the problem facing clients but to focus on what the client can contribute to her or his own care. Table 3.2 lists Cowger and Snively's (2002) 12 guidelines for a strengths assessment.

The second aspect is the use of language. The strengths perspective requires the social worker to use language purposefully (Saleebey, 2013b). Social workers are encouraged to talk in the language of strengths, possibilities, aspirations and hopes. Conversely, social workers are encouraged to de-emphasize problem-saturated talk and labelling or diagnosing (Saleebey, 2001). When clients return to problem-oriented talk, De Jong and Miller (1995, p. 735) suggest, 'the worker listens, empathizes, and gently returns them to defining their goals for a more desirable future'. Social workers can utilize solution-focused questions (see Chapter 10) to continue the use of strengths

Table 3.2 Twelve guidelines for a strengths assessment

1	Give pre-eminence to the client's understanding of the facts as the client is the expert in her or his experiences
2	Believe the client as clients are ultimately trustworthy
3	Discover what the client wants from the work together
4	Move the assessment towards personal and environmental strengths and away from problems and obstacles
5	Make assessment of strengths multidimensional, assessing on the personal, interpersonal and socio-political levels
6	Use the assessment to discover the uniqueness of each client
7	Use the client's words when writing an assessment and defining strengths
8	Make assessment a joint activity between worker and client
9	Reach a mutual agreement on the assessment, which is to be opened and shared
10	Avoid blame and blaming as this focuses on problems and not strengths and stalls the process from moving forward
11	Avoid cause-and-effect thinking as this leads to blaming
12	Assess; do not diagnose

Source: Cowger and Snively (2002, pp. 221–5).

language (De Jong and Miller, 1995; Greene et al., 2006). Such questions can include the following: (1) survival questions – identifying past and current survival or coping skills ('How have you managed to survive thus far?'); (2) support questions – identifying the support networks/people in the client's life ('Who have you been able to rely upon?'); (3) exception questions – identifying when things were better in the client's life, or the problem was reduced ('When were things going just a little better for you? What was different during those times?'); and/or (4) possibility questions – identifying the client's hope, dreams, goals and aspirations ('What do you want for your life? Where do you want to be in five years?') (Saleebey, 2009, pp. 102–3).

Case example: applying the strengths perspective to practice

Sally, a white British female, was 23 when she was diagnosed with schizophrenia. She was told by her treating psychiatrist that her symptoms were treatable with medication, but the diagnosis was not curable and she would be unlikely to work. Her psychiatrist recommended she see a community mental health social worker. You are the community mental health social worker who works from the strengths perspective. At your first meeting with Sally, she describes her experience of being diagnosed with a mental illness. She states that the voices had started 20 months earlier and that they scared her. While being diagnosed with schizophrenia gave her an answer to her fears, the diagnosis was itself fear inducing. She describes her past success in school and in the workforce and her ability to participate in social activities, but discusses how this all 'went out the window' when she began to hear voices. You begin to assess that Sally has several strengths, such as intelligence and the ability to do well in school and the workforce (*competencies and possibilities*), a clear insight into her presenting problem (*competencies and possibilities*) and her resilience to her experience of hearing voices (*resilience; CPR of strengths*). The mere fact that Sally had agreed to meet with you and discuss her experiences shows hope for a positive future.

To further delve into Sally's strengths and resources, you ask about the voices (*in the struggle – the harbingers and hints of strengths*). 'The voices,' Sally said, 'told me that I was alone in the world and not to trust anyone. They said that I needed to become self-reliant.' You ask Sally, 'How did you manage to cope with hearing the voices?' (*survival questions*) Sally reports that now that she looks back on the experience, she realizes that she managed to keep her life together despite hearing the voices. She reports that she spent a lot of time alone and often thought about harming herself, but the thought of leaving her family and friends stopped her. You then ask, 'When are there times the voices are not so troubling?' (*exception questions*) Sally stated that she did not hear the voices as often once she started the medication and she never heard the voices when she was with her family or playing on the computer. Inquisitively, you ask her to describe what it was about being around her family that lessened the impact of the voices (*stimulate the discourse and narratives of resilience and strengths*). Sally said that she believed that being around her family scared the voices. Her family has always been a strong support in her life, and the voices would be lying to her if they said she was alone. You then ask if this was true when she was around other people (*support questions*). Sally stated that the voices got worse when she was in big crowds, but better when she was with her closest friends. Searching for the strengths in Sally's social network, you ask how often she visits with friends and family (*stimulate the discourse and narratives of strengths*). Sally had moved home with her parents, but spent most of her time in her room alone. As for her friends, she rarely saw them. Building on Sally's strengths and resources, you encourage Sally to spend just a little more time with her family and friends (*acting in context: the project*).

At your next meeting with Sally, you ask about the time she had spent with family/friends (*stimulate the discourse and narratives of resilience and strengths*). Sally stated that she actually reconnected with her friend Andy and they talked about what had been going on in her life. Andy agreed to remain in contact and to be of whatever help he could to Sally. In addition, she stated that she spent less time in her room and more time helping her father cook and clean the house (*acting in context: the project*). She openly stated that the voices were less troublesome when she helped her father and was with her friend Andy.

Realizing Sally's strengths of motivation, insight, resilience and external support, you turn the conversation over to discussion of future goals. In tears, Sally states that she has given up on doing much more than just living. You respond by asking, 'What did you want to do before you were diagnosed?' (*possibility question*). Sally reports she wanted to be a graphic designer. You point out to Sally her past successes in school and in the workforce, and remind her that she had said that playing on the computer was one way to combat her voices. You ask Sally if she would be interested in revisiting her goal of becoming a graphic designer. Sally states that she would. Over the next several months, you and Sally put together a plan for Sally to go back to school (*acting in context: the project*). The plan is completed in consultation with Sally's psychiatrist and with her family. You and Sally involve Andy and her family in transportation to and from school. Sally earns a degree in graphic design. In consultation with Sally and colleagues, Sally applies for open positions at several local graphic design shops. You and Sally practise her interviewing skills together in preparation for the interview and discuss how Sally might capitalize on her strengths when in the workforce (*move towards normalizing and capitalizing on one's strengths*).

Strengths and limitations

There are several identified strengths and limitations to utilizing the strengths perspective in social work practice. The strengths include:

- The strengths perspective is an empowerment-based approach. Strengths-based practice is developed on principles and assumptions that view each client, family and community as having strengths and the ability to grow and develop. The approach requires a collaborative partnership between social worker and client to assess for strengths, address problems and difficulties, and capitalize on existing or newly found strengths and resources that can be utilized in the future.
- The strengths perspective can be used in combination with other theories and methods. The general principles and assumptions of the strengths perspective can serve as a foundation for the work that social workers conduct with clients. For example, social workers may utilize the strengths perspective when conducting an assessment and then implement motivational interviewing in an attempt to help a client change a specific behaviour.
- The strengths perspective seeks to assess strengths and resources on the individual, interpersonal and socio-political levels. This multidimensional assessment enables social workers and clients to determine any structural oppression or discrimination that is contributing to the client's problem or prohibiting the client from attaining a goal. Social workers often take an advocacy or brokerage role in working with clients to utilize the necessary strengths and resources to reach goals.
- Strengths-based practice can be utilized in a variety of settings and with clients who present with a variety of problems. Strengths-based practice is implemented in community practice, the criminal justice system, substance abuse settings, with older adults and with individuals through case management.

Saleebey (1996) articulates four major criticisms of the strengths perspective and responds to each as follows:

- The strengths perspective is merely positive thinking in disguise. Rather than being a series of phrases or ideas a person repeats to them, the strengths perspective utilizes personal and environmental strengths to create a meaningful future for clients.

- The strengths perspective is really reframing misery. The strengths perspective acknowledges the pain, misery and reality of clients' lived experiences. Rather than merely reframing clients' misery and/or deficits, the strengths perspective helps clients 'to develop an attitude and language about the nature of possibility and opportunity and the nature of the individual beneath the diagnostic label' (Saleebey, 1996, p. 302).

- The strengths perspective is absurdly optimistic. The strengths perspective recognizes that there are persons who may be beyond help. However, the strengths perspective recognizes that individuals have within themselves the ability to grow and change. Rather than first assuming that a client is beyond help, the strengths perspective encourages social workers to start with a view of the client in front of them that is based on possibilities and change.

- Another criticism of the strengths perspective is that it ignores the reality of client problems. While the strengths perspective focuses on using client and community strengths to help clients reach a preferred future, the perspective does not deny the cathartic value of hearing client's painful stories or the need to evaluate client's problems. However, understanding client's problems is not enough. In the conversations clients and social workers have with each other, including conversations about clients' problems, the social worker seeks out clients' strengths that can be used to rectify the presenting problem and move clients towards their desired goals.

- Gray (2011) argues that the strength perspective is rooted in a neoliberal view of reality that diminishes the responsibility of the state welfare system to care for clients. Individuals are responsible for creating change. As a result of this view, the strengths perspective, 'fails to take account of the evidence of the relationship between structural inequalities, such as race and class, or of mental illness, poverty, and so on' (p. 8). Rather than working to change or challenge structures of oppression that are the root causes of many client problems, the strengths perspective requires that individuals find solutions to their own problems without considerations of the larger cultural and community contexts of the problem. For example, persons who are unemployed, including highly employable individuals, living in an impoverished community may find it hard to find work unless businesses are attracted to the community. Social workers will need to engage in system-level change efforts to increase employment opportunities.

Ethical and cultural considerations

A core belief of a strengths-based social worker is a positive view of human nature and of human society. Rather than ignoring culture, the strengths perspective recognizes that strengths can be found in different cultural traditions. Lee (2003, p. 387) writes: 'Clinicians operating from a strengths perspective should be curious about and appreciative of the cultural strengths in clients. They can assist the client to fully recognize and utilize their cultural strengths and resources in the treatment process'.

Social workers should be open to the way in which clients' cultures define strengths, particularly as one culture's strength may be another culture's weakness. Therefore, the collaborative relationship between social worker and client is essential as the client is the expert on her or his life, experiences and culturally specific strengths and resources.

One important aspect of culture is spirituality. Eichler et al. (2006) have written of the importance of recognizing spirituality as a source of great strength. They articulate a number of principles that can be used in understanding a strengths-based under-standing of spirituality the following two of which are relevant for this discussion: (1) 'Respect the diverse religious and nonreligious expression of spirituality in client's life context' (Eichler et al., 2006, p. 70). Rather than ignoring a client's lived religious or spiritual experiences, a strengths-based practice embraces the role of spirituality as a strength that can be drawn on to help clients move towards desired goals; and (2) 'Establish cooperative patterns of referral and collaboration with spiritual leaders and mentors in the community as relevant to clients' spiritual perspective' (Eichler et al., 2006, p. 70). Social workers practising from a strengths-based approach need to help the client recognize the strengths that exist within their religious communities. This includes integrating spiritual and cultural contexts of religion and spirituality in both the strengths assessment and goal development phases of treatment. The Church of Jesus Christ of Latter-Day Saints (LDS), which is one of the fastest growing religions in the world, has developed strong helping networks to ensure that members of the LDS faith have support during times of hardship (Walton et al., 2011). The LDS church has a built-in welfare system to help individuals and families who may need material or social support. Utilizing indigenous religious support can enable individuals to develop long-lasting plans for positive growth and change.

Anti-oppressive practice and the strengths perspective

A core principle of the strengths perspective is that all individuals have the capacity to grow and change. The focus of practice and assessment under the strengths perspective should be on clients' strengths not their deficits (Kisthardt, 2013). Therefore, social workers need to believe in the inherent ability of all clients to change and help clients identify, amplify and utilize their inherent strengths. Social workers begin this process through a collaborative relationship with the client where the client is viewed as the expert in her or his experiences and perspectives. Social workers should conduct a multidimensional strengths assessment where they assess the strengths and resources on individual, interpersonal and socio-political levels. Clients may experience blocks to resources on interpersonal and/or socio-political levels, due to poverty, structural oppression, discrimination and/or racism, and in such situations social workers and clients will need to take action to combat the blocks and attempt to create access.

Blocks to resources are often a result of stigma or oppression. One group of clients that has been historically stigmatized is persons with mental illness, including self-stigmatization (Kondrat and Teater, 2009). The strengths perspective recognizes that this discriminated against group has strengths and the inherent capacity to grow

(Greene et al., 2006). Strengths-based social workers are responsible for emancipating persons from the labels. Saleebey writes:

> The number of people who suffer from disorder and disorganization in their mental and interpersonal life suffer enough without having to experience an iatrogenic push towards chronicity and a social nudge towards alienation. As social workers, given our value commitments, we must do what we can to leaven the intense preoccupation with symptoms and labelling with an equally intense preoccupation with understanding life's real problems and the virtues of people who suffer them. The work of constructing an institutional edifice of the possible and the promising, of virtues and visions, must begin now and must be taken seriously.
>
> (2001, p. 186)

Clearly, the strengths perspective pushes the social worker to look beyond stereotypes and focus on the capabilities of all clients to move towards a meaningful future. In addition, the strengths perspective seeks to emancipate clients from the negative aspects of oppression, discrimination, racism and labels and accompanying stereotypes.

Research on the strengths perspective

Strengths-based practice has been applied to work with a number of client populations, and research has been conducted to evaluate the effectiveness of this approach with these populations. Though applied to multiple areas of social work practice, including child welfare (Early and GlenMaye, 2000), ageing and long-term care (Fast and Chapin, 1996; Sullivan and Fisher, 1994), child welfare/child mental health (Early, 2001; Early and GlenMaye, 2000), social policy and community development (Chapin, 1995; Weick and Saleebey, 1995), run away/homeless youth (Lindsay et al., 2000), and corrections (Clark, 2001), the most convincing research on strengths-based practice comes from the mental health literature. Community-based mental health case management is one area in which strengths-based practice has been applied (Rapp and Goscha, 2011). Research suggests that when applied to work with persons with major mental illnesses, strengths-based practice is an effective approach. Using the strengths-based approach to working with persons with severe mental illness, Rapp and Chamberlain (1985) found that 61 per cent of client goals were achieved and Rapp and Wintersteen (1989) found that 79 per cent of client goals were achieved. Björkman et al. (2002) found that strengths-based case management was superior to treatment as usual for clients with severe mental illness in relation to satisfaction with treatment, number of hospital days and number of hospital admissions. Finally, Barry et al. (2003) found that clients in a strengths-based programme had more positive perceptions of their quality of life and reduced symptom severity compared with clients receiving assertive community treatment, which is the dominant model of community care for persons with a severe mental illness. Despite the research on strength-based practice, no randomized clinical trial has examined the effectiveness of this model of care. In order to determine the true impact of the strengths approach to practice, rigorous experimental research is needed.

Summary

The strengths perspective is a social work theory and method that honours and respects the potential of all humans. As an approach, strengths-based practice assumes that all humans and communities have strengths that can be used to help clients achieve their aspirations and desired goals. Unlike most approaches to practice, strengths-based practice focuses on what clients are already successfully doing and seeks to utilize these strengths to help clients achieve their full potential. At the crux of the strengths-based approach is the strengths-based assessment that encourages both the social worker and client to focus on what the client is already doing or has the capacity to do to help the client achieve self-determined goals. While not forgetting that clients have problems, the strengths-based approach focuses on clients' strengths to help clients counter their problems and move towards a self-defined satisfying life.

Case study

Toby is a 16-year-old, white British male, who has been having trouble in school and with his family. Toby's mother reports that he has been spending too much time with his friends engaged in 'illegal activities'. His mother believes that Toby is using marijuana and other illegal substances. Toby admits to using marijuana, but states that his passions are for football and fixing cars. Toby does not like school and believes that he should join the workforce. Toby still lives with his parents, but hopes to move out soon. He does not think that school is a priority and wants a job. He has tried to apply for a few jobs, but has been unsuccessful so far. Describe how you could approach this situation utilizing the strengths perspective.

Further reading and web resources

De Jong, P. and Miller, S.D. (1995) How to interview for client strengths, *Social Work*, 40(6): 729–36.
    Provides readers with an operationalization of the strengths perspective by connecting it to solution-focused practice.
Glicken, M.D. (2004) *Using the Strengths Perspective in Social Work Practice: A Positive Approach for the Helping Professions*. Boston, MA: Pearson Education.
    Explores the basic premises of the strengths perspective and provides examples of how to apply this approach to practice.
Rapp, C.A. and Goscha, R.J. (2011) *The Strengths Model: A Recovery-oriented Approach to Mental Health Services*. New York: Oxford University Press.
    A discussion of the strengths perspective to working with persons with mental illness.

Saleebey, D. (ed.) (2013) *The Strengths Perspective in Social Work Practice*, 6th edn. Boston, MA: Pearson Education.

    A collection of essays that describe the principles and practices of the strengths perspective in general terms and with different client groups.

The University of Kansas Strengths Institute: http://data.socwel.ku.edu/strengths/

References

Barry, K.L., Zeber, J.E., Blow, F.C. and Valenstein, M. (2003) Effect of strengths model versus assertive community treatment model on participant outcomes and utilization: two-year follow-up, *Psychiatric Rehabilitation Journal*, 26(3): 268–77.

Björkman, T., Hansson, L. and Standlund, M. (2002) Outcome of case management based on the strengths model compared to standard care. A random controlled trial, *Social Psychiatry and Psychiatric Epidemiology*, 37(4): 147–52.

Blundo, R. (2001) Learning strengths-based practice: challenging our personal and professional frames, *Families in Society*, 82(2): 296–304.

Chapin, R.K. (1995) Social policy development: the strengths perspective, *Social Work*, 40(4): 506–14.

Clark, M.D. (2001) Influencing positive behavior change: increasing the therapeutic approach of juvenile courts, *Federal Probation Quarterly*, 65(1): 18–27.

Cowger, C. (1994) Assessing client strengths: clinical assessment for client empowerment, *Social Work*, 39(3): 262–8.

Cowger, C.D. and Snively, C.A. (2002) Assessing client strengths, in A.R. Roberts and G.J. Greene (eds), *Social Worker's Desk Reference*. New York: Oxford University Press.

De Jong, P. and Berg, I.K. (2008) *Interviewing for Solutions*, 3rd edn. Belmont, CA: Thompson.

De Jong, P. and Miller, S.D. (1995) How to interview for client strengths, *Social Work*, 40(6): 729–36.

Early, T.J. (2001) Measures for practice with families from a strengths perspective, *Families in Society*, 82(3): 225.

Early, T.J. and GlenMaye, L.F. (2000) Valuing families: social work practice with families from a strengths perspective, *Social Work*, 45(2): 118–30.

Eichler, M., Deegan, G., Canda, E.R. and Wells, S. (2006) Using the strengths assessment to mobilize spiritual resources, in K.B. Helmeke and C.F. Sori (eds), *The Therapist's Notebook for Integrating Spirituality in Counseling: Homework, Handouts, and Activities for Use in Psychotherapy*. Binghamton, NY: Hawthorn Press.

Fast, B. and Chapin, R. (1996) The strengths model in long-term care: linking cost containment and consumer empowerment, *Journal of Case Management*, 5(2): 51–7.

Gallo, K.M. (1994) First person account: self-stigmatization, *Schizophrenia Bulletin*, 20(2): 407–10.

Glicken, M.D. (2004) *Using the Strengths Perspective in Social Work Practice: A Positive Approach for the Helping Professions*. Boston, MA: Pearson Education.

Gray, M. (2011) Back to basics: a critique of the strengths perspective in social work, *Families in Society*, 92(1): 5–11.

Greene, G.J. and Lee, M.Y. (2002) The social construction of empowerment, in M. O'Melia and K.K. Miley (eds), *Pathways to Power: Readings in Contextual Social Work Practice*. Boston, MA: Allyn and Bacon.

Greene, G.J., Kondrat, D.C., Lee, M.Y., Clement, J., Siebert, H., Mentzer, R.A. and Pinnell, S.R. (2006) A solution-focused approach to case management and recovery with consumers who have a severe mental disability, *Families in Society*, 87(3): 339–50.

Kisthardt, W.E. (2013) Integrating the core competencies in strengths-based, person-centered practice: clarifying purpose and reflecting principles, in D. Saleebey (ed.), *The Strengths Perspective in Social Work Practice*, 6th edn. Boston, MA: Pearson.

Kondrat, D.C. and Teater, B.A. (2009) An anti-stigma approach to working with persons with severe mental disability: seeking real change through narrative change, *Journal of Social Work Practice*, 23(1): 35–47.

Lee, M.Y. (2003) A solution-focused approach to cross-cultural clinical social work practice: utilizing cultural strengths, *Families in Society*, 84(3): 385–95.

Lindsay, E.W., Kurt, D., Jarvis, S., Williams, N.R. and Neckerud, L. (2000) How runaway and homeless youth navigate troubled waters: personal strengths and resources, *Child and Adolescent Social Work*, 17(2): 115–40.

Link, B.G., Cullen, F.T., Struening, E., Shrout, P.E. and Dohrenwend, B.P. (1989) A modified labeling theory approach to mental disorders: an empirical assessment, *American Sociological Review*, 54(3): 400–32.

McMillen, J.C., Morris, L. and Sherraden, M. (2004) Ending social work's grudge match: problems versus strengths, *Families in Society*, 85(3): 317–25.

Rapp, C.A. and Chamberlain, R. (1985) Case management services for the chronically mentally ill, *Social Work*, 30(5): 417–22.

Rapp, C.A. and Goscha, R.J. (2004) The principles of effective case management of mental health services, *Psychiatric Rehabilitation Journal*, 27(4): 319–33.

Rapp, C.A. and Goscha, R.J. (2011) *The Strengths Model: A Recovery-oriented Approach to Mental Health Services*. New York: Oxford University Press.

Rapp, C.A. and Wintersteen, R. (1989) The strengths model of case management: results from twelve demonstrations, *Psychosocial Rehabilitation Journal*, 13(1): 23–32.

Rapp, C.A., Saleebey, D. and Sullivan, W.P. (2005) The future of strengths-based social work, *Advances in Social Work*, 6(1): 79–90.

Saleebey, D. (1996) The strengths perspective in social work practice: extensions and cautions, *Social Work*, 41(3): 296–305.

Saleebey, D. (2001) The diagnostic strengths manual?, *Social Work*, 46(2): 183–7.

Saleebey, D. (2009) Introduction: power in people, in D. Saleebey (ed.), *The Strengths Perspective in Social Work Practice*, 5th edn. Boston, MA: Allyn and Bacon.

Saleebey, D. (2013a) The strengths approach to practice: beginnings, in D. Saleebey (ed.), *The Strengths Perspective in Social Work Practice*, 6th edn. Boston, MA: Pearson.

Saleebey, D. (2013b) Introduction: power in people, in D. Saleebey (ed.), *The Strengths Perspective in Social Work Practice*, 6th edn. Boston, MA: Pearson.

Stein, L.I. and Test, M.A. (1980) Alternative to mental hospital treatment: I. conceptual model, treatment program, and clinical evaluation, *Archives of General Psychiatry*, 37(4): 392–7.

Sullivan, W.P. and Fisher, B.J. (1994) Intervening for success: strengths-based case management and successful aging, *Journal of Gerontological Social Work*, 22(1–2): 61–74.

Walter, J.L. and Peller, J.E. (1992) *Becoming Solution-focused in Brief Therapy*. New York: Brunner/Mazel.

Walton, E., Limb, G.F. and Hodge, D.R. (2011) Developing cultural competence with latter-day saint clients: a strengths-based perspective, *Families in Society*, 92(1): 50–4.

Weick, A., Rapp, C., Sullivan, W.P. and Kisthardt, W. (1989) A strengths perspective for social work practice, *Social Work*, 34(4): 350–4.

Weick, A. and Saleebey, D. (1995) Supporting family strengths: orienting policy and practice toward the 21st century, *Families in Society*, 76(3): 141.

4   Empowerment and use of language

Introduction

A prominent aim within social work is to work with clients to gain or regain power and control over various aspects of their lives. In attempting to combat this lack of power, or the inability to obtain resources to meet one's wants and needs, social workers participate in the process of empowerment. Whereas power 'involves the capacity to influence for one's own benefit the forces that affect one's life space' (Hopps et al., 1995, p. 44), empowerment is a 'process involving the creative use of one's personal resources to gain and use power to control one's life circumstances, achieve personal goals and improve relational and communal good' (Greene et al., 2005, p. 268). Empowerment involves individuals and communities obtaining resources that will increase their spiritual, political, social or economic strength in order to obtain greater control over their environment and move towards their personal or communal aspirations (Hasenfeld, 1987). The empowerment approach can be utilized collaboratively with individuals, groups or communities. This chapter explores the empowerment approach by discussing the basic premises and characteristics, the use of language and the application of the approach to social work practice.

The origins of empowerment

The ideas of empowerment have existed for centuries. Empowerment, or self-help, can be found in the mutual aid and friendly societies in Britain, which date back to the eighteenth century (Leadbetter, 2002). Such groups allowed poorer people to deposit money into a friendly society to save for the future, and to pay for their funeral or to borrow money through the not-for-profit society (Adams, 2009). The settlement movement, particularly the work of Jane Addams, women's clubs and social reform clubs of African Americans of the nineteenth century in the United States are all evidence of an empowerment-based approach (Lee and Hudson, 2011). Hull House, one of the settlement homes in Chicago, Illinois, consisted of women and men working with oppressed groups in order to share resources and mutually provide for basic needs (Lee and Hudson, 2011). Empowerment was more widely evidenced in the United States in the late 1960s with social and political activism of oppressed groups (Leadbetter, 2002) particularly the civil rights movement and the work of Dr Martin Luther King Jr.

Empowerment theory in social work is relatively new and has drawn from other social science disciplines, such as political science, psychology, sociology, economics and religion (Lee and Hudson, 2011). The major theorists of the empowerment approach in social work, such as Barbara Bryant Solomon (1976), Ron Mancoske and Jeanne Hunzeker (1989), all stressed that empowerment involves individuals taking control of their lives and influencing their surroundings in order to obtain the necessary resources. Empowerment is a process and an outcome and, while social workers can participate and help in this process with clients, the process ultimately resides with the client (Lee and Hudson, 2011).

The empowerment approach is grounded in the ecological perspective (see Chapter 2) as theorized by Gitterman and Germain (2008), which makes connections between the person and her or his environment and highlights the interdependence of social and economic justice and individual pain and suffering (Lee and Hudson, 2011). In examining the interdependence and interaction between the person and environment, the empowerment approach can be utilized collaboratively with individuals, groups, communities and/or society.

Empowerment explained

Empowerment can be viewed as both a theory and a method. Empowerment as a theory holds that individuals who have power and control over their lives, in the sense that they are able to access the necessary resources to meet their needs and rights, are able to thrive and develop. Empowerment as a method is defined in the Dictionary of Social Work as 'any process whereby those lacking, comparatively, in power become or are helped to become more powerful' (Pierson and Thomas, 2010). This definition highlights that empowerment as a method consists of challenging those individuals and systems who are currently preventing individuals, groups and/or communities from holding the power and control over the aspects that are crucial to meeting their own needs and rights and, thus, shifting this power and control to those who are marginalized or oppressed (Leadbetter, 2002). Empowerment as a concept is best defined as: 'The capacity of individuals, groups and/or communities to take control of their circumstances, exercise power and achieve their own goals, and the process by which, individually and collectively, they are able to help themselves and others to maximise the quality of their lives' (Adams, 2008, p. 17). This definition stresses the ability of those who are marginalized or oppressed to obtain power and control over their lives, often termed 'self-empowerment' (Adams, 2008), and dictate the necessary routes they need to travel in order to help themselves obtain a quality of life.

According to Greene et al. (2005) the presence of empowerment in individuals, groups or communities is evidenced by a high degree of self-determination, self-esteem, competence in living, self-efficacy and an internal rather than external locus of control. Therefore, a lack of empowerment can be evidenced by a low self-esteem, learned helplessness and an external rather than internal locus of control. Table 4.1 provides

Table 4.1 Psychological terms explained

Term	Definition
Self-esteem	A person's sense of self-worth
Self-efficacy	A person's belief in her/his ability to succeed in situations (Bandura, 1997)
Learned helplessness	Over time, persons learn to be helpless because they see no connection between actions and outcomes; they believe they have no control over situations (Seligman, 1975)
Locus of control	The attitudes of people about the control they have over their life circumstances (Rotter, 1954)
External	Persons believe their life is controlled by external forces, such as fate, chance or powerful others
Internal	Persons believe they control their life

definitions for these psychological concepts. Parsons (2002) identifies specific presenting problems that demand empowerment-based practice, such as isolation, depression, alienation, feeling hopeless, learned helplessness and/or a need for community connections.

When faced with an individual, group or community who expresses these characteristics and/or who are being marginalized or oppressed, social workers should implement an empowerment-based approach. The goal of the approach is to increase the personal, interpersonal and political power of the individual, group or community in order to have them feel empowered rather than powerless and therefore take control over their situation and/or self (Greene et al., 2005). According to Lee and Hudson (2011, p. 163), there are three interconnected dimensions of empowerment, which consist of the following: (1) 'the development of a more positive and potent sense of self; (2) the construction of knowledge and capacity for more critical comprehension of the web of social and political realities of one's environment; and (3) the cultivation of resources and strategies, or more functional competence, for attainment of personal and collective social goals, or liberation'. Therefore, individuals, groups or communities are to be critically conscious and have knowledge of the oppression they experience and are to nurture a healthy personality development, including a heightened sense of self-esteem, identity and direction, which leads to power and the ability to influence others (Lee and Hudson, 2011).

Basic assumptions

The empowerment approach holds the following four basic assumptions, the first three of which are described by Lee and Hudson (2011):

1   *Oppression is a structurally based phenomenon that affects individuals and communities.* Oppression can lead to many negative outcomes on individuals

and communities, such as death due to inadequate healthcare, homicide and suicide or other forms of violence, individuals being more readily targeted for incarceration or even an increase in general hopelessness leading to self-doubt, despair or false beliefs. When such structural oppression is recognized, one must attempt to tackle both the self and the environment. This type of structural oppression is best represented through Thompson's (2012) PCS model (see Chapter 1) which highlighted how discrimination and oppression against an individual is often embedded in the individual's cultural and societal norms, values, customs and structures. Interventions can include forming strong support networks for people of the community with similar experiences in order to alleviate the negative self-perceptions and gain a sense of unity. Negative community thoughts and beliefs can be challenged and reframed into more valid, positive realities that are acceptable to the self and/or community (Lee and Hudson, 2011).

2   *People and communities have strengths and resources to solve immediate problems and are resilient to the effects of institutionalized oppression and the structures that maintain it.* All individuals, groups and communities are seen as having strengths and resources to combat their problems, although their environment may be limiting or blocking access to certain resources. The goal is to acknowledge and foster the strengths of the individuals or community in order to overcome existing problems, combat the oppression and discrimination, and create routes to utilize the previously blocked resources.

3   *Empowerment involves focusing on individuals and their environment.* When using an empowerment-based approach, individuals must address their personal strengths and resources and participate in empowerment work, but the empowerment work must also address the environment within which the individuals live, which is highlighted through Thompson's PCS model (see Chapter 1). As the person and environment are seen as being independent and interconnected, empowerment-based work must address both systems. If empowerment work aims to challenge the oppression from the environment that is negatively affecting individuals, then the work must target both the oppressed and the oppressor to truly create positive change (Lee and Hudson, 2011).

4   *Empowerment is a process and an outcome.* Empowerment work, or the process of individuals, groups or communities gaining power and control over their lives, leads to an end goal of being empowered and having the necessary strengths, resources, power and control in order to grow and develop. This end goal is ultimately achieved through social change and justice (Howe, 2009). In this sense, empowerment is not just something that you do, nor is it just something that you work towards, but rather empowerment is a process and an outcome (Greene et al., 2005). The empowerment approach is a developmental process that can begin with the individual, yet seeks to end with social change that prohibits future oppression and enables individuals to access resources and hold power and control over their lives (Parsons, 1991).

Applying empowerment to practice

To apply the empowerment-based approach to practice, one must acknowledge that every individual, group or community has strengths and resources and the current lack of power is a result of a block to or non-use of resources, particularly due to direct and indirect discrimination and oppression. Therefore, an empowerment-based approach works on a multisystem level to focus on the strengths and resources of the individual, interpersonal and environmental levels in order to restore power and self-efficacy to oppressed and disempowered populations (Parsons, 2002). The focus includes an assessment of the person:environment interactions and how individuals are affected by their environments and environments affected by individuals and where interventions are necessary in order to restore power to individuals, group or communities so they can meet needs, gain rights and achieve goals.

The empowerment process involves a collaborative approach where clients self-define their problems, actively engage in interventions to acknowledge and combat oppression, and participate in joint decision-making. Lee and Hudson (2011, p. 163) state that 'the empowerment process resides in the person, not the helper'.

There are two specific stages in the empowerment approach, which often overlap: (1) assessment and (2) intervention. Each of these stages are discussed in turn.

Assessment

In adhering to the ecological perspective, as well as Thompson's (2012) PCS model, which acknowledges the interdependence and interactions of persons and their environments, social workers are to assess and attempt to foster change in three areas of the client's life: (1) personal, (2) interpersonal and (3) socio-political (Parsons, 2002). The assessment of the person would include examining attitudes, values and beliefs about self-efficacy, self-esteem, self-worth and their belief in having rights as a person or a member of a larger entity. The interpersonal assessment includes an examination of how the person views themselves in relation to others, such as work, the ability to form networks and systems of mutual aid, and the necessary knowledge and skills in order to interact and participate with others. Finally, the socio-political assessment includes an examination of clients' actions and participation in society and their ability to influence the larger environment (Parsons, 2002). The social worker must assess power, powerlessness, strengths and resources in relation to these three areas of the client's life.

The assessment process is not a matter of ticking boxes, but rather is obtained through clients telling their stories. Clients' stories may include the oppression they are experiencing at the present time, but can also include a description of the oppression of their past. The social worker views the client as the expert in her or his situation and therefore should seek to obtain the problem as defined by the client. Although the presenting problem may not specifically be 'oppression', the experience of oppression should be included as one of the areas for intervention when utilizing the empowerment-based approach (Lee and Hudson, 2011).

Intervention

The empowerment-based approach does not specify a time limit for working with clients, and the interventions can vary depending on the assessment and the number of systems that require a change. The empowerment approach can also serve as one of several methods in working with clients. For example, a social worker might include the empowerment approach when working with a client involved in a drug and alcohol treatment centre where motivational interviewing is being used to assist the client in moving through the stages of change, and the empowerment approach is being used to combat the discrimination and stigma received by the client due to her or his drug use. Therefore, the type of intervention, the estimated length of involvement and the systems that are the focus of intervention should be decided in collaboration with the client and jointly agreed.

As stated above, the assessment needs to be multifaceted to include the individual, interpersonal and socio-political levels. Once the assessment is complete and areas for intervention identified, the social worker and client are to jointly agree what type of interventions are necessary. Additionally, when keeping the ecological perspective as the foundation of the empowerment-based approach, the social worker and client are to consider interventions at both the individual and environmental levels. When examining the individual level, Gitterman and Germain (2008) reminds us that there are certain attributes that individuals need in order to grow and develop in interaction with the environment. The following attributes, as described by Lee and Hudson (2011), should advise our interventions and be connected to the end goals:

1   *Motivation.* Social workers can assist in fostering motivation by adhering to some of the basic principles of the person-centred approach (Rogers, 1959), such as unconditional positive regard, empathy and congruence (see Chapter 7). The social worker should encourage the client to identify and define her or his problems as well as future goals and should provide support, empathy and understanding of the oppression that clients experience. Motivation is enhanced and sustained by the supportive social worker–client relationship as well as the client's environment when positive consequences and incentives are received. Once motivation exists, the individual can only sustain it through receiving the necessary resources, such as food, clothing, shelter, and financial and emotional support. Therefore, the social worker and client work towards overcoming identified problems and accessing and sustaining the strengths and resources from the person and environment (Lee and Hudson, 2011).

2   *Problem-solving skills.* Once the client has identified and defined the problem(s), the social worker and client work together to create solutions to combat the problem and identify skills that could be used to address future problems. The problem-solving skills not only include addressing the presenting problem, but also any connected problems that contribute to oppression (Lee and Hudson, 2011). These skills can include either of the following techniques:

(a) *Consciousness raising.* This technique focuses on addressing the reality of oppression by identifying actual situations within the environment and discussing how these situations directly or indirectly affect the individual. This technique is often combined with critical education, which involves exploring and questioning how individuals view oppressive situations and how they can possibly view them in new ways. For example, if working with a female who is oppressed within her work situation, the social worker may provide information on the wage differences between men and women to initiate a discussion of how this client has been personally affected by this type of oppression. By identifying and analysing these situations individuals become more aware of how the oppression affects them and others around them and ways in which they can combat them; this results in a change in thinking and doing. The worker's responsibility includes providing the information to stimulate discussion in order to raise the conscious acknowledgement of oppression and to provide understanding and empathy in regard to the feelings and experiences of the client.

(b) *Cognitive restructuring.* Cognitive restructuring (Berlin, 1983) may need to take place where the normal ways in which the clients view themselves or their situations is restructured into something more positive for them (Lee and Hudson, 2011). For example, a woman in recovery from substance misuse may believe that she is not capable of attending university because she has 'failed at everything I do'. The social worker can attempt to reconstruct this negative view by highlighting the ability of the woman to overcome her substance misuse and how this strength to cope with difficulties can serve as a tool to completing university work.

3 *Maintenance of psychological comfort.* Social workers and clients work together to identify the oppression being experienced and how this has affected the clients' thoughts and feelings about themselves and their identified community or group. Any negative thoughts and feelings are explored and the social worker and clients evaluate their validity and place the negative effects of oppression on the correct system. This process allows the client to reduce feelings of self-blame and replace them with an acknowledgement of her or his strengths, accomplishments and resources, which enhances self-esteem (Lee and Hudson, 2011).

4 *Self-esteem.* Maintaining a good level of psychological comfort and being able to manage feelings can lead to a good level of self-esteem. Self-esteem can be enhanced by workers validating clients' feelings and experiences with oppression, and by the worker identifying and acknowledging client achievements and attributes, which the client is then able to own (Lee and Hudson, 2011).

5 *Self-direction.* Clients establish a sense of self-direction where they have more control over the events in their life and how they respond or react to such events. Clients are able to access the resources necessary for their growth and development and to meet their defined future goals (Lee and Hudson, 2011).

Therefore, interventions focused at the individual level should seek to incorporate end goals of increasing motivation, consciousness-raising, psychological comfort, self-esteem and self-direction and could include acknowledging and supporting strengths, challenging false beliefs, fostering pride, identifying and solving problems, engaging in dialogue about problems, beliefs and solutions, and building collectivity (Lee and Hudson, 2011). Interventions at the interpersonal and socio-political levels can include consciousness-raising, critical education and cognitive restructuring, as well as political advocacy where direct and indirect oppression are highlighted and alternative methods of interaction suggested. One simple way to create an environment conducive to supporting empowerment at the individual, interpersonal and/or socio-political level is through the social worker's use of language.

The use of language in social work practice

The use of language in social work practice is one simple way of either empowering or oppressing a client. As language is the primary means of interaction between individuals, social workers should evaluate the extent to which their language can be interpreted by clients. Greene et al. (2005) discuss how the meaning of words is arbitrary and vague. Certain words, such as angry, depressed, excited, sad and happy all mean something different to each person, and each person will experience feelings and emotions differently. Therefore, words can often be subject to misinterpretation and misunderstanding. As social workers use language in assessment and interventions, they should be cautious to explore the potential meaning to the words they use.

Empowering clients through language

Greene et al. (2005) specify five areas or ways in which social workers can empower clients through the use of language:

1   *The language of collaboration versus the language of help*. Social workers and clients working in collaboration is a fundamental aspect of the empowerment approach. Therefore, the social worker should use words that emphasize the collaborative relationship versus a relationship where the social worker is seen as the expert and the client as one who is seeking help. For example, the use of the phrase, 'How can I help you?' can send a message that there are two people in the relationship: a helper (the social worker) and a helpee (the client). Greene et al. (2005, p. 271) suggest that in order to foster a collaborative relationship, acknowledge that the client is the expert in her or his experiences and share the power in the relationship, the social worker should ask questions such as, 'What do you want for yourself today?' or 'What can we work on together to achieve what you want for your family?'.

2   *The language of ownership*. In creating an empowering environment, social workers should give clients the credit they deserve, which includes the

ownership of their strengths and ability to make changes in their lives versus believing that change can only occur through external forces. Clients who are disempowered or oppressed will often not take ownership of their accomplishments and strengths. For example, a student who receives positive feedback on a piece of work in her social work placement may state that she only received the positive feedback because the placement supervisor is friendly and kind ('My placement supervisor gave me positive feedback because she is friendly and kind'). The student is not taking credit for the good work she did, but rather is giving the credit to an external force (the placement supervisor). In such situations, the social worker should encourage the client to use the word 'I' and take credit for her accomplishments ('I received positive feedback on my work because I worked hard and was effective in my practice'). Greene et al. (2005, p. 272) suggest using phrases such as 'What do you want to accomplish by coming here today?' versus 'What problems bring you in today?' or 'How do you feel about that?' versus 'How does that make you feel?'.

3   *The language of possibilities.* Social workers should create an environment of possibilities versus blocks for clients. In communicating with clients, social workers may need to use reframing where they take a phrase, word or description used by the client and reframe or interpret it into something more positive and acceptable to the client. For example, if a client states 'I'm a bad mum because I have to work two jobs and can't stay home with my kids', the social worker could reframe this as, 'you really care about your children and you're making sure you provide for them'. Reframing can encourage clients to see the positives and strengths in their lives, and to see alternatives or possibilities to their problem situations.

4   *The language of solutions.* Social workers and clients should use language that focuses on solutions versus problems. As Greene et al. (2005, p. 272) state, focusing on solutions points clients in the direction of 'noticing, identifying, amplifying and reinforcing their existing strengths, competencies, resources and potentials'. Asking the clients how they have coped in the past can provide valuable lessons and strategies for how to cope in the future. Using solution-focused questions, such as 'When are there times that you are feeling just a little less depressed than usual?' allows clients to acknowledge past coping strategies and enables them to formulate plans for addressing current and future problems.

5   *The language of elaboration and clarification.* Encouraging clients to elaborate and clarify situations allows for social workers and clients to fully explore the clients' stories and the evidence for and against their current belief systems. For example, Greene et al. (2005) state that disempowered or oppressed clients can often use language of deletion, where certain aspects or traits of a client are deleted while others are overemphasized ('I'm too lazy to go back to school'), or generalization, where a client generalizes a negative experience or trait to all aspects of her or his life ('I'm a failure at everything'). When such language is used, social workers should encourage elaboration and

clarification about the evidence for and against these traits in an attempt to emphasize how the client may be falsely criticizing or oppressing her- or himself.

Exercise box 4.1   Your thoughts on empowerment

1   From your personal or professional experience, discuss how language has made you feel empowered or disempowered.
2   Should social workers self-disclose their own experiences with oppression?
3   How do you envisage using empowerment in your social work practice?
4   Identify a constraint to empowerment and how you would attempt to overcome this barrier.

Case example: an empowerment-based approach to practice

Hannah is a 24-year-old, white British female who has recently entered an alcohol and drug residential treatment centre after her son, Sam (aged 7), was taken into care. Hannah has completed a detox programme for alcohol use and is beginning a 12-week inpatient programme. You are the social worker at the alcohol and drug treatment centre and are aware of the oppression and stigma often experienced by individuals who misuse substances. You have an initial meeting with Hannah to discuss her life and future. As you adhere to an empowerment approach, you begin your work with Hannah by conducting an assessment that examines power, powerlessness, strengths and resources on the personal, interpersonal and socio-political levels.

You allow her to talk and tell her story (*client self-defines problems and goals*). Hannah discloses that she started using alcohol when she was 12 years old after her mother's boyfriend, Paul, had sexually abused her. Hannah remembers telling her mother about the abuse, but her mother stated she was making it up to get attention and told Hannah she never wanted to hear her mention it again. Hannah reports that the abuse continued throughout her teenage years and she used alcohol to 'numb the pain'. She states she left home when she turned 16 and moved into her boyfriend's home (Mark, aged 30 at the time). Hannah describes how Mark was physically and emotionally abusive. After Hannah had their son, Sam, she left Mark and moved back in with her mother, who had since separated from Paul.

Hannah reports that her alcohol use 'spiralled out of control' after her mother unexpectedly passed away and Hannah fell into a state of depression. She continued to become more reliant on alcohol and reports that she would drink throughout the day, often 'passing out' and leaving Sam alone. Children and Family Services became involved after the school reported concerns over Sam's appearance and comments about his mum sleeping all day long. Children and Family Services worked with Hannah to keep Sam with her, but she was unable to control her alcohol use and Sam was taken into care. Hannah reports she desperately wants Sam back with her, but she isn't sure that will happen as she fails at everything she does. You make a mental note of the motivation Hannah is expressing in that her ultimate goal is to have Sam back and living with her.

You encourage Hannah to elaborate on the evidence that she fails at everything she does (*language of elaboration/clarification*). Hannah recalls how she dropped out of school, was in a bad relationship with Mark, her mother never believed her about the abuse from Paul, and she lost her son. You empathize with Hannah about these very difficult experiences, but you also remind her that she has successfully completed detox and has voluntarily entered treatment, which is a great accomplishment. Hannah reports feeling sad and alone and states she has little to look forward to without Sam in her life. You ask Hannah to describe the times since being in treatment when she has felt a little less sad than usual (*language of solutions*) and she describes feeling better when receiving a letter from Sam or when she counts the number of days since she has been sober and thinks about being with Sam again. You acknowledge that these could be useful tools for Hannah as she works towards her recovery and to her goal of reuniting with Sam (*language of possibilities*).

In this assessment process, you are able to identify that Hannah is currently feeling helpless and has a low sense of self-worth and self-esteem. Hannah feels that she does not have control over her life, and you assess that she has experienced oppression from her interpersonal relationships and is self-stigmatizing. You also realize that Hannah is working to deadlines set by Children and Family Services to regain custody of Sam, which feels overwhelming and, sometimes, unrealistic for her. Despite this, Hannah presents as a strong survivor of physical, sexual and emotional abuse from her mother, Paul and Mark. Hannah does not have any siblings or close friends to draw support from, but she is actively engaged in the treatment centre and is bonding with other females in her group activities. Additionally, Hannah has been open and honest with you and is fully engaged in the treatment process; she is clearly showing signs of motivation to regain custody of her son.

You ask Hannah what she would like the two of you to work on together while she is at the treatment centre (*language of collaboration*) and what she would like to accomplish for herself (*language of ownership*). Hannah has decided that she would like to establish the following goals for herself: (1) finish the inpatient treatment and continue to remain sober; (2) get a job to support herself and Sam; (3) get accommodation where she and Sam can live together; and (4) have Sam come home. In addition to these goals, you and Hannah agree to work on the perception that Hannah has of herself as a 'bad mother who fails at everything she does'. This will be accomplished by exploring the actions that Hannah is taking to regain custody of Sam and the progress she is making (*language of possibilities/solutions*). You will provide Hannah with information about alcohol addiction and recovery and examine how the skills and strengths she is obtaining while in recovery can be transferred to her life with Sam outside of alcohol misuse (*problem-solving skills*). You both plan to meet twice a week for at least 30 minutes each time to work towards these goals (*collaboration*).

The interventions agreed by both you and Hannah include the following: (1) individual counselling, where you and Hannah can discuss her thoughts and feelings about her past experience, future plans and sense of self (*increase motivation, psychological comfort, self-esteem and self-direction*); (2) task-centred practice, where you and Hannah work towards exploring educational and training opportunities, job skills and opportunities for employment once she leaves the centre; and (3) advocacy work and problem-solving skills, where you and Hannah work with Children and Family Services to document the progress Hannah is making and work to reunite Hannah and Sam, as well as work on skills that Hannah can take forward with her in the future.

Strengths and limitations

There are several identified strengths and limitations to utilizing empowerment in social work practice. The strengths include:

- Clients are the experts in their experiences and situations. The empowerment approach views the clients, not the social workers, as the experts on the clients' experiences and situations, and therefore, seeks to give clients the power and control they need in order to foster positive growth and development. The work of the social worker and client is to be conducted in collaboration with a relationship that is egalitarian in nature.
- Empowerment-based approaches are anti-oppressive in nature. The actual use of the empowerment-based approach is a form of anti-oppressive practice as it seeks to give clients the power and control to tackle the oppression that is limiting or blocking clients from needed resources.
- The approach provides skills and tools for clients to use after the social work involvement has ceased. Owing to empowerment being a process and an outcome, the work of the social worker and client, such as formulating coping skills, consciousness-raising, political advocacy and identification of strengths, resources and accomplishments should continue on the part of the client after the social worker has ended involvement.
- The empowerment approach can be used simultaneously with other methods. A thorough use of the empowerment approach would involve connecting with the client on the individual level and building a relationship that validates the person's experiences, but then considering interventions on multiple levels to unblock access to resources and challenge discrimination and oppression. For example, a social worker may utilize cognitive behavioural therapy with a child who misbehaves in the classroom, but may utilize empowerment approaches to explore the child's sense of self-worth and self-esteem, and the impact of the school's approach towards his behaviour.

The limitations include:

- Empowerment may be diluted to enablement (Adams, 2003; Leadbetter, 2002). Empowerment is evidenced by people having power and control over their lives and the ability to access resources in order to support their growth and development. When utilizing an empowerment-based approach, social workers should strive to give power and control to clients in order for them to make decisions and provide for themselves rather than social workers doing so for clients and creating a dependent relationship or continuing an oppressive environment.

- Empowerment may not be the same for everyone. What one individual or group may see as empowering, another individual or group may find disempowering (Adams, 2003). This limitation highlights the necessity to work in collaboration with clients and elicit from clients what they would find to be empowering given their experiences and situations.
- The empowerment process may be taken too far (Adams, 2003). There may be some situations where social workers are seeking to provide empowering environments for clients, yet in the process lose sight of the individual needs of the clients. Social workers need to be mindful of the type and amount of work that can be handled without losing any of the quality or depth of work.
- Social work practice is not always empowering (Adams, 2008; Lee and Hudson, 2011). Many social workers will work in agencies where clients are mandated to receive services, such as child protection or substance misuse. In such circumstances the very nature of the work can appear disempowering for the mandated clients as they are being 'forced' to work with the social workers and may not agree the identified goals in the work together. Social workers should attempt to minimize the extent to which the experience is disempowering for clients by attempting to build a relationship with them, collaborating with and involving them in decision-making, and being open and honest about the social worker's and agency's role.

Ethical and cultural considerations

The empowerment-based approach is considered appropriate for anyone who experiences issues of oppression as long as the individual has cognitive and emotional abilities to complete the work (Lee and Hudson, 2011). The social worker must consider the cultural implications for empowerment as one individual or group's definition of empowerment might be another individual or group's disempowerment (Adams, 2003). Therefore, the social worker and client must work collaboratively to address the problem as defined by the client and to meet the goals as established by her or him. The goals should be in adherence to the social work profession's values, principles and ethics.

Lee and Hudson (2011) stress that social workers need both clinical and political knowledge in order to use an empowerment-based approach. Social workers need to understand the oppression and struggles that individuals face, due to individual experiences, such as mental illness or substance misuse, as well as oppression from the environmental or political systems, such as sexism, racism and/or stigma. Social workers should participate in self- and critical-reflection to evaluate how their own experiences of oppression may affect their work with clients from both similar and different backgrounds. Supervision and/or peer support is crucial in ensuring that social workers are not participating in countertransference and are using self-disclosure only when appropriate (Lee and Hudson, 2011).

Empowerment-based approach and anti-oppressive practice

The empowerment-based approach is a form of anti-oppressive practice. When utilizing the empowerment-based approach, the social worker is attempting to challenge the oppression and lack of resources as experienced by clients and to work collaboratively with clients in order to strengthen their power and control over their lives. There is a 'preference for working with people who are poor, oppressed and stigmatized to strengthen individual adaptive potentials and promote environmental/structural change through individual and collective action' (Lee and Hudson, 2011, p. 166). The work is to be completed in partnership where the client is viewed as the expert in her or his life and is to define the problem and goals that is the focus of the work together. As Thompson's (2012) PCS model highlights (see Chapter 1), anti-oppressive practice must involve a consideration of the personal, cultural and societal processes and structures, and how the three are embedded with one another. Social workers and clients can participate in an empowerment-based, anti-oppressive approach on an individual, interpersonal and/or socio-political level in order to fully address the oppression that is negatively affecting clients. Social workers will need to have multiple perspectives – such as historical, ecological, feminist, critical, cultural and global – to fully assess clients' situations and determine the most appropriate intervention (Lee and Hudson, 2011). Social workers may carry this work beyond the individual work with a client by promoting policies, programmes and agency procedures that are anti-oppressive and empowering for the clients who are affected by the policies or are recipients of the services.

Research on empowerment

Empowerment as a stand-alone method is difficult to research as empowerment-based approaches are often combined with other methods, such as groupwork or community educational or service programmes. Empowerment can also be seen as an outcome of other programmes or models of working, such as the recovery model in mental health services (Sowers, 2012) or the personalization agenda (Gardner, 2011), although the latter has been disputed as being empowerment-based (see Dodd, 2013). The majority of research on the effectiveness of empowerment-based approaches has included some aspect of groupwork. For example, women who have experienced intimate partner violence were found to have lower levels of traumatic stress after participating in the Moms' Empowerment Program (MEP) (Graham-Bermann and Miller, 2013); yet a meta-analysis of the extent to which Youth Empowerment Programs (YEPs) impacted on self-esteem, self-efficacy and other social, emotional and behavioural outcomes were inconclusive, with the authors highlighting the need for more rigorous research to determine the true effectiveness of the programmes (Morton and Montgomery, 2013). Empowerment-based educational programmes are increasingly being used within healthcare settings to help increase knowledge of health-related issues and enhance quality of life. An empowerment-based educational programme for individuals with Type II diabetes was found to enhance quality of life and physical activity, and reduce the negative impacts of diabetes (Molsted et al., 2012). Alternatively, numerous studies examine the extent to which particular programmes enhance the empowerment of those individuals involved. For example, peer support and buddy programmes for people living with HIV/AIDS reported greater personal growth and empowerment (Marino et al., 2007); parents of children with disabilities involved in a group-based manualized parent education group reported more empowerment than that of a control group (Farber and Maharaj, 2005); and a community service intervention was found to enhance African American custodial grandmothers' knowledge, advocacy and self-efficacy as measured by the Family Empowerment Scale (Whitley et al., 2011).

Valid and reliable scales that measure empowerment are useful tools when determining if an intervention is effective in enhancing empowerment. Such scales include the Empowerment Scale (Rogers et al., 2010), the Family Empowerment Scale (Koren et al., 1992), Women's Empowerment Scale (Nanda, 2011), and the Organizational Empowerment Scale (Matthews et al., 2003). Generally, empowerment can be evidenced by a greater self-image, self-worth, sense of control, improvement in problem-solving skills, and a greater sense of knowledge about the effects of the environment on the individual (Itzhaky and York, 2000; Segal et al., 1995).

Summary

The empowerment-based approach seeks to address the oppression and lack of power and control of individuals, groups or communities. Empowerment is considered a process and an outcome where social workers and clients collaborate to challenge oppression and gain greater access to resources within the environment to assist the clients to better meet their needs. Social workers can utilize the empowerment-based approach in assessments by exploring the power, powerlessness, strengths and resources at the individual, interpersonal and socio-political levels. Interventions can target any or all of these systems with an ultimate goal of the client having an increase in motivation, psychological comfort, self-esteem, self-direction and the ability to problem-solve in order to access needed resources.

Case study

Tom is a 46-year-old male of dual heritage who was referred to an adult social services physical disabilities team after experiencing a permanent spinal injury from a car accident. Tom has been told he will not be able to walk again. He is ready to be discharged from hospital, and you are the social worker assigned to assess his needs to live at home. The hospital notes on Tom show he is a biology teacher, divorced, and has two children (aged 16 and 14) who live with their mother. Tom's parents live in the same town as Tom. You enter Tom's hospital room and the first thing he says is, 'My life is over. I don't know how I will ever be able to cope like this.'

Discuss how you could employ the empowerment approach in your work with Tom. Consider assessing and intervening on the personal, interpersonal and socio-political areas of Tom's life.

Further reading

Adams, R. (2008) *Empowerment, Participation and Social Work*, 4th edn. Basingstoke: Palgrave Macmillan.

Examines empowerment and participation at the individual, group, community, organization and political levels.

Lee, J.A.B. and Hudson, R.E. (2011) Empowerment approach to social work practice, in F.J. Turner (ed.), *Social Work Treatment: Interlocking Theoretical Approaches*, 5th edn. Oxford: Oxford University Press.

An overview of the history and basic assumptions of empowerment as well as case studies of how to use empowerment approaches in practice.

Mullender, A. (2013) *Empowerment in Action*. Basingstoke: Palgrave Macmillan.

Explores the use of an empowerment approach in groupwork.

References

Adams, R. (2003) *Social Work and Empowerment*, 3rd edn. Basingstoke: Macmillan.

Adams, R. (2008) *Empowerment, Participation and Social Work*, 4th edn. Basingstoke: Palgrave Macmillan.

Adams, R. (2009) Advocacy and empowerment, in R. Adams, L. Dominelli and M. Payne (eds), *Critical Practice in Social Work*, 2nd edn. Basingstoke: Palgrave Macmillan.

Bandura, A. (1997) *Self-efficacy: The Exercise of Control*. New York: Freeman.

Berlin, S. (1983) Cognitive behavioral approaches, in A. Rosenblatt and D. Waldfogel (eds), *The Handbook of Clinical Social Work*. San Francisco, CA: Jossey-Bass.

Dodd, S. (2013) Personalisation, individualism and the politics of disablement, *Disability and Society*, 28(2): 260–73.

Farber, M.L.Z. and Maharaj, R. (2005) Empowering high-risk families of children with disabilities, *Research on Social Work Practice*, 15(6): 501–15.

Gardner, A. (2011) *Personalisation and Social Work*. Exeter: Learning Matters.

Gitterman, A. and Germain, C.B. (2008) *The Life Model of Social Work Practice: Advances in Theory and Practice*, 3rd edn. New York: Columbia University Press.

Graham-Bermann, S.A. and Miller, L.E. (2013) Intervention to reduce traumatic stress following intimate partner violence: an efficacy trial of the Moms' Empowerment Program (MEP), *Psychodynamic Psychiatry*, 41(2): 329–49.

Greene, G.J., Lee, M.Y. and Hoffpauir, S. (2005) The language of empowerment and strengths in clinical social work: a constructivist perspective, *Families in Society*, 86(2): 267–77.

Hasenfeld, Y. (1987) Power in social work practice, *Social Service Review*, 61(3): 469–83.

Hopps, J.G., Pinderhuges, E. and Shankar, R. (1995) *The Power to Care: Clinical Practice Effectiveness with Overwhelmed Clients*. New York: Free Press.

Howe, D. (2009) *A Brief Introduction to Social Work Theory*. Basingstoke: Palgrave Macmillan.

Itzhaky, H. and York, A.S. (2000) Empowerment and community participation: does gender make a difference?, *Social Work Research*, 24(4): 225–34.

Koren, P.E., DeChillo, N. and Friesen, B.J. (1992) Measuring empowerment in families whose children have emotional disabilities: a brief questionnaire, *Rehabilitation Psychology*, 37(4): 305–21.

Leadbetter, M. (2002) Empowerment and advocacy, in R. Adams, L. Dominelli and M. Payne (eds), *Social Work: Themes, Issues and Critical Debates*, 2nd edn. Basingstoke: Palgrave Macmillan.

Lee, J.A.B. and Hudson, R.E. (2011) Empowerment approach to social work practice, in F.J. Turner (ed.), *Social Work Treatment: Interlocking Theoretical Approaches*, 5th edn. Oxford: Oxford University Press.

Mancoske, R.J. and Hunzeker, J.M. (1989) *Empowerment Based Generalist Practice: Direct Services with Individuals*. New York: Cummings and Hathaway.

Marino, P., Simoni, J.M. and Silverstein, L.B. (2007) Peer support to promote medication adherence among people living with HIV/AIDS: the benefits to peers, *Social Work in Health Care*, 45(1): 67–80.

Matthews, R.A., Diaz, W.M. and Cole, S.G. (2003) The organizational empowerment scale, *Personnel Review*, 32(3): 297–318.

Molsted, S., Tribler, J., Poulsen, P.B. and Snorgaard, O. (2012) The effects and costs of a group-based education programme for self-management of patients with type 2 diabetes: a community study, *Health Education Research*, 27(5): 804–13.

Morton, M.H. and Montgomery, P. (2013) Youth empowerment programs for improving adolescents' self-efficacy and self-esteem: a systematic review, *Research on Social Work Practice*, 23(1): 22–33.

Nanda, G. (2011) *Compendium of Gender Scales*. Washington, DC: FHI 360/C-Change.

Parsons, R.J. (1991) Empowerment: purpose and practice principles in social work, *Social Work with Groups*, 14(2): 7–21.

Parsons, R.J. (2002) Guidelines for empowerment-based social work practice, in A.R. Roberts and G.J. Greene (eds), *Social Workers' Desk Reference*. New York: Oxford University Press.

Pierson, J. and Thomas, M. (2010) *Dictionary of Social Work: The Definitive A to Z of Social Work and Social Care*. Maidenhead: Open University Press.

Rogers, C.R. (1959) A theory of therapy, personality, and interpersonal relationships as developed in the client-centered framework, in S. Koch (ed.), *Psychology: A Study of Science: Formulations of the Person and the Social Context*. New York: McGraw-Hill.

Rogers, E.S., Ralph, R.O. and Salzer, M.S. (2010) Validating the empowerment scale with a multisite sample of consumers of mental health services, *Psychiatric Services*, 61(9): 933–6.

Rotter, J.B. (1954) *Social Learning and Clinical Psychology*. New York: Prentice-Hall.

Segal, S.P., Silverman, C. and Temkin, T. (1995) Measuring empowerment in client-run self-help agencies, *Community Mental Health Journal*, 31(3): 215–27.

Seligman, M.E.P. (1975) *Helplessness: On Depression, Development and Death*. San Francisco, CA: W.H. Freeman.

Solomon, B.B. (1976) *Black Empowerment: Social Work in Oppressed Communities*. New York: Columbia University Press.

Sowers, W.E. (2012) Recovery and person-centered care: empowerment, collaboration, and integration, in H.L. McQuistion, W.E. Sowers, J.M. Ranz and J. Maus Feldman (eds), *Handbook of Community Psychiatry*. New York, NY: Springer.

Thompson, N. (2012) *Anti-discriminatory Practice: Equality, Diversity and Social Justice*, 5th edn. Basingstoke: Palgrave Macmillan.

Whitley, D.M., Kelley, S.J. and Campos, P.E. (2011) Perceptions of family empowerment in African American custodial grandmothers raising grandchildren: thoughts for research and practice, *Families in Society*, 92(4): 110–19.

5 Social constructivism

Introduction

Social constructivism is a recently developed theory that gained wide attention after Berger and Luckman (1966) wrote *The Social Construction of Reality* in which they examined the sociology of knowledge and reality creation. Berger and Luckman explored how individuals create knowledge, make sense of the world around them, and construct reality and a view of themselves. Reality refers to the state of things as they actually exist and includes everything that is observable and comprehensible. Reality in this sense refers to how people view and understand the world around them, how they make sense of themselves and what they see, feel and believe to be real. This process is explained by Berger and Luckman:

> Man is biologically predestined to construct and to inhabit a world with others. This world becomes for him the dominant and definitive reality. Its limits are set by nature, but once constructed, this world acts back upon nature. In the dialectic between nature and the socially constructed world the human organism itself is transformed. In this same dialectic man produces reality and thereby produces himself.
>
> (1966, p. 168)

Social constructivism is a relatively new system of thought within social work and can also be found in disciplines such as psychology, counselling, sociology, philosophy and linguistics. Social constructivism is used to explain social problems and reality construction, and to address individual and family therapy, social problems and research. The theory of social constructivism was built on social constructionism, which Gergen (2003, p. 15) describes as being 'principally concerned with explicating the processes by which people come to describe, explain, or otherwise account for the world (including themselves) in which they live'. Building on social constructionism, social constructivism attempts to explain individuals' reality and how these realities are constructed based on the social context, interaction with other individuals and perceptions of the world. Before continuing in the discussion of social constructivism, one should acknowledge that there are several different approaches or degrees that exist within social constructivism, such as social constructionism, strict constructionsim, constructivism, feminist constructionism, and radical constructivism, some of which will be described in more detail below. This chapter explores the main theory of social constructivism (oftentimes referred to as critical constructionism in the literature) by examining the history and basic premises of the theory, the assumptions about human behaviour, functioning and the role of the social environment, and the application of the theory to social work practice.

The origins of social constructivism

The basic ideas of social constructivism can be traced back to philosophical developments that flourished several hundred years ago (Carpenter, 2011; Witkin, 2012). The philosophers Giambattista Vico, Hans Vaihinger, Immanuel Kant, Friedrich Nietzsche and Karl Marx, and psychologists Lev Vygotsky, Jean Piaget and George Kelly were instrumental in initiating thought around knowledge development and the influence of psychological, cognitive or sociological factors in this process. Carpenter (2011) acknowledges more modern day theoreticians, such as Paul Watzlawick, Ernst von Glaserfeld and Heinz von Foerster as contributing to the development of social constructivist ideas particularly through their examination of 'realness' or 'reality as observer-dependent'. The theory of social constructivism penetrated other disciplines after Berger and Luckman (1966) wrote *The Social Construction of Reality*, at which time the idea began to be used in social problems theory in the 1960s and 1970s. The theory's basic principles were identified in other sociological theories such as Schutz's (of whom Berger was a student) phenomenological sociology, which examines the social experiences of individuals and how they make them meaningful, and Garfinkle's ethnomethodolgy, a research methodology which explores the way in which people make sense of the world, interact and communicate with others and assist in the creation of social order. The basic theory proposed by Berger and Luckman purports that social problems are also socially constructed and therefore this theory has been used in social problems theory within sociology (Franklin, 1995). Elements of social constructivism have been incorporated in theories used in social work for a number of years, such as the strengths perspective, solution-focused practice, person-centred approach and narrative therapy, but only recently has been formally recognized within social work (Carpenter, 2011).

The original ideas proposed by Berger and Luckman have since been refined or separated into several sub-theories and understanding the similarities and differences between these adapted theories is necessary in determining what theory best fits with social work values. For example, as Table 5.1 indicates, social constructionism emphasizes the influence of the use of language within interpersonal relationships in creating one's reality as well as the influence of history, society and culture (Franklin, 1995; Gergen, 2003; Greene and Lee, 2002). Constructivism places the emphasis of reality construction on one's biology, developmental processes and cognitive structures (Franklin, 1995; Greene and Lee, 2002). Finally, social constructivism, as discussed in this chapter, posits 'that while the mind constructs reality in its relationship to the

Table 5.1 Clarifying terms

Social constructionism	• Reality is constructed through the use of language in interactions with society; social processes are essential to reality construction
Constructivism	• Reality is constructed by one's biology, processes and cognitive structures; the human mind is essential to reality construction
Social constructivism	• Reality is equally constructed by both individual and social factors

world', this mental process is significantly informed by influences from social relationships' (Gergen, 1999, p. 60). More simply stated, social constructionism focuses on the sociological aspects that influence and help shape or create reality for a person (more of an influence of nurture) and constructivism focuses on the psychological and neurological aspects of an individual and how these assist and create reality for the person (more of an influence from nature). Social constructivism acknowledges that the psychological, neurological and sociology aspects work in combination (a joint influence of nature and nurture) and help to create and shape an individual's reality.

Social workers should practise from a systems theory or ecological perspective (Gitterman and Germain, 2008) where there is a knowledge that individuals interact with their physical, social and cultural environments and a change in one of these systems can cause a change in another. Based on this foundational knowledge, social constructivism is more closely aligned with social work by acknowledging the influence that both the individual and the environment play on reality construction. According to Carpenter (2011), social constructivism should be viewed as a philosophical-behavioural-methodological thought system. From this thought system, the philosophical underpinnings of social constructivism is concerned with 'the nature of reality and being (metaphysics and ontology) and the nature and acquisition of human knowledge (epistemology)', the behavioural aspect is concerned with 'certain understandings of human perception and cognition, personal and interpersonal dynamics, and the nature and execution of change' (p. 117–18). Finally, the philosophical and behavioural thoughts provide the rationale to a methodological approach to social work practice (described later in this chapter).

Social constructivism explained

Social constructivism believes that 'human beings do not find or discover knowledge so much as we construct or make it . . . we do not construct our interpretations in isolation but against a backdrop of shared understandings, practices, language, and so forth' (Schwandt, 2000, p. 197). People come to know the world by interacting with other people, organizations and institutions, and if we accept this presumption then we need to acknowledge that these experiences are different from person to person (Greene et al., 1996). When taking a social constructivist approach, we value each person's life experiences and acknowledge that each individual can experience situations very differently, particularly when one is influenced by social and/or cultural values (Greene and Lee, 2002). If we acknowledge that everyone has a distinct and unique view of reality, then how do we come to know and understand others' view of reality? We can attempt to begin to understand another's view of reality through the use of language. The basic premises of social constructivism are detailed below.

Basic premises

These are as follows:

1   *Individuals have their own reality and their own way of viewing the world.* An individual's reality is created by the individual and no other individual has the same reality. No one can experience or fully understand another individual's reality directly as it is developed by the events experienced in the world and the individual's values and beliefs about these experiences, which are influenced by the culture of which she or he is a member (Laird, 1993; Middleman and Wood, 1993). As individuals experience the world, and therefore mould their reality accordingly, the individuals attempt to describe their reality to others using words, either verbally or non-verbally (Laird, 1993).

2   *'People are active participants in developing their knowledge of the world, rather than passive recipients of stimulus–response interaction with their environment'* (Greene and Lee, 2002, p. 180). Individuals do not create their view of reality on their own, nor do they become passive and allow society to completely form their views of reality. Rather, individuals participate in this process of reality construction by interacting with the environment and processing these experiences through their own cognitions (Gergen, 1985; 2003). Individuals' realities are continually changing and adapting to the various experiences which they are encountering in their life. Despite experiencing events that are out of their control, individuals are able to help shape their reality of the event. For example, there is no denying that there was a bomb at the Boston marathon on the 15th of April, 2013 resulting in several people dead and hundreds injured, but what we do not know is how different people experienced this tragic event. Even two people that were together during the event will have different realities; they will have different feelings, recollections and views of what happened. Their realities have been changed due to this experience and those who did not experience the Boston marathon bombing will never know exactly what that experience was like.

3   *An individual's reality and knowledge is placed in a historical and cultural context; the reality is developed through social interactions within these historical and cultural contexts* (Gergen, 1985). This premise focuses on the historical and cultural environment that has an influence on how an individual will interpret an experience, and how this experience will shape the individual's reality. Individuals experience and interpret the world, as well as developing knowledge and meaning, based on the current social processes and the

current values and beliefs of their culture or subculture (Dean and Fleck-Henderson, 1992; Franklin, 1995; Middleman and Wood, 1993). These values and beliefs are usually determined by the dominant members of society and thus if an individual's reality does not agree with the dominant culture she or he is considered abnormal. Through social interchange within a culture or subculture, knowledge and meaning are created and are influenced and sustained by the various institutions within that culture (Dean, 1993; Witkin, 1995). Therefore, individuals construct their own reality based on their experiences, but these experiences take place within a historical and social context, which influence the interpretation of their experiences. For example, if you talk to someone who lived in the UK during the Second World War when sugar was rationed you might discover that this individual has stocked up on sugar and has several bags in the pantry. You can then talk to others who did not experience this historical event and ask them how they view and use sugar; the perceptions will most likely be different and such differences can be attributed to experiencing historical events.

4   *Language is used to express an individual's reality.* Language is the means by which individuals, with their own constructed reality, attempt to explain their reality and attempt to understand the reality of others (Witkin, 2012). Words are arbitrary. Agreement on the meaning of terms used in language develops based on actions in society that individuals agree to express or describe using a particular term; this differs by social class and sector of society. For example, the majority of individuals in society agree on the socially constructed term 'anger' which is often expressed by the raising of one's voice or shouting, fast movement of arms and hands, or a furrowed brow or clinching of the jaw. Therefore, when individuals see someone who exhibits one or more of these visual or verbal traits they believe the person to be angry. Yet, we really do not know how anger is felt internally from person to person, and the only way to attempt to understand how anger is really felt and experienced by another is for the person to express this through language.

5   *'Reality is what "we" agree on; Truth is agreement'* (Carpenter, 2011, p. 121). With individuals constructing their own reality, which no one else is able to completely understand, there is an argument that an objective external world may exist, but we cannot 'know this world directly but only indirectly through the filtering mechanisms of perception, cognitive, affect, belief systems, and language' (Carpenter, 2011, p. 120). The term 'objective' means based on observed facts and, according to this theory, individuals cannot bypass their reality to understand an objective world. This is best explained by Greene and Lee (2002, p. 180), 'There is no such thing as an objective observer because the very act of observing changes that which is being observed'. Individuals' constructed realities determine how they view the world and therefore cannot view the world without their reality, values and beliefs shaping their perceptions (Dean, 1993). 'Reality is what "we" agree on [where] the "we" can refer a unit as small as a dyad or as large as a society' (Carpenter, 2011, p. 121) and, therefore, truth is agreed upon by individuals in which they specify that

something will be viewed in a particular way. The agreed upon truth is usually determined by the dominant group within a culture, which comes about based on their experiences and does not represent the truth for all individuals (Middleman and Wood, 1993).

Social constructivism, human behaviour and individual functioning

Social constructivism addresses human behaviour and functioning as well as the impact that the social environment plays on individual functioning. Individual functioning is determined by the interpretation of an individual's experiences. From the experiences of the individual, a reality is created and the individual then views future experiences through this reality (Dewees, 1999). Individuals will view their experiences differently based on their interpretations of previous experiences, which thus determines how they understand the world (Middleman and Wood, 1993). Through individuals' understanding of the world they gain knowledge of the world and draw upon this knowledge when faced with new experiences, therefore, prior knowledge is a foundation on which future knowledge can be built (Mailick and Vigilante, 1997).

Individual functioning is determined by the culture and environment, which have an influence on the individual (Dewees, 1999). The environment, culture and subculture of individuals influence the belief and value systems of the individuals and therefore impacts how they view the world and process experiences. Individuals function and behave according to their beliefs and value systems and therefore interpret the world through this lens.

Language influences individual functioning and behaviour. Language is the source of attempting to understand another's reality and is seen as central in shaping meaning (Witkin, 2012). Individual behaviour is influenced by how individuals interpret the meaning of terms. Individuals will use actions and language to express their behaviour or their reality when faced with different experiences. The actions and the language which individuals choose have been agreed upon in advance to mean something specific, usually determined by the dominant members of the culture or subculture. Individuals' interpretations of the world and ability to express their reality are shaped by the type of language forms available to them (Witkin, 2012).

The use of language as a way of expressing reality is difficult based on the social constructivist belief that no one will ever fully know another's reality. When individuals are expressing their reality to an observer through language, the observer is attempting to understand the reality through their own lens created by values and beliefs. Individuals attempt to understand someone's reality as it relates to their own life or the lives of someone they know (that is, concrete comparisons), yet find it difficult to allow others to have their own experiences and their own reality (Middleman and Wood, 1993). Even if observers wanted to allow others to have their own experiences, social constructivism theorizes that this is impossible due to the observers' values, beliefs and perceptions. Franklin (1995, p. 396) best states this phenomenon, 'operations of human cognitive structures and processes and the nature of language and social processes, in particular, make it impossible for us to know an objective reality completely'.

Human behaviour and functioning is not the same for each individual. Individuals react to the experiences in the world based on how they view the world. Differences in individual functioning could be explained by the environment, culture or subculture in which the individual functions. The power structures within environments shape how individuals view the world. Meanings within individuals' environments are socially constructed and are subject to change with time and change across environments (Middleman and Wood, 1993). Knowledge that is obtained by individuals' interaction with the environment has been influenced by the social and political institutions that dominate that environment (Dean and Rhodes, 1998) and is historically situated and thus evolving (Mailick and Vigilante, 1997). Therefore, the environment in which an individual is situated plays a critical and ever-evolving role in shaping an individual's reality.

Exercise box 5.1 Exploring social constructivism

In pairs or a small group, take turns answering the following questions. Consider how your family, friends, community, culture and history affect your answers.

1 What is the most significant holiday of the year to you?
2 Should families routinely sit down and eat dinner together?
3 Do you believe people should remain abstinent from sex before marriage?
4 How would you view a parent who allows their 15-year-old son to drink at home?
5 What is your favourite sport and why?

A social constructivist approach to practice

When conceptualizing social constructivism and understanding the application, one can come to realize that 'all we can ever know is ourselves and the impacts on ourselves of different persons and situations' (Dean, 1993, p. 134). Thus, how can we know another, and how can social constructivism be applied in practice? Carpenter (2011) states, 'people behave and lead *their* lives based on what they believe to be true and real, and this is where the practitioner must initially meet her or his clients if effective help is to be given' (p. 122).

Greene and Lee (2002; Lee and Greene, 2009) have identified six aspects or skills that would enable a social worker to apply the basic premises of social constructivism to practice. They stress that social constructivism is not a separate approach, but more a meta-framework that assists social workers in thinking and organizing practice with clients. The six aspects are described below.

1 *Develop collaborative relationships with clients*. This first aspect involves the social worker and client sharing power as they work together (Dean, 1993; Dean and Rhodes, 1998). The social worker and client should maintain an

egalitarian relationship versus a relationship where the social worker is viewed as the expert who is there to help the client by applying learned theoretical knowledge to the client's situation (Greene and Lee, 2002). Taking a collaborative approach mandates that the social worker acknowledge clients as experts in their own reality and therefore the social worker should attempt to understand clients' realities versus attempting to have clients conform to the reality of the social worker. In fostering a collaborative relationship the social worker should continually assess for client strengths and resources, which reinforces the client as the expert and validates her or him as a collaborative partner (Greene and Lee, 2002). Through this collaborative relationship the client and social worker can begin to develop a plan that both the client and social worker find meaningful and are motivated to pursue.

2   *Focus on and work towards client-defined goals.* This aspect involves clients specifying and defining the problem from their reality and defining and setting goals that are personally meaningful. Clients are less likely to be motivated to work towards goals that are externally imposed on them versus working towards goals which clients find relevant to their needs and situations (Lee and Greene, 2009). This does not negate the fact that clients will occasionally have externally imposed goals, for example, a court order for a parent to attend parenting classes or a client to attend a drug and alcohol education programme. When goals are externally mandated, the social worker and client should participate in a dialogue where the client and social worker acknowledge this goal as a mandate and attempt to have the client find routes to reach that goal which are defined by and are personally meaningful to the client.

3   *Take a position of curiosity.* When coming from a social constructivist framework, the social worker acknowledges that clients have their own version of reality which needs to be discovered by the social worker. This aspect specifies that the social worker can attempt to discover the reality of the client by taking a position of curiosity versus assuming the client's version of reality (Gergen, 2009; Lee and Greene, 2009). The social worker should be genuine in pursuing the way in which clients view their life, their problems, their strengths and resources, and their daily routines. For example, the social worker could simply state, 'What is a typical day like for you?' or 'Tell me, what is it like to be the full time carer for your father?' By taking a position of curiosity the social worker is showing the client that the social worker truly values and is interested in the client (Greene and Lee, 2002). According to Gergen (2009) to show curiosity is to show affirmation.

4   *Take a 'not-knowing, non-expert' position.* When using the theory of social constructivism, one should acknowledge that the client is the expert in her or his own life (Franklin, 1995). As a social worker, one should take a not-knowing, non-expert stance and allow clients to express their realities through their own words instead of the social worker making assumptions about clients' situations. This approach should enable the social worker to work collaboratively with clients in attempting to understand their reality and acknowledging that the clients can teach the social worker about their competencies, strengths,

resources, problems and solutions (Lee and Greene, 2009). The social worker should attempt to utilize empathy and see herself or himself from the client's viewpoint (Dean and Rhodes, 1998). According to Mailick and Vigilante (1997, p. 362) when utilizing social constructivism when working with families, the social worker should 'shift the focal point from what the social worker needs to know in order to help the client to what the family knows about their own situation and how the family and social worker participate in a process of mutual discovery'. Therefore, the client, rather than the social worker, is seen as the expert, and thus the social worker and client work collaboratively. Greene and Lee (2002, p. 185) note that this approach does not suggest that the social worker should be passive when the client asks a question or for an opinion, but rather the social worker should 'give an honest answer, as long as the social worker's position is presented as one of many possible ideas'.

5   *Learn and use the client's language.* In further validating the client as the expert in her or his situation, the social worker should attempt to learn and use the client's language and the meanings she or he gives to concepts (Lee and Greene, 2009). Social workers should be careful to limit the amount of professional jargon that is used with a client and instead should use language and concepts that are best understood by the client.

6   *Co-construct reality through dialogue.* According to Greene and Lee (2002, p. 186), 'social workers are in the business of facilitating change'. Therefore, when clients have a view of reality that is disempowering, stigmatizing or harmful to them, the social worker should participate in a dialogue with the client in an attempt co-construct a new reality that is more positively accepted by the client. A social constructivist approach allows clients to express their reality and experiences in an attempt to help clients to view their realities as influenced by the dominant culture and encourages clients to look at alternative interpretations of stories (Greene and Lee, 2002). This can involve the use of narrative therapy approaches such as 'externalizing the problem' (White 1989; 2002), which aims to separate the problem from the client; the 'person is not the problem – the problem is the problem' (Madigan, 2013, p. 455). Through conversation, questioning, and exploring and revising the client's story, the social worker and client move from a 'problem' narrative to a more 'preferred' narrative (Madigan, 2013). Although, the social worker will never fully understand the client's reality, therapy can be used to allow the client to express her or his reality and the difficulties she or he is experiencing through the use of language and storytelling. Through this expression, the client and social worker work together to develop a more fulfilling reality for the client.

When applying the theory of social constructivism, social workers must understand that clients are the experts. Social workers must 'learn to listen to their clients, to learn from them about their pain, and to explore together ways to alleviate it' (Middleman and Wood, 1993, p. 134). Social worker and client share their meanings and interpretations about events and social workers view themselves as equal with the client.

Case example: applying social constructivism to practice

Marjorie is a 45-year-old, black British female who lives with her husband, Al, and their two children, Toni (age 16) and Michael (age 14). Marjorie's widowed mother, Grace (age 72), was diagnosed with dementia two years ago and had been able to live in her own home with support from social services and Marjorie and Al's assistance. Six months ago, the medical doctor diagnosed Grace as having advanced dementia and recommended 24-hour-care or residential assistance. Marjorie refused to admit Grace to a care home and moved Grace in with her and Al. Marjorie is spending the majority of her days caring for Grace and has had to quit her job due to the caring demands. The stress and strain of the 24-hour care has led to relationship problems with Al, and Toni and Michael report they 'wish they had their mother back'. Grace's medical doctor has referred Marjorie to social services for a carers assessment. As a social worker who practises from a social constructivist framework, you participate in a dialogue with Marjorie about her past experiences, current situation and future aspirations in an attempt to understand Marjorie's reality and develop a support plan that is meaningful to Marjorie and built upon a collaborative relationship.

By incorporating the six aspects of a social constructivist approach, as outlined by Greene and Lee (2002), you would first *develop a collaborative relationship* with Marjorie. You understand that by being a professional social worker, Marjorie could view you as someone who could assess her ability to care for her mother and might make judgements about her and her family. Despite your undeniable professional position, your first visit with Marjorie is one that attempts to foster collaboration, listen to her story and solicit her defined needs and goals. You want to understand Marjorie as a person whose reality has been shaped by her past and current experiences, particularly in relation to her mother, her culture, family and society. You begin the dialogue by asking Marjorie to inform you of her current situation and *take a position of curiosity* by asking her to tell you what a typical day is like for her, focusing on what she is feeling and thinking throughout the day. Marjorie explains the events leading up to Grace's diagnosis and her subsequent move into the family home and you ask her to tell you what this experience has been like for her.

In continuing with the collaborative relationship you ask Marjorie to explore what she would like for herself and to describe her preferred future, which begins to take the discussion to a *focus on client-defined goals*. Marjorie openly discloses that she has been feeling very exhausted and lacks the energy to carry out daily activities let alone provide all the care Grace needs. Marjorie discloses how her relationship with Al has been strained since Grace moved in and how their conversations only consist of what is needed for Grace. Marjorie explains that she feels guilty that is not being a 'good' mother and wife and describes feeling torn between her family and caring for her mother. Marjorie describes how it is not common within her culture to place one's parent in a care home as care is viewed as being the best at home and with family. Instead of immediately discussing with Marjorie suggestions of how to improve her situation, you *take a non-knowing, non-expert position* and listen to how Marjorie is currently dealing with and experiencing her situation. You can ask Marjorie to tell you what it is like for her to experience these feelings of responsibility and guilt and ask her to tell you some possible solutions to her identified problems.

Marjorie discloses that her ultimate goal is to be there for her husband and for her children, especially as they are teenagers and will most likely move out in a few years time. She also wants her mother to be properly looked after, but realizes that Marjorie, herself, needs to be physically and mentally healthy in order to do so. You complete the carers assessment in collaboration with Marjorie and *use her words* in specifying her needs and goals. You incorporate some narrative therapy questions with Marjorie in an attempt to have her explore her expectations of her caring roles and how these could be *co-constructed and reframed through dialogue* into more positive, acceptable explanations. In particular, you ask Marjorie to explore her thoughts about her culture's expectations of her caring role and how this is working and not working for her. In this process, Marjorie begins to acknowledge that she has set expectations for herself that are unrealistic and are causing her 'to fail'. She reframes her idea of 'caring for my mother' from one of 'care has to be by myself in the home' to 'I need help in caring for my mother.' In this sense, Marjorie creates a new reality of her 'caring role'.

Since your involvement, Marjorie has worked with social services to provide care in the home on a daily basis. Marjorie also has agreed to short respite breaks where Grace spends a weekend a month in a care home. The extra support that Marjorie has accepted has enabled her to spend more time with her family while also ensuring that Grace stays close to home.

Strengths and limitations

There are several strengths and limitations of social constructivism that are worth exploring before incorporating this theory into practice. Some strengths of the theory and its approach are as follows:

- The theory embraces empowerment-based practice by encouraging collaboration with clients and acknowledging that clients are experts in their reality, problem definitions and solutions.
- The power and control lie with the client and not the social worker. This enables social workers to realize that they are not responsible for defining or achieving goals for clients, but that the power and control lie with the clients. The social worker is to facilitate the process, but the success, or failure, in reaching those goals ultimately lies with the client.
- The theory embraces anti-discriminatory, anti-racist and anti-oppressive practice. Social workers are to be curious about clients' realities and explore how their culture, society and history influence their reality. Social workers are to embrace clients as being experts in their reality and are not to influence the clients to take on the reality of the social worker.
- The theory takes a strengths-based approach and challenges the identification of deficits. There is no support for diagnoses or a deficit model, which

are often defined by the dominant culture or society and do not fit in with everyone's reality.

Some of the limitations of social constructivism are as follows:

- The inability of social workers to strictly adhere to the theory when working with clients who have externally mandated goals. This limitation could be lessened by collaborating with the client and asking the client to define how she or he would like to reach this mandated goal.
- The view of extreme subjectivity where the belief that we cannot directly know the external world is taken to mean that social workers can never know their clients and can never empathize with clients. Social workers should understand that the theory is basically calling for one to take a step back and take a 'not-knowing, non-expert' stance, as well as attempt to put oneself in another's situation. Therefore, a client's reality can be understood through empathy, intuition and meaning, often expressed by the client through language and dialogue (Atherton, 1993).
- Allowing the client to be the expert in their own experiences and reality could be difficult for social workers to grasp. The social worker and client need to work together in understanding each other's realities and neither individual has an expert view on the other's (Dean and Rhodes, 1998). Social constructivism challenges the social worker to examine their own views, beliefs and theories when working in collaboration with the client to open up the possibility of reaching mutual discovery.
- If we acknowledge that everyone has their own view of reality and we are to value these different perspectives, how do we make sense of realities that are discriminatory in nature? The theory can assist social workers in attempting to understand one's reality and the cultural, societal and historical influences on the reality, but this does not mean that social workers should embrace attitudes and beliefs that are harmful to others. As social workers, we have professional values, principles and ethics to follow, and when we combat attitudes and beliefs that go against these we can acknowledge the basis for that person's reality but do not have to embrace them, and we should attempt to co-construct a new reality with that person that is less harmful to others.

Ethical and cultural considerations

The theory of social constructivism contains numerous values, tacit and explicit, pertaining to individuals and the social environment. Social constructivism values cultural diversity as the theory states that individuals' realities are formed within their cultural context and no one's reality or experiences are more true than another (Dewees, 1999; Laird, 1993; Mailick and Vigilante, 1997). Therefore, when taking a social constructivist framework, a social worker should value the ethnicities and cultures of clients that help to shape their reality. Social workers must realize that their culture is no more or less true or correct than the client's culture and should be conscious not to impose meanings, assumptions, values or understandings of the social worker's culture onto the client.

Despite this basic assumption, one must acknowledge that a culture is socially constructed. When taking a social constructivist framework, social workers must understand and appreciate that they will work with clients from different ethnicities and cultures and must reflect on how this will impact their work together. Social workers should be careful to not make assumptions about cultures and should acknowledge that even two people from the same culture might interpret situations and experiences very differently.

In valuing the culture of which clients are members, social workers must take the position of curiosity and participate in a dialogue with the client about how the ethnicity and culture shapes and influences the client's actions and behaviours (that is, both positively and negatively). This process of understanding takes place through communication where the social worker learns from the client about the culture and the meanings ascribed to the words and concepts used in the language of the culture. Some clients might believe, or feel, that they do not fit in with their culture or may experience actions from their culture that are discriminatory or oppressive in nature. Social workers should listen to what the client is experiencing and have the client define the problem and the solution from her or his perspective. The social worker may need to intervene into the cultural system to assist in alleviating the discrimination and oppression and/or may assist the clients in reconstructing their view of themselves to something that is more acceptable and less oppressive to them.

Using a social constructivist framework suggests that social workers value the reality of a client. In some situations, social workers may come across ethical dilemmas where the client or the client's culture possesses norms and values that are not consistent with social work profession's values, principles or ethics. For example, a mother may believe she has a right to 'punish' her child with a belt leaving welts and bruises in an attempt to teach the child a lesson. The mother's culture and community supports her actions. In such ethical situations, the social worker would need to make her or his values explicit and inform the mother of the legal duty to report the mother's actions. Acknowledging and valuing another's reality does not mean that social workers do not have ethical and legal obligations which they are mandated to follow. Ironically, these are also socially constructed and determined by a dominant culture within society and the social work profession.

Social constructivism and anti-oppressive practice

Social constructivism is an example of anti-oppressive practice as it values the dignity and worth of each individual and acknowledges that each has a separate and distinct reality that is to be valued (Dewees, 1999). An individual's reality cannot conform to another's reality and one reality is not to be perceived as superior to another (Middleman and Wood, 1993). Therefore, individuals hold their own constructed reality based on their experiences, which although it cannot be completely understood by another is to be equally valued. Social constructivism is also an empowering approach as social workers are not to assume they know a client's reality and are to take a not-knowing, non-expert position and one of curiosity that focuses on the client defining the problem and solution. Social workers should learn and use the language of the client rather than having the client learn the language of the social worker.

In using social constructivism and anti-oppressive practice, social workers must begin to assess their own values, biases and agendas when working with clients who possess different realities. A social constructivist approach requires that social workers remove stereotypes and assumptions about clients and treat each client as a unique individual with a uniquely shaped reality. In some social work situations, the social worker may have an undeniable position of authority, yet the social worker is not to be oppressive in practice, but rather move towards a collaborative relationship where the goals and motives of the social worker are made explicit to the client.

Social constructivism stresses the importance of the use of language and dialogue between the social worker and the client. When working in an anti-oppressive way, social workers should be mindful of the use of language and how the choice of words can be interpreted by clients.

Lastly, social workers may find that the client's culture is actually oppressive or discriminatory in nature. As stated previously, social workers are in the business of facilitating change and promoting social justice, therefore social workers working from a social constructivist framework and in an anti-oppressive way should confront discrimination and oppression, and attempt to reconstruct the reality of the system that is discriminatory in nature in order to prevent future harm.

Research on social constructivism

Social constructivism is a conceptual framework or a theory for social workers to use when approaching and working with clients and can inform certain practice approaches (Lee and Greene, 2009), such as narrative therapy (see Madigan, 2011) and solution-focused practice (see Chapter 10). Based on the nature of social constructivism as a theory or framework, the effectiveness of this approach is difficult to determine without some techniques or specific practice approaches to test or evaluate. There is also a debate within the constructivist field about whether empiricism is actually valid given the belief that we each construct our own reality through our own lens. Determining the effectiveness of the use of social constructivism in practice should begin with a look at the research on practice approaches that incorporate social constructivist beliefs. Chapter 10 provides an overview of the effectiveness of solution-focused practice.

Summary

Social constructivism is a theory that values each person's reality as being uniquely shaped by her or his environment, culture, society, history, developmental processes and cognitions. Lee and Greene (2009) stress that social constructivism is a metaframework from which to organize work with clients and therefore is not a separate approach to social work practice. Aspects of social constructivism can be seen in other theories and methods, such as the strengths perspective (Saleebey, 2012), solution-focused brief therapy/practice (de Shazer et al., 1986), person-centred therapy/approach (Rogers, 1957) and narrative therapy (Madigan, 2011; White and Epston, 1990).

When taking a social constructivist framework, the social worker explores the client's version of reality and attempts to understand this reality through a dialogue and use of language that is used and understood by the client. The theory enables social workers to take a position of curiosity with the client to fully understand the client's definition of the problem, goals and possible solutions. This theory encourages the social worker to explore this reality versus struggling to have the client view the reality of the social worker as shaped by professional knowledge. The theory promotes collaboration and challenges social workers to put all assumptions (professional and personal) aside when beginning work with a client. The client and social worker are to explore each other's realities in the process of reaching mutual discovery and participate in a relationship that is working towards personally meaningful goals as defined by the client.

Case study

Sam is a 15-year-old, white British male who has recently been arrested for shoplifting. Sam has never been in trouble with the police before, but due to the value of the items he shoplifted, he has been referred to social services' youth offending team. At your first meeting with Sam as his youth offending social worker, Sam acknowledged that he had shoplifted and showed remorse. He stated that his 'life is over', he has disappointed his parents and he will always be known as an 'offender'. He feels as if he has failed in life. You and Sam are court ordered to meet weekly for the next ten weeks. How can you approach your work with Sam from a social constructivist framework?

Further reading

Berger, P.L. and Luckman, T. (1966) *The Social Construction of Reality.* Garden City, NY: Doubleday.
   The original piece of work that brought social constructivism to the forefront of social work.
Gergen, K.J. (2009) *An Invitation to Social Construction*, 2nd edn.
   Thousand Oaks, CA: Sage Publications. A comprehensive review of social constructionism.
Lock, A. and Strong, T. (eds) (2010) *Social Constructionism: Sources and Stirrings in Theory and Practice.* Cambridge: Cambridge University Press. Provides an introduction to the different theorists and schools of thought that have contributed to the development of social constructionism.

Witkin, S.L. (ed.) (2012) *Social Construction and Social Work Practice*. New York: Columbia University Press. An exploration of the ways in which social constructionism can be applied in social work practice in various settings and across client groups.

References

Atherton, C.R. (1993) Empiricists versus social constructionists: time for a cease-fire, *Families in Society*, 74(10): 617–24.

Berger, P.L. and Luckman, T. (1966) *The Social Construction of Reality*. Garden City, NY: Doubleday.

Carpenter, D.E. (2011) Constructivism: a conceptual framework for social work treatment, in F.J. Turner (ed.), *Social Work Treatment: Interlocking Theoretical Approaches*. Oxford: Oxford University Press.

De Shazer, S., Berg, I.K. and Lipchik, L. (1986) Brief therapy: focused solution development, *Family Process*, 25(2): 207–21.

Dean, R.G. (1993) Constructivism: an approach to clinical practice, *Smith College Studies in Social Work*, 63(2): 127–46.

Dean, R.G. and Fleck-Henderson, A. (1992) Teaching clinical theory and practice through a constructivist lens, *Journal of Teaching in Social Work*, 6(1): 3–20.

Dean, R.G. and Rhodes, M.L. (1998) Social constructionism and ethics: what makes a 'better' story?, *Families in Society*, 79(3): 254–62.

Dewees, M. (1999) The application of social constructionist principles to teaching social work practice in mental health, *Journal of Teaching in Social Work*, 19(1/2): 31–46.

Franklin, C. (1995) Expanding the vision of the social constructionist debates: creating relevance for practitioners, *Families in Society*, 76(7): 395–406.

Gergen, K.J. (1985) The social constructionist movement in modern psychology, *American Psychologist*, 40(3): 266–75.

Gergen, K.J. (1999) *An Invitation to Social Construction*. Thousand Oaks, CA: Sage Publications.

Gergen, K.J. (2003) Knowledge as socially constructed, in M. Gergen and K.J. Gergen (eds), *Social Construction: A Reader*. London: Sage Publications.

Gergen, K.J. (2009) *An Invitation to Social Construction*, 2nd edn. Thousand Oaks, CA: Sage Publications.

Gitterman, A. and Germain, C.B. (2008) *The Life Model of Social Work Practice: Advances in Theory and Practice*, 3rd edn. New York: Columbia University Press.

Greene, G.J., Jensen, C. and Jones, D.H. (1996) A constructivist perspective on clinical social work practice with ethnically diverse clients, *Social Work*, 41(2): 172–80.

Greene, G.J. and Lee, M.Y. (2002) The social construction of empowerment, in M.W. O'Melia and K.K. Miley (eds), *Pathways to Power: Readings in Contextual Social Work Practice*. Boston, MA: Allyn and Bacon.

Laird, J. (1993) Family-centered practice: cultural and constructionist reflections, *Journal of Teaching in Social Work*, 8(1/2): 77–109.

Lee, M.Y. and Greene, G.J. (2009) Using social constructivism in social work practice, in A.R. Roberts (ed.), *The Social Workers' Desk Reference*, 2nd edn. New York: Oxford University Press.

Madigan, S. (2011) *Narrative Therapy – Theory and Practice*. Washington, DC: American Psychological Association.

Madigan, S. (2013) Narrative therapy, in M. Davies (ed.), *The Blackwell Companion to Social Work*, 4th edn. Chichester: John Wiley & Sons.

Mailick, M.D. and Vigilante, F.W. (1997) The family assessment wheel: a social constructionist perspective, *Families in Society*, 78(4): 361–9.

Middleman, R.R. and Wood, G.G. (1993) So much for the bell curve: constructionism, power/conflict and the structural approach to direct practice in social work, *Journal of Teaching in Social Work*, 8(1/2): 129–46.

Rogers, C.R. (1957) The necessary and sufficient conditions of therapeutic personality change, *Journal of Consulting Psychology*, 21(2): 95–103.

Saleebey, D. (2012) *The Strengths Perspective in Social Work Practice*, 6th edn. London: Allyn and Bacon.

Schwandt, T.A. (2000) Three epistemological stances for qualitative inquiry: interpretivism, hermeneutics and social constructionism, in N.K. Denzin and Y.S. Lincoln (eds), *Handbook of Qualitative Research*, 2nd edn. Thousand Oaks, CA: Sage Publications.

White, M. (1989) The externalizing of the problem and re-authoring of lives and relationships. Dulwich Centre Newsletter, Summer. Reprinted in M. White and D. Epston (eds) (1990) *Narrative Means to Therapeutic Ends*. New York: W.W. Norton.

White, M. (2002) Addressing personal failure, *International Journal of Narrative Therapy and Community Work*, 3: 33–76.

White, M. and Epston, D. (eds) (1990) *Narrative Means to Therapeutic Ends*. New York: W.W. Norton.

Witkin, S.L. (1995) Family social work: a critical constructionist perspective, *Journal of Family Social Work*, 1(1): 33–45.

Witkin, S.L. (2012) An introduction to social construction, in S.L. Witkin (ed.), *Social Construction and Social Work Practice: Interpretations and Innovations*. New York: Columbia University Press.

6   Feminist theory and practice

Introduction

Feminist theory and practice address specific issues and ways of understanding women, although the principles and approaches of feminist theory can be implemented with men and children. Feminist theory seeks to explain the differences between men and women, particularly as they develop throughout the lifespan, and feminist practice seeks to implement approaches that are tailored to address these differences and with a goal of empowerment. The theory and approach aim to increase consciousness of the oppression of women and in turn provide avenues by which women can gain control of their lives. The theory is congruent with the ecological perspective, which examines the interconnection and interdependence of the person and the environment (Gitterman and Germain, 2008). The approach, therefore, seeks to intervene in either the individual and/or the environment in order to create change, increase personal empowerment and promote positive growth and development.

Feminism is particularly appropriate for social work as the majority of social workers are women and women are often clients or connected to clients of social services (Orme, 2009a). Due to this connection, feminism within social work is termed feminist social work. Although variations exist in feminist social work ideologies, the commonalities among feminist social workers include the following: (1) to end patriarchy; (2) to empower women; (3) to view the person-in-environment (that is, the personal is political); and (4) to raise the consciousness of women and society as a whole in regard to the structural gender inequalities (Bricker-Jenkins and Hooyman, 1986; Dominelli, 2002).

In understanding feminism, one must first distinguish between the terms *sex* and *gender*. Sex is used to refer to the biological differences between females and males whereas gender is used to refer to the sociological differences, such as thoughts, beliefs and attitudes about women and men (Sharf, 2012). Gender is socially constructed and therefore varies from cultures and across time (Valentich, 2011). Additionally, *gender roles* are the roles assigned to and seen as appropriate for women and men that are created and reinforced by the dominant culture and society. This chapter explores the theory and practice of feminism by examining the history and basic premises of the theory, the techniques of the approach, and the application of the theory and approach to social work practice.

The origins of feminist theory

The late 1800s and early 1900s saw the existence of first-wave feminism where women fought and won the right to vote. The work of the first-wave feminists led to the second wave of feminism: from the 1960s to the 1990s were there was a concern with the way women were portrayed – at the present time and historically – and the way in which women's views and needs were consolidated with the views and needs of men. Women were not considered to be of the same status as men and this was evident in society in numerous ways. For example, the male-as-normative theme was prominent where 'mankind', 'man' and the pronoun 'he' referred to both men and women (Hyde and Else-Quest, 2013). Such language was used by Carl Rogers in his writings about the person-centred approach and is often still used in the writing of legislation. Many socio-logical, psychological and social work theories, such as psychoanalytic and psychody-namic approaches, were based on studies of white men or 'pathological' women (Valentich, 2011). Historically, men made the rules and established norms for both men and women (Sharf, 2012). Through these acknowledgements of inequality, women became concerned with the effects on women and the need for change that considered women as valuable.

The feminist movement was prominent within the academic disciplines, such as social work, psychology and sociology, which began to address the unequal relation-ships within the helping professions, such as man as therapist and expert, and woman as helpee. Feminist groups began to establish shelters for battered and sexually assaulted women to receive support and counselling (Valentich, 2011). Additionally, the feminist movement was penetrating the political arena through women's organizations – such as the National Organization for Women (NOW), and the emergence of the Women's Health Movement in the United States – who sought to fight for women's rights with political issues, such as employment practices, and enable women to take control of their physical and mental health. Through these collectives emerged the consciousness-raising (CR) groups which aimed to bring women together to end isola-tion and fight collectively to bring about social change (Enns, 2004; Sharf, 2012). Consciousness-raising groups provided a forum for women to express the oppression and discrimination they had experienced with other women who had similar experi-ences and, therefore, were able to collaborate in their efforts to combat the discrimina-tion and create positive change. The CR groups were run on feminist principles, which consisted of a non-competitive and leaderless group that was emotionally supportive (Valentich, 2011).

A major criticism of the second-wave feminist movement was the dominance of white, middle-class women as the forerunners and theorists, which addressed women as one homogenous group without acknowledging the diversity among women, such as race, ethnicity, sexual orientation, age and class. Additionally, feminism began to be criticized for failing to keep up the momentum in terms of theory and practice develop-ment, and there were arguments that feminism was dead (Valentich, 2011). Since this time, third-wave feminism has emerged and third-wave feminists have expanded the definition and application of feminism to encapsulate broader cultural and global issues, such as antiracism, global social justice, disability and heterosexism, with a focus on 'intersectionality' (Hyde and Else-Quest, 2013). Intersectionality is defined as 'an approach that simultaneously considers the meaning and consequences of multiple categories of identity, difference and disdvantage' (Hyde and Else-Quest, 2013, p. 55). This new perspective views 'women' not as a homogenous group, but rather as a group that differs based on ethnicity, social glass, sexual orientation and cultural beliefs. Therefore, current feminism focuses more on being ethnically sensitive and better suited to all women by focusing on eliminating all forms of oppression, exploitation and discrimination.

The second and third waves of feminists have lead to the emergence of numerous perspectives on feminism, particularly in regard to the criticism of feminism initially being developed by white, middle-class women. The various perspectives all aim to create equality and promote empowerment for women, but there remains slight variations in the origins of the inequality and how to reach the end goal of empowerment and emancipation. Table 6.1 provides a list of the various feminist perspectives and a brief explanation of each.

Table 6.1 Variations of feminism

Feminist type	Description
Liberal feminism	Women and men should have equal access to resources and opportunities. Examines the personal interactions of women and men and supports changes through political and legal reform. Men can be involved in supporting women in the fight for equal rights
Radical feminism	Patriarchy, the social organization that advantages men, has led to men putting their interests over those of women. Therefore, men through the use of social systems are able to control women. Radical feminism actively participates in changing social institutions and systems that lead to a patriarchy. Less likely to believe that men can be supportive in women's fight for equal rights
Marxist and socialist feminism	The economic forms of power enable men to control women. Theorists are critical of the failure of Marx to deal with the inequality of women. Dismantling capitalism and ending economic and cultural sources of oppression is a way to liberate women
Black/Hispanic feminism	Critical of original feminism as it was developed by white, middle-class women and only addressed sexism. Examines classism, sexism and racism in conjunction. Hispanic feminism has particularly emerged in the United States
Lesbian feminism	Challenges heterosexuality as an institution. Politically and personally resists patriarchal power and domination
Womanism	Created to be different to black feminism in that womanism focuses on culture, family and the mutually supportive relationships between men and women, in addition to racism and sexism. Focuses on the struggles of both black men and women
Global feminism	Focuses on women's rights on a global scale while acknowledging locally and culturally specific challenges for women

(Continued)

Table 6.1 *Continued*

Feminist type	Description
Psychoanalytic feminism	Argues that gender is developed and learned and, therefore, aims to challenge the patterns, relationships and language that reinforce masculinity and femininity
Cultural feminism	Has evolved from radical feminism and aims to build a women's culture that values and celebrates the biological and cultural differences and qualities between men and women

Sources: Enns (2004), Hyde and Else-Quest (2013), Sharf (2012), and Worell and Remer (2003)

Feminist theory explained

Theories and methods that traditionally inform social work practice – such as psychodynamic approaches, person-centred approaches, cognitive and behavioural theories and theories of life-stage development – were predominately created by men, and based on the life experiences, development, views and needs of men; yet they were often presumed to be gender neutral. With the emergence of the feminist movement, theorists began to examine how women differed from men in development and life experiences and took these differences into account when practising social work.

Gender differences between women and men can be found across the lifespan and are often categorized into childhood, adolescents and adulthood. In childhood, gender differences begin to emerge at birth with the assignment of pink clothes to girls and blue clothes for boys. Little girls are supposed to play with dolls and wear dresses, and boys are to play with trucks and cars and get their clothes dirty. If the children do not adhere to these gender norms, a boy may be referred to as a 'sissy' and a girl as a 'tomboy'. By the creation of these gender norms, as predominantly imposed by adults, children learn to adopt the different gender-role expectations (Sharf, 2012). In adolescence, puberty occurs, which can cause females additional stress with the societal expectations of the female body as thin and physically attractive. Males may experience pressure to be tough and have a strong, masculine appearance. Adolescent girls and boys have different expectations in regard to sexual activity with girls having to learn to control their sexual activity and take more responsibility for the use of contraception (Sharf, 2012). The gender role differences continue through adulthood where women deal with the role of motherhood, which not only means experiencing pregnancy, but also having to face decisions about work and caretaking responsibilities. Within the workforce, women are continually paid less than men (Le and Miller, 2010; Scott et al., 2008) and are more likely to experience discrimination and sexual harassment (Sharf, 2012).

These differences as dictated by the dominant society are necessary considerations when practising social work with women and men. From an understanding of these differences, social workers acknowledge a need to tailor interventions to the specific needs of women, which are different from those of men. Additionally, the feminist approach is congruent with the ecological perspective and empowerment approach, and requires social workers to challenge the oppression of women by society and the socially constructed terms that negatively segregate women from men. Therefore, social workers are attempting to meet the needs of individuals and the environment. Feminist social workers strive to integrate the woman's personal and political dimensions of life, transform social and structural relations, respect diversity, promote egalitarian relationships and empower women through social work practice (Orme, 2009a; 2009b; Valentich, 2011).

Feminist theories

There are several theories that can guide social work practice, two of which are discussed in more detail below.

1 *Gender schema theory.* This theory (Bern, 1981; 1983) examines how society influences individuals to view gender in a specific way based on the established roles and norms attached to the gender type. The theory proposes that children are conditioned to learn from society the definition and roles of a female and a male, which then shape their future development of self and their views of how others should conduct themselves. Some individuals are theorized to view situations more from a gender perspective than others, which is often based on the rules and norms that society has placed on the specific gender (Sharf, 2012). For example, my mother and I took my 10-year-old nephew to the emergency room after he had fallen on his arm during a school activity. We were waiting for the doctor to enter the room when my nephew stated, 'When will *he* come in here?' My mother asked, 'Why do you think the doctor is a he?' My nephew replied, 'Because doctors are hes and nurses are shes'.

   Gender schema theory purports that one's view of gender is shaped and influenced by the dominant society, hence why many individuals believe little girls should wear pink and play with dolls and little boys should wear blue and play with trucks, and why many individuals will automatically assume that doctors are male as described in the example above. These assumptions and norms not only shape how individuals view gender, but can limit how they view themselves (Sharf, 2012).

2 *The relational-cultural model.* The relational-cultural model was developed by several female psychotherapists working at the Stone Centre at Wellesley College in the United States. The theory was originally proposed by Miller (1976) and further refined by other female theorists who together examined and explored the development of women (Comstock, et al., 2008; Jordan, 2010). The theorists postulate that women's growth and development occurs out of the connections and relationships that women have in their lives that consists of mutual empathy and mutual empowerment. A women's sense of identity and self-worth is based on the types of relationships that she encompasses. A growth-fostering connection or relationship, referred to as *relational resilience*, will result in empowerment, a clear sense of self, the other and the

relationship, a better sense of self-worth and a desire for multiple positive relationships (Jordan, 2010; Miller, 1988). When disconnections in relationships occur, such as relational violations, injuries, insults or a lack of empathy, the woman should be able to express her feelings regarding the disconnection, referred to as *relational competence*, and feel the effects of creating positive change through mutual empathic responses, thus fostering positive growth and development (Jordan, 2010). If an unempathic response or lack of understanding is received then the woman will change the dynamics of the relationship and incorporate strategies of disconnection or survival (that is keep a part of herself out of the relationship) in order to maintain the relationship (Miller, 1988). This can often be seen by women attending to the emotional and physical needs of others before attending to their own. The woman becomes less authentic, loses her sense of self-worth and identity, and her positive growth and development is halted.

As the presence of relationships are viewed as a strength to a woman's growth and development, the theory proposes interventions that foster a woman's ability to assert their own needs within the relationship where all parties support mutual empowerment and empathy, and, thus, relational resilience and relational competence are present and fostered (Comstock, et al., 2008; Jordan, 2010). This theory focuses on the relationships at the personal, interpersonal and socio-political levels, and takes into account the effects of racism, sexism, heterosexism and classism on a woman's ability to engage in relationships that lead to positive growth and development.

Feminist methods

There are numerous methods or approaches to social work practice. Often, feminist social workers will adapt existing methods such as cognitive behavioural therapy, empowerment, groupwork, solution focused practice or political advocacy to alleviate or diminish presenting problems while adhering to the aims of feminist social work. Feminist social work should encompass the ultimate goal of empowering the woman to utilize the existing personal, interpersonal and socio-political strengths and resources to meet her needs. This goal can be reached through interventions with the woman, couple, family, community and/or society. A collaborative relationship between social worker and client is critical as there should be a focus on breaking down power differentials and imbalances and fostering positive, healthy relationships (Jordan, 2010; Valentich, 2011). Sharf (2012) defines the goals of feminist practice based on the work of Klein (1976), Sturdivant (1980) and Enns (2004) as consisting of:

1 *Symptom removal.* Practice with women should involve addressing both the symptoms of a problem as well as the problem itself. Merely masking a symptom, such as depression, with a prescription medication does not address the underlying problem that is causing the depression. Practice should focus on both symptoms and the cause(s).

2   *Self-esteem and body image and sensuality*. Practice with women should focus on creating a positive self-esteem and body image that comes from within the woman and is not based on the views and perceptions of others. Decisions regarding sex and sexuality should be made by women and not based on coercion from others.

3   *Quality of interpersonal relationships*. In adhering to the relational-cultural theory, practice with women should focus on creating more direct and assertive relationships that foster mutual empathy and empowerment versus a relationship that fosters dependency or control.

4   *Attention to diversity*. Practice with women should consider the cultural differences that can shape women's view of themselves and the goals they establish for themselves.

5   *Political awareness and social action*. Both social worker and woman should raise their consciousness to the discrimination and oppression that women experience from society and should work together to change these social standards.

As the goals illustrate, feminist social work practice seeks to empower a woman within a gender-oppressive environment by focusing on the woman's desires and goals for herself. This should result in the woman accepting herself versus allowing others to dictate what she should be and challenging the environment that is prohibiting the woman from reaching her full potential. Feminist social work strives for an environment where women and men have relationships and rights that are equal. In reaching these goals, Sharf (2012, pp. 500–7) provides some feminist theory techniques, which could include applying one or more of the following:

1   *Gender-role analysis*. This technique involves the social worker and woman identifying a situation where the woman has experienced a clear gender-role message (that is, working mums are selfish for not staying at home with their children). The social worker and woman begin the process with an analysis of the message and how it has affected the woman. The social worker and woman then attempt to create a change that is more appropriate, true and positive for her. Based on the gender-role message, the social worker and woman may progress through the following steps in conducting the analysis: (a) identify the consequences of the gender-role message and specifically how this message affects the woman (that is, women with children feel guilty about working. 'I may not be providing enough love and care for my child because I am working'); (b) social worker and woman decide how they want to change this message to better fit the reality and experience of the woman (what is the evidence that you aren't providing enough love and care for your child? What are the benefits to your child because you are working?); (c) the social worker and woman reframe the situation to be more positive and acceptable to the woman ('I would not be able to provide for my child if I was not working. I am considering both my needs and my child's needs in working'). Through the gender-role analysis the woman is able to interpret the message through her

own reality and experiences versus those imposed on her by others (Worell and Remer, 2003).

2   *Gender-role intervention.* This technique is similar to consciousness-raising where the social work provides information related to the gender-role messages that can assist the woman in reframing the socially constructed gender-role stereotype into something more positive. Gender-role intervention aims to alleviate any presenting problems and promote empowerment through education and acknowledgements of societal oppression. This process should provide the woman with evidence that although the gender-role may be prominent in society its mere existence can also oppress or discriminate against women. In our example above, the social worker may provide the woman with statistics as to the number of working mothers demonstrating that the woman is not alone in her situation. Additionally, the social worker and woman can discuss how men are not looked down upon for working or following a career, as women can be, and how the social worker and woman can challenge this established norm.

3   *Power analysis and intervention.* The steps of power analysis are similar to those in the gender-role analysis where the woman identifies a situation where there is a power difference (that is, financial, physical, employment) and then discusses ways in which power and power strategies can be used to bring about change (Sharf, 2012). The goal of power analysis is to explore how the power differences between men and women are contributing to the woman's presenting problem and through this process identify areas that require change. For example, if a woman is experiencing discrimination within her place of employment where she is receiving less pay for like work compared with men, the social worker could provide information on legislation and case law that illustrates the unlawful discrimination of her employer and together identify steps to remedy the problem.

4   *Assertiveness training.* This technique involves the social worker and woman discussing and practising assertiveness skills, often through the use of role-play. According to Sharf (2012, p. 505), assertiveness 'refers to standing up for one's rights without violating the rights of others. Assertive behaviour is a clear direct (no sarcasm or humour) statement or request'. This is particularly helpful in situations where women have lost control and power over their lives and are being oppressed or discriminated by others. Despite the end goal of becoming more assertive, society tends to view assertiveness as a 'male trait', and female assertiveness may be viewed more negatively than male assertiveness (Enns, 2004; Sharf, 2012).

5   *Reframing and relabelling.* This is a technique that involves rephrasing or relabelling a negatively loaded word, phrase or situation into a word, phrase or situation that is more positive and acceptable to the woman. For example, a woman states she is worried she is a selfish mother because she works and receives negative comments from other stay-at-home mums, such as 'at least I can say I have always been there for my kids'. The social worker could reframe this situation by stating to the woman, 'you are working to provide a good life

for your children and although some women may justify their reasons for staying home, that does not mean that they can explain your reasons for not'. Reframing takes the blame away from the woman and places it in the correct location, which is usually society (Sharf, 2012).

The above techniques may be incorporated into feminist social work practice, or the social worker may adjust other theories and methods to fit with feminist values and goals. When incorporating feminist values and goals in the delivery of other theories or methods, the social worker would first need to explore the history, development of terms and use of language in order to determine if the theory or method is gender or culturally biased. Then, the social worker would need to ensure that, after the elimination of any gender or cultural bias, the theory or method is still compatible for the situation and with the goals and aims of feminist theory (Worell and Remer, 2003). Sharf (2012) and Worell and Remer (2003) identify several theories and methods that have been adapted to incorporate feminist values and goals; these include feminist psychoanalytic theory, feminist behavioural and cognitive therapy, feminist gestalt therapy and feminist narrative therapy.

Feminist theory and men

Feminist social work practice is not just for women; it can also be used with men. Men can also experience negative consequences due to societal expectations of their gender role. For example, men may experience some stress due to society's expectations of achievement, performance and masculinity (Levant, 1996), which are constantly reinforced through the patriarchal system. The patriarchal system is seen to reinforce men as powerful and in need of controlling their emotions, which can have negative effects for men who need to deal with feelings and emotions or are among those who are denied power or access to resources. Men can also experience discrimination and oppression due to race, ethnicity, class, age or sexual orientation.

The extent to which feminist theory can be applied to men depends on the ideological perspective of the social worker. For example, radical feminists would not work with men as they believe it would drain the female of all her energy and reinforce her role as a carer (Dominelli, 2002). Yet other feminists, such as liberal feminists, would work with men in an anti-sexist way in order to enable men to explore relationships and power imbalances or to express feelings and emotions that society often prohibits them from exploring. Working in an anti-sexist way requires 'a commitment not to impose gender stereotypes on either men or women and thereby limit their scope to experience the entire range of emotional experiences and work opportunities' (Dominelli, 2002, p. 97). Therefore, the goals and techniques of feminist theory discussed above could be applied to men in social work practice. For example, gender-role analysis can be used with a man who is experiencing external pressure not to pursue a career that is predominantly held by women by exploring the socially established gender role and an alternative way of viewing the situation that is more positive and acceptable to the man. Alternatively, problem-solving skills can be used with men to teach new ways of working with others that involve more collaboration, listening and negotiation skills instead of competition or dominance (Sharf, 2012).

Exercise box 6.1   Thoughts on feminist theory

In pairs or small groups discuss the following:

1   Explain a situation where you could incorporate the feminist techniques with women. What about with men?
2   What are the gender-role stereotypes that could be oppressive or discriminatory for women? What about for men?
3   Can male social workers practise feminist social work? Explain.

Case example: applying feminist theory to practice

Jessica is a 29-year-old, white British female who has come to see you at a community mental health agency specifically for women, due to struggling with anorexia. Jessica has ended a two-year marriage with Nick and has moved to a town several hours away from him to start a new life. Since her move, Jessica's anorexia has greatly increased and she realizes that she is ready to address the issue before she ends up hurting herself. Jessica discloses to you that she began having some difficulty with her eating habits when she married Nick and the problem had got progressively worse during their marriage together. Jessica has always been concerned with being thin and often watched her calorie intake and exercised at least five days a week. Nick always told Jessica that one of the reasons he married her was because she was thin and attractive. Nick would tell her, 'I won't let you get fat' and discussed how he would make sure she exercised if she ever became pregnant to prevent gaining too much weight. Nick took pride in Jessica's appearance and began to purchase provocative clothing for her, which he expected her to wear in public when with him. Jessica discloses to you that she felt as if Nick was controlling her life and she was losing her identity. Jessica and Nick divorced after two years due to Nick's infidelity, which left Jessica feeling as if she was not good enough for Nick. Jessica began to be increasingly concerned with her weight and now believes she has a problem that needs to be addressed.

You are a social worker who works from a feminist perspective. Based on the information that Jessica has disclosed, you theorize that Jessica has received messages from society and her relationships that tell her she is not attractive or worthy unless she is thin (*gender schema theory*). Her relationship with Nick has further validated this schema, due to his continual reminders that she needs to be thin. In the relationship with Nick, Jessica aimed to please him by watching her weight, exercising and wearing the clothes that he purchased, yet felt as if she was losing her sense of self and was becoming more of what Nick wanted her to be. Jessica reports that she often felt depressed, powerless and lonely in the relationship, and continues to feel this way despite the divorce from Nick (*relational-cultural model*). Jessica states that she does not really know who she is any more and controlling what goes into her body makes her feel comfortable by being able to control at least one aspect of her life.

Based on the information that Jessica has provided, combined with the feminist theoretical perspectives, you and Jessica decide that you will work towards increasing her sense of self-worth and self-esteem by exploring the messages and experiences that are contributing to her anorexia (*symptom removal*). The end goal of the work together is to eliminate the anorexia for Jessica and to have her feel worthy, empowered and in control of her life (*self-esteem and body image*). Jessica would like to explore how to have future relationships where she does not lose herself and is able to feel in control (*quality of interpersonal relationships*).

In order to achieve these goals, you and Jessica work through several feminist perspective techniques. You begin with a *gender-role analysis* where you ask Jessica to identify the consequences of the gender-role message, 'I must be thin in order to be attractive', and how this message has affected her. Jessica discusses how she has always looked at magazines and admired how thin the celebrities appeared and how she aimed to look like them. After meeting Nick, the desire to be thin was stronger particularly as he was attracted to thin women and he wanted her to be thin. Jessica admits that her anorexia is a way for her to ensure that she remains thin, yet she realizes that this is causing great harm to her body and is not giving her the happiness she had anticipated. Jessica states that all the messages she received, from the media and from Nick, have caused her a lot of harm. You and Jessica then decide how you can change this message to better fit her experiences and reality. You combine this step with another technique, *gender-role intervention*, where you give Jessica information about healthy weights, healthy women, the negative effects of anorexia and the way in which the media edits pictures to create a flawless image. Jessica begins to acknowledge that her thoughts about thinness are unhealthy and that beauty does not lie in someone's weight. Jessica explores the characteristics and traits of women in her life that she believes to be beautiful and begins to challenge the gender-role message that has caused her harm. Jessica ends the gender-role analysis by stating that beauty is actu-ally being healthy, both physically and mentally.

You and Jessica also participate in *assertiveness training* where you have Jessica discuss her experiences of losing herself in the relationship with Nick. Jessica explores how she was passive in the relationship with Nick and attempted to please him at the cost of ignoring her needs and wants. Jessica would like to have a relationship in the future, but wants one where both she and her partner feel comfortable and happy. You and Jessica practise how she could express her thoughts and desires to a partner, particularly during difficult situations, and discuss how being assertive would feel for her. Through the work together, Jessica is able to explore the underlying messages that were contributing to her presenting problem of anorexia. By exploring and challenging these messages, Jessica is able to learn from her past experiences and reframe the messages into ones that are more positive and acceptable to her. Jessica is able to prac-tise how to deal with future situations that could contribute to the presenting problem and reports feeling healthy, both physically and mentally, when the work together comes to an end.

Strengths and limitations

There are several strengths and limitations of feminist social work that are worth exploring before incorporating this theory into practice. Some strengths of the theory and its approach are as follows:

- The theory and practice is anti-oppressive in nature. Feminist social work practice has a commitment to social change where women and men are given equal access to opportunities and resources. The approach seeks to challenge gender-role stereotypes that oppress women, and to eliminate inequality by focusing on both the personal and political (Valentich, 2011). Additionally, women are not considered one homogenous group, but rather there is a focus on intersectionality where the diversity among women is considered in addition to sexism, such as racism, sexual orientation, ageism and classism.
- Feminist social work can be used in conjunction with other theories and methods, such as psychoanalytic theory, cognitive behavioural therapy, gestalt therapy, narrative therapy, solution-focused practice, empowerment and advocacy, crisis intervention and person-centred therapy. Social workers must first explore the theory to remove any gender biases that might impede the goals of feminist practice.
- Feminist social work practice is empowerment based. Social workers seek to work with women to challenge the inequalities and oppression experienced in relationships and in society. The goal is to empower women to utilize the strengths and resources available on the personal, interpersonal and societal level and to eliminate any boundaries that are prohibiting such use.

The limitations of feminist social work are as follows:

- Various feminist approaches may be in conflict with one another and thus lose sight of the true values and goals of feminist social work. Owing to the variance in feminist approaches and their underlying theoretical positions, some practitioners may be in opposition to one another. For example, radical feminists may criticize liberal feminists for allowing men to participate in the feminist approach, and liberal feminists may criticize radical feminists for self-disclosing with the woman client. Social workers should recognize that the approach is diverse and, therefore, should provide a clear rationale for their specific theoretical framework and approach (Bricker-Jenkins and Netting, 2009).
- Feminist social work is difficult to implement within managed care and state-run social services where social workers are faced with organizational rules, masculine language and cutbacks in funding (Valentich, 2011). As feminism seeks to challenge inequalities and power imbalances between men and women, the approach often requires intervening in the individual, interpersonal and the socio-political levels. The approach may be difficult to fully implement within all agencies or organizations where the emphasis of work is

solely on the individual, and there is no support, and limited resources, to advocate or intervene in larger societal systems.

Ethical and cultural considerations

Feminist social work practice primarily comes from western and developed countries, such as Australia, Canada, the United States and the UK, and therefore is more compatible with the societal norms and views of these cultures. This does not mean that feminist theorists and practitioners do not acknowledge the oppression of women from other cultures, but rather the theories and approaches may need to be adapted to fit with these cultures and societies (Valentich, 2011). Due to cultural differences, modern feminist theorists and practitioners are careful to consider cultural diversity and are reluctant to make generalizations about issues such as race, class, ethnicity, age and sexual orientation (Sharf, 2012). For example, the writings from the Stone Centre at Wellesley College have considered how to approach women from various cultures and classes (Jordan, 2010) and stress considering these issues in conjunction with sexism and not separately. When working with women who experience other forms of oppression, the social worker may want to consider groupwork for the client to receive support and help from other women with similar experiences. Additionally, feminist social work practice is also shown to be used with men, children and families, and therefore is not for women only (Orme, 2009a).

An important ethical guideline of feminist practice is the use of power by the social worker. As feminist practice seeks to challenge and diminish the power inequalities within society, social workers should maintain a relationship with the client that is collaborative and egalitarian in nature (Jordan, 2010; Sharf, 2012; Valentich, 2011). There should be no issues of power and the social worker is not viewed as the expert but, rather, clients are experts in their own situations and experiences. Additionally, ethical issues include the use of self-disclosure by the social worker, which should be limited and only used in accordance with agency guidelines and the principles and values established for the social work profession.

Feminist theory and practice and anti-oppressive practice

Feminist social work practice is anti-oppressive in nature. Feminist theories challenge the existing stereotypes and gender roles that are established by the dominant members of society as they are seen to oppress women and limit the ability to access resources and opportunities for equality with men. Women are not viewed as a homogenous group, but, rather, the diversity of women is considered in terms of ethnicity, social class, sexual orientation, culture and age (e.g. intersectionality). Feminist theory challenges existing sociological, psychological and social work theories that have been created by men and primarily for men, yet marketed as being gender neutral. The feminist perspective seeks to provide social work practice from an anti-oppressive approach that empowers women to access and receive resources and opportunities that originally have been limited or blocked. Empowerment is a critical feature of feminist social work and involves the social worker intervening collaboratively with the client on the personal, interpersonal and socio-political levels to challenge the oppression and provide opportunities for equality.

Research on feminist theory

The effectiveness of feminist theory is difficult to establish as the principles, values and techniques of feminist practice are often incorporated with other methods, such as cognitive behavioural therapy, solution-focused practice, empowerment, groupwork or advocacy work. The feminist approach, relational-cultural therapy – based on the relational-cultural model – has been found to be effective, both short and long term, with women who attend a community-based mental health centre (Oakley et al., 2013), with adolescent incarcerated females (Lenz et al., 2012), in terms of relational power and engagement with others, and is argued to be effective when working with individuals with eating disorders (Trepal et al., 2012) and when working with children who have experienced trauma (Vicario et al., 2013). Other research has attempted to measure the extent to which feminist principles and values are being integrated into therapy sessions. For example, McGeorge et al. (2013) sought to validate the Feminist Couple Therapy Scale (FaCTS), which measures the extent to which therapists incorporate feminist principles and values when working with heterosexual couples. The authors found that therapists had an underlying belief in addressing patriarchy and power differentials between men and women in their practice with heterosexual couples.

An integrative review of the effectiveness of feminist practice by Gorey et al. (2003) provides evidence that feminist methods were more effective in changing larger systems than other practice models and, in particular, radical feminist approaches were more effective than liberal approaches. This review compared 35 studies of feminist interventions with 44 studies of other social work interventions. Of the 35 feminist interventions, 22 were considered liberal approaches and tended to target the individual and 13 were radical and tended to target larger systems. The majority of the interventions (83 per cent) consisted of groupwork. The findings revealed that approximately 17 out of every 20 women who participated in the feminist social work practice were better off than the average woman receiving alternative methods, and those women who received the radical feminist approaches were better off than the women who received the liberal approaches. The findings indicate that interventions based on feminist theory and the specific needs of women are more effective than non-feminist approaches and that intervening in larger systems creates better change than intervening on behalf of the individual.

Summary

Feminist social work practice is a method of working that focuses on the power imbalance and inequalities between women and men. The approach is influenced by the ecological perspective, which views the interdependence and interconnection between a person and her or his environment. The approach acknowledges the differences between women and men in regard to relationships, power, gender roles, development and experiences and seeks to challenge the oppression and inequalities that society places on women. The approach works towards an end goal of empowerment and equality for women by intervening into the personal, interpersonal and socio-political systems. Although the approach was initially developed for work with women, it can be used with men and children.

Case study

Ayesha is a 28-year-old, Pakistani British female who has called a women's refuge after fleeing her husband, Umar, with her two children (aged 6 and 2). Ayesha states that Umar punched and kicked her last night, causing her to fall down the stairs with her 2-year-old daughter in her arms; both appeared to be unhurt physically. Umar then left the house in a rage, and Ayesha packed a single bag of clothes for her two children and fled to her cousin's house. She tells you that her cousin has asked that she leave soon as they are fearful that Umar will find her, and hiding Ayesha and her children would look bad on the whole family. You arrange for Ayesha and her two children to be picked up by taxi and brought to the women's refuge. Once there, Ayesha begins to question whether she has done the right thing. She mentions how she fears disgracing her and Umar's families as they have very strong cultural beliefs about marriage and staying together. Ayesha states that maybe she has overreacted and coming to the refuge will cause more harm than good. She says she would like to leave Umar to protect herself and her children, but does not know how she will survive financially or how her family will react. Describe how you would utilize feminist theory and practice in your work with Ayesha.

Further reading and web resources

Affilia, The Journal of Social Work with Women.
> A peer-reviewed journal that publishes articles on social work practice and issues involving women.

Enns, C.Z. (2004) *Feminist Theories and Feminist Psychotherapies: Origins, Themes, and Diversity*, 2nd edn. New York: Haworth.
> Provides a historical overview of feminist practice, explores feminist theories, and illustrates the application of theories to practice.

Feminist.com:
> http://www.feminist.com – a website that provides resources on women's issues, such as legislation, activism, anti-violence, books, articles and speeches.

Feminist Majority Foundation:
> http://www.feminist.org – a website that provides resources on women's issues and global feminism.

Hyde, J.S. and Else-Quest, N. (2013) *Half the Human Experience: The Psychology of Women*, 8th edn. Belmont, CA: Wadsworth.
> Provides an overview of the psychology of women and addresses feminist theories and topics around gender. Includes a chapter on the psychology of men and male roles.

White, V. (2006) *The State of Feminist Social Work*. London: Routledge.
> Explores how to incorporate feminist theory into various systems, such as statutory social work, education, relationships and management.

References

Bern, S.L. (1981) Gender schema theory: a cognitive account of sex typing, *Psychological Review*, 88(4): 354–64.

Bern, S.L. (1983) Gender schema theory and its implications for child development: raising gender-aschematic children in a gender-schematic society, *Signs*, 8(4): 598–616.

Bricker-Jenkins, M. and Hooyman, N.R. (eds) (1986) *Not for Women Only: Social Work Practice for a Feminist Future*. Silver Spring, MD: National Association of Social Workers.

Bricker-Jenkins, M. and Netting, F.E. (2009) Feminist issues and practices in social work, in A. Roberts (ed.), *Social Workers' Desk Reference*, 2nd edn. New York: Oxford University Press.

Comstock, D.L., Hammer, T.R., Strentzsch, J., Cannon, K., Parson, J. and Salazar, G. (2008) Relational-cultural theory: a framework for bridging relational, multicultural, and social justice competencies, *Journal of Counseling & Development*, 86(3): 279–87.

Dominelli, L. (2002) *Feminist Social Work Theory and Practice*. Basingstoke: Palgrave Macmillan.

Enns, C.Z. (2004) *Feminist Theories and Feminist Psychotherapies: Origins, Themes, and Diversity*, 2nd edn. New York: Haworth.

Gitterman, A. and Germain, C.B. (2008) *The Life Model of Social Work Practice: Advances in Theory and Practice*, 3rd edn. New York: Columbia University Press.

Gorey, K.M., Daly, C., Richter, N.L., Gleason, D.R. and McCallum, M.A. (2003) The effectiveness of feminist social work methods, *Journal of Social Service Research*, 29(1): 37–55.

Hyde, J.S. and Else-Quest, N. (2013) *Half the Human Experience: The Psychology of Women*, 8th edn. Belmont, CA: Wadsworth.

Jordan, J.V. (2010) *Relational-Cultural Therapy*. Washington, DC: American Psychological Association.

Klein, M.H. (1976) Feminist concepts of therapy outcome, *Psychotherapy: Theory, Research, and Practice*, 13: 89–95.

Le, A.T. and Miller, P.W. (2010) Glass ceiling and double disadvantage effects: women in the US labour market, *Applied Economics*, 42(5): 603–13.

Lenz, A.S., Speciale, M. and Aguilar, J.V. (2012) Relational-cultural therapy intervention with incarcerated adolescents: a single-case effectiveness design, *Counselling Outcome Research and Evaluation*, 3(1): 17–29.

Levant, R.F. (1996) The new psychology of men, *Professional Psychology: Research and Practice*, 27(3): 259–65.

McGeorge, C.R., Carlson, T.S. and Toomey, R.B. (2013) Establishing the validity of the feminist couple therapy scale: measuring therapists' use of feminist practices with heterosexual couples, *Journal of Couple & Relationship Therapy*, 12(1): 3–21.

Miller, J.B. (1976) *Toward a New Psychology of Women*. Boston, MA: Beacon Press.

Miller, J.B. (1988) Connections, disconnections, and violations, *Work in Progress*, no. 33. Wellesley, MA: Stone Center Working Paper Series.

Oakley, M.A., Addison, S.C., Piran, N., Johnston, G.J., Damianakis, M., Curry, J., Dunbar, C., and Welgeldt, A. (2013) Outcome study of brief relational-cultural therapy in a women's mental health center, *Psychotherapy Research*, 23(2): 137–51.

Orme, J. (2009a) Feminist social work, in M. Gray and S. Webb (eds), *Social Work Theories and Methods*, 2nd edn. London: Sage.

Orme, J. (2009b) Feminist social work, in R. Adams, L. Dominelli and M. Payne (eds), *Critical Practice in Social Work*, 2nd edn. Basingstoke: Palgrave Macmillan.

Scott, J.L., Dex, S. and Joshi, H. (2008) *Women in Employment: Changing Lives and New Challenges*. Cheltenham: Edward Elgar Publishing.

Sharf, R.S. (2012) *Theories of Psychotherapy and Counseling: Concepts and Cases*, 5th edn. Belmont, CA: Brooks Cole.

Sturdivant, S. (1980) *Therapy with Women*. New York: Springer.

Trepal, H.C., Boie, I., Kress, V.E. (2012) A relational-cultural approach to working with clients with eating disorders, *Journal of Counselling & Development*, 90(3): 346–56.

Valentich, M. (2011) Feminist theory and social work practice, in F.J. Turner (ed.), *Social Work Treatment: Interlocking Theoretical Approaches*, 5th edn. New York: Free Press.

Vicario, M., Tucker, C., Smith, S.A. and Hudgins-Mitchell, C. (2013) Relational-cultural play therapy: re-establishing healthy connections with children exposed to trauma in relationships, *International Journal of Play Therapy*, 22(2): 103–17.

Worell, J. and Remer, P. (2003) *Feminist Perspectives in Therapy: Empowering Diverse Women*, 2nd edn. Hoboken, NJ: Wiley & Sons.

7 Person-centred approach

David C. Kondrat

Introduction

Carl Rogers developed the person-centred approach, or therapy, and the person-centred theory of personality from his direct work with clients in a therapeutic setting. His therapy and theory of personality evolved from the humanistic school of psychology. Like other humanistic theories, person-centred theory holds at its core a basic belief in the growth-oriented nature of human development (DeCarvalho, 1990). Person-centred theory asserts that humans wish to grow and to discover their true self. Environmental forces, and the ensuing psychological responses to the environmental forces, often disrupt persons from discovering their true self to the point where their psychological growth can become stifled. Despite this disruption, the person remains capable of growth and development and able to undergo personality change (Ziegler, 2002).

The goal of the person-centred approach is to help clients discover their true self, a self which has been hidden from the client's awareness (Sharf, 2012). Goals for the client include: (1) the ability to discover the internal freedom that is embedded in each individual, which can be used to make choices about how to live; (2) a recognition that the individual is responsible for her or his life; and (3) a realization that the individual is capable of making such important decisions (Rogers, 1961). This chapter explores Rogers' theory of personality, the person-centred approach and the sufficient and necessary conditions to facilitate change and foster human growth and development.

Origins of the person-centred approach

The person-centred approach traces its origins to humanistic psychology, and humanistic psychology traces its roots back to older philosophical traditions that emerged in the sixteenth century and the Renaissance (Crain, 2011). At that time, humans were viewed as sinful and in need of submitting themselves to the will of God. Humanism emerged as a criticism of a church-dominated view of the person as sinful. A strong sense of individualism permeated the writings of humanistic philosophers of the

Renaissance. Humans beings, themselves, began to be viewed as good and valued, and were seen as existing for their own sake and not just for God's.

Like the humanistic thinkers of the Renaissance, humanistic psychology emerged as a reaction to the deterministic and limited view of humanness that was the hallmark of the two dominant schools of psychological thought: psychodynamic theory and behaviourism (Crain, 2011; DeCarvalho, 1990). To early humanists, classical psycho-analytic theories focused too narrowly on the role of the unconscious and erotic moti-vation in determining behaviour, which led to a pessimistic and fatalistic view of the human condition. Behaviourists, similarly, were critiqued for having too narrow a view of human behaviour and motivation as early humanists did not agree that behaviour was solely determined in some derivation of a stimulus–response relationship. Consequently, humanism and humanists believe that theory building and practice should start with and focus on the human being. Humanism holds that, 'human beings supersede the sum of their parts (a holistic perspective including "body", "soul" and "mind"), that they live consciously, have the free will to decide and live towards aims' (Schmid, 2007, p. 31).

Carl Rogers' person-centred approach, or therapy, is part of the humanistic movement in psychology. His first job, after graduating from Teachers College, Columbia University, was as a psychologist at the Child Study Department of the Society for the Prevention of Cruelty to Children (Rogers, 1961). His work with children and families serendipitously moved him towards his view of person-centred therapy. While Rogers (1961) describes a number of influences on his view of therapy, one story stands out. Rogers was working with a woman whose child was described as a 'hellion' and Rogers, as well as the client, realized that therapy was not working. The woman asked if Rogers did personal therapy and he agreed to see the woman. When she arrived, he let her talk about her frustrations with life, her family and her husband. Rogers argued that it was letting her tell her story that resulted in treatment success:

> This incident was one of a number which helped me to experience the fact – only fully realized later – that it is the client who knows what hurts, what directions to go, what problems are crucial, what experiences have been deeply buried. It began to occur to me that unless I had a need to demonstrate my own cleverness and learning, I would do better to rely upon the client for the direction of movement of the process.
>
> (Rogers, 1995, pp. 11–12)

According to Sharf (2012), it was during this time that Rogers developed his non-directive approach to therapy. Over time, and at many different locations, such as The Ohio State University, the University of Chicago and the University of Wisconsin, Rogers and his colleagues developed and refined a person-centred approach to practice. Rogers is credited with moving counselling from being psychiatrist and psychoanalyst driven to being accessible and utilized by all other helping professions, including social work (Kirschenbaum and Henderson, 1984).

The person-centred approach explained

A person-centred view of self: Rogers' theory of personality

Carl Rogers' (1959) theory of personality developed out of his direct work with clients in therapy. The development of this theory was through a post hoc consideration of the personality mechanisms and client experiences that led his clients to seek treatment. The theory is deeply steeped in Rogers' own experiences as a therapist and researcher of the therapeutic process. Central to understanding his theory of personality is the concept of the self, commonly referred to as self-concept. Rogers (1959, p. 200) defined the self as 'the organized, consistent conceptual gestalt composed of perceptions of the characteristics of the "I" or "me" and the perceptions of the relationship of the "I" or "me" to others and to the various aspects of life, together with the values attached to these perceptions'. The self is the platform from which an individual perceives and symbolizes her or his world and place within this world. Every experience and feeling is screened by the self to determine its place within conscience awareness.

According to Rogers (1959), in addition to the differentiation of the self from others there is a need for positive regard, which is experienced and felt through making a difference in the life of another. Positive regard is often associated with the direct or indirect perception of praise or affirmation that an individual receives from another. The need for positive regard represents a universal striving for all individuals and to fulfil this need, individuals look outside themselves for positive affirmation from others who are present in the individual's field of awareness.

Positive regard from another is often conditional where only those actions that the other individual values are praised and encouraged (Rogers, 1959). In many situations, individuals put restraints on the positive regard that they provide to others. For example, parents often praise the behaviours of their children that they regard as good and worthy, yet parents will not provide positive regard (that is, affirmation, praise) for those behaviours that are deemed inappropriate or disappointing. Consequently, individuals tend to act in such ways that maximize the amount of positive regard that they receive from others.

One can argue that the need for positive regard acts as a motivational system. Individuals engage in activities that lead to positive regard from others and abstain from those activities that do not. The need for positive regard from another can potentially overpower individuals in the sense that they begin to act in ways that please others and not necessarily themselves. This can often be observed in abusive or controlling relationships where individuals act in ways to appease or make the abuser/ controller happy instead of acting in ways that benefit themselves. This process can lead to a deterioration of the individual's positive self-regard.

Positive regard, as received by others, develops in concert with one's self-regard (Rogers, 1959). Self-regard is the internalization of the positive regard, conditional or unconditional, that the individual experiences from others. Self-regard can be viewed as an individual's sense of self-worth or esteem and is influenced by the way in which others perceive and react to the individual. As a particular experience becomes symbolized in awareness as worthy of regard from others, the experience becomes internalized by individuals as worthy of regard for themselves. Thus, positive self-regard is often directly associated with the positive regard given by another.

Self-regard becomes another motivational system for the individual. Experiences symbolized as worthy of self-regard serve as the criteria for judging all experiences, therefore, individuals become more selective of experiences that fit with and confirm their sense of self-regard. In this process, individuals are setting up conditions of worth, which serve as a tool for individuals to determine which experiences to avoid and which to engage in. For example, if a woman is told she is not a good public speaker, she may feel frightened when having to speak in public and will avoid any public engagements that require speaking. This behaviour is in contrast to a woman who is repeatedly praised for her clear and informative speeches who then actively seeks situations where she speaks publicly.

Incongruence between self and experience

As individuals develop conditions of worth, the perceptions they have about any experience become filtered through the conditions of worth (Rogers, 1959). Experiences that are in line with one's conditions of worth are accurately perceived in awareness (that is, accurately acknowledged), and experiences which are not in line with one's conditions of worth are distorted or ignored. Considering our example above, the woman presents in a public place where she immediately believes she gave a horrible speech. She is praised by someone for the speech, yet ignores this comment and believes the person is 'just being nice'. As this example illustrates, incongruence develops between the self of the person and her or his experiences. Behaviours that are congruent with the conditions of worth are recognized as coming from the self and behaviours that are not congruent with the conditions of worth are not recognized as originating in the self. Let us consider another example: Tina was always overshadowed by her older sister, Hilary, who was the shining star of the family. Hilary was an excellent student, singer and athlete. Tina's parents always bragged about Hilary and would consistently make comments such as, 'Hilary's our bright child', 'We are so proud of Hilary' and 'Do it like Hilary does' (lack of positive regard). Therefore, Tina always believed that she was not worthy of praise as she could never live up to her sister's abilities and accomplishments (self-regard) and therefore never enrolled in after school functions or sporting events as she did not believe she was good enough (conditions of worth). Tina always attributed any of her accomplishments to luck or fate (distorted conditions of worth). After Tina finished university, she applied for a job at a successful marketing firm in London and received an offer for a prestigious position. Tina immediately thought that she was the only one who applied for the position as there was no way she could have been selected for the position on her own merits. In this case, Tina's behaviours and actions (applying and receiving the job) were not congruent with her conditions of worth, therefore, the firm's offer must have been based on external factors (assumptions that no one else applied) versus her own merits.

Individuals with large amounts of conditions of worth often have a rigid sense of self, and are often inflexible to new experiences that are not in line with their sense of self (Rogers, 1959). Rogers has used the term intentionality to describe the behaviours and perceptions of such persons. When individuals act with intentionality they 'see experiences in absolute and unconditional terms, to over generalize, to be dominated by concept or belief, to fail to anchor his reactions in space and time, to confuse fact and evaluation, to rely upon abstractions, rather than upon reality-testing' (Rogers, 1959, p. 204). Such an individual can be said to be closed rather than open to new experiences.

Experiences that are incongruent with a person's sense of self are often subceived by the self as being a threat (for example, noticed by the person without the incongruence being accurately acknowledged). As a result, the person often develops defences such as fantasy or projection, or develops paranoid types of thoughts or phobias to keep the experiences from being accurately perceived (Rogers, 1959). An accurate perception of these experiences would lead to greater levels of anxiety, disorganized behaviour and dysfunction on the part of the individual, or it can lead to a change in the self-concept.

Great amounts of incongruence between individuals' self-concepts and their experiences, coupled with a sudden realization of the incongruence by individuals, will overwhelm their defences and a complete breakdown will ensue (Rogers, 1959). Basically, the individuals recognize the incongruence because their defences are no longer adequate to ward off awareness of the incongruence. The complete breakdown is characterized by a 'tension between the concept of self (with its included distorted perceptions) and experiences which are not accurately symbolized or included in the concept of self' (Rogers, 1959, p. 229). Thus, the individual is unable to discern how to perceive a particular experience. What often results are dysfunctional or irrational behaviours that the person is unable to control (Rogers, 1959). When individuals are able to re-establish their defences after this breaking point, they are often left feeling as if they are unable to control their lives and their sense of self is changed to account for this feeling of inadequacy.

Goals of intervention: who emerges from therapy?

Rogers (1959; 1961; 1969) articulated an ideal picture of the person who emerges from therapy, or any person who is in the process of becoming. It is important to note that what follows is an ideal and not a real picture of the person that is in the process of becoming; most individuals will not meet this ideal but will simply approximate it. This ideal representation of the person who emerges from therapy describes the direction of human growth and a person who holds a sense of self that is unique and distinct from others. This is represented by the following four components as defined by Rogers (1961, pp. 115–23):

1 *An individual is open to experience.* Such an individual is able to experience life as it exists at any moment without distorting it or forcing it into preconceived structures – structures that are congruent with their distorted self-concept. The person acts with extensionality versus intentionality.

2 *An individual is able to gain trust in her or his own organism.* Because such an individual is open to experience, she or he is able to see the self as a

trustworthy decision-maker. An individual who is in the process of becoming is able to weigh her or his perception of the self and experience to make accurate decisions about how to live a satisfying life. Further, such individuals actually perceive themselves as able to make choices that will meet their own needs and desires.

3   *An individual develops an internal locus of evaluation.* Individuals often develop a self-concept that is rooted in other peoples' expectations and ideas of them. However, individuals in the process of becoming recognize the importance of their own evaluation of the perceptions of self and of experiences. Such an evaluation enables a person to make accurate decisions and judgements about how to proceed with life in a way that is congruent with whom he or she really is. Basically, the person uses her or his organismic valuing process as the criterion for making decisions rather than using conditions of worth.

4   *An individual engaged in the process of becoming recognizes that life and the discovery of self are processes and not end points.* Individuals who are engaged in discovering their real self realize that they are 'a stream of becoming, not a fixed and static entity; a flowing river of change, not a block of solid material; a continually changing constellation of potentialities, not a fixed quantity of traits' (Rogers, 1961, p. 122).

Necessary and sufficient conditions

Rogers (1957; 1959) asserts that there are six necessary and sufficient conditions of the therapeutic process. When present, these six conditions, irrespective of any other therapeutic technique, milieu or client characteristic, will foster personality and behavioural change in clients. The six necessary and sufficient conditions include the following: (1) there is contact between client and therapist; (2) the client is experiencing incongruence; (3) the therapist is congruent in the relationship; (4) the therapist expresses and experiences unconditional positive regard towards the client; (5) the therapist experiences empathetic understanding of the client and her or his perception of experiences; and (6) the client perceives, at least minimally, the conditions of empathy and unconditional positive regard. Each of these conditions is explained below as described by Rogers (1957; 1959). Although Rogers uses the term 'therapist', we acknowledge this term to be used interchangeably with psychologist, counsellor and social worker, therefore, we use the terms 'therapist' or 'practitioner' throughout this chapter.

1   *The therapist and client must be in personal or psychological contact.* To be in contact, both the therapist and the client must be aware of the relationship and to be aware of the contact, 'each must make a perceived difference in the experiential field of the other' (Rogers, 1957, p. 96). The perception of contact is required for therapy to work.

2   *The client must be in a state of incongruence.* The client must be in a state of incongruence, perceived or subceived, between the client's concept of self and

her or his experiences. Basically, the client must be in a state of anxiety or other psychological or emotional distress. Rogers has postulated that a client who is minimally aware of the incongruence, rather than not aware of the incongruence, will be more willing to be involved in the therapeutic process. As clients become more aware of this incongruence, they become more willing to enter into the therapeutic process.

3   *The therapist must be congruent in the therapeutic relationship.* Congruence occurs when the therapist 'is freely and deeply himself, with his actual experience accurately represented by his awareness of himself' (Rogers, 1957, p. 97). Congruence is often used interchangeably with genuineness. Therapists are keenly aware of the experiences of being with the client in a relationship and their feelings about or towards the client. What the therapist is thinking and feeling on the inside is what is being displayed on the outside. Being congruent in the relationship does not mean that the therapist tells the client about her or his feelings. Only when the therapist's feelings about the client or the therapeutic situation could diminish the therapeutic relationship must the therapist communicate these feelings to the client. An important note: Rogers (1957) has argued that the therapist need only be congruent in the therapist–client relationship; it is not necessary that she or he be congruent outside the therapeutic milieu.

4   *The therapist must experience and express to the client unconditional positive regard.* As previously written, individuals who experience unconditional positive regard do not develop conditions of worth and tend to be more psychologically well adjusted. The job of the therapist is to unconditionally accept clients for who they are and what they are experiencing. The therapist must accept both the positive and negative feelings of the client. As Rogers (1957, p. 98) has written of this condition: 'It means a caring for the client, but not in a possessive way or in such a way as simply to satisfy the therapist's own needs. It means a caring for the client as a *separate* person, with permission to have his own feelings, his own experiences' (original emphasis).

5   *The therapist must experience accurate empathetic understanding of the client.* The therapist must be aware of the client's sense of self and her or his perceptions of experience as it relates to the concept of self. The therapist must enter the client's world without losing sight of her or his own world. By experiencing empathetic understanding of the client, the therapist is able to communicate to the client aspects of the client's experiences and sense of self for which the client has both awareness and limited awareness.

6   *The client must perceive, at least minimally, the conditions of empathy and unconditional positive regard.* The therapist not only needs to empathize with the client and provide the client with unconditional positive regard, but the client must also experience these conditions in a way that are accurately recognized in awareness. Basically, the client must feel accepted and understood by the therapist. Without the perception on the part of the client of accurate empathy and unconditional positive regard, the client will not engage in the therapeutic relationship. Table 7.1 summarizes the six necessary and sufficient conditions.

Table 7.1 The six necessary and sufficient conditions

- The therapist and client are in contact
- The client is in a state of incongruence
- The therapist is congruent/genuine
- The therapist experiences unconditional positive regard towards the client
- The therapist experiences an empathic understanding of the client's experiences
- The client perceives the therapist's congruence, unconditional positive regard and empathy

As Rogers (1957; 1959) has made clear, each of these six conditions is a matter of degree. That is, each condition is not an all or nothing proposition. For example, a therapist will not always provide unconditional positive regard towards a client. At some point the therapist will, wittingly or unwittingly, experience and communicate positive or negative regard towards the client, thus the conditions serve as ideals. The therapist holds the job of fostering a therapeutic relationship that closely approximates the six core conditions.

When the six conditions are present, the therapeutic process will ensue (Rogers, 1959). This process is characterized by clients becoming increasingly aware of their concept of self and of their experiences. Basically, clients are able to more accurately perceive experiences that were once distorted or denied in awareness. This happens through the process of the client becoming more aware of her or his incongruence. The client feels safe in exploring the incongruence, due to the therapist's communication of unconditional positive regard and expressing empathetic understanding to the client. As a result of this exploration, the client increasingly becomes able to use her or his organismic valuing process instead of her or his conditions of worth as the criterion for evaluating experiences. Clients become keenly aware of their responsibility for their own life and the freedom that they have to make decisions. Because of the six necessary and sufficient conditions, clients are able to engage in the process of treatment.

Exercise box 7.1 Exploring the necessary and sufficient conditions

In pairs or a small group, take turns answering the following questions:

1   Who has provided you with unconditional positive regard? How did this make you feel?
2   Who has provided you with conditional positive regard? What were the conditions? How did this make you feel?
3   As a social worker, how would you know if your client was experiencing you as being empathetic, congruent and providing unconditional positive regard?
4   Are Rogers' necessary and sufficient conditions necessary? Are they sufficient?
5   How would you use the necessary and sufficient conditions in practice with persons mandated to treatment?

Current trends

The early formulation of person-centred therapy has left an indelible mark on individual practice. The 'necessary and sufficient' conditions undergird many modern
approaches to direct practice, including practices that provide a more directive
approach to therapy than person centred. Practitioners understand the importance of
developing a strong working alliance and recognize that Roger's conditions are essential for achieving this end. For example, few persons would discount the importance of
empathy in developing a strong working relationship (Watson, 2001). While many
forms of psychotherapy have adopted the practices of person-centred therapy, it has
also adapted to meet the demands of current practice.

Person-centred care has found a home in work with people with dementia (Brooker,
2005; Kitwood, 1993). Kitwood (1993) recognized that the system that cared for people
with dementia was dehumanizing. He also recognized that dementia could not be
reduced to a medical explanation; rather, dementia involves a delicate interplay
between ones personality, biography, physical health status, neurological impairment
and social psychology (pp. 541–2). His person-centred approach was built on his multi-
faceted understanding of people with dementia.

Brooker (2003, p. 216) summarizes Kitwood's person-centred treatment philosophy
as '(1) Valuing people with dementia and choosing to care for them; (2) Treating people
as individuals; (3) Looking at the world from the perspective of the person with
dementia; and (4) A positive social environment in which the person living with
dementia can experience relative well-being'. Central to Kitwood's treatment philosophy is reclaiming the person with dementia. People with dementia must not be reduced
to their illness, should be viewed as people fully capable of interacting with their environment, and should be valued as wholly human (Brooker, 2003). Kitwood understood
the need for using best practices in the treatment of people with dementia, just not at
the expense of taking away the personhood of clients (Dewing, 2008).

Also central to Kitwood's (1993) theory is the environment that cares for people
with dementia. Kitwood was particularly troubled by the treatment environments and
the tactics used by treatment providers, for example, using treachery, lying to people
with dementia to gain compliance, or invalidating the lived experience of the person
with dementia. Professionals and the treatment milieu are often part of the problem.
Providing state-of-the-art treatment in an environment that is dehumanizing can be
iatrogenic. The social environment needed to foster a sense of humanity requires 'assertion of desire, emotional ambience, initiation of social contact, showing affection,
sensitivity to others' feelings, self-respect, acceptance of other emotional sufferers,
humour, creativity, helpfulness, taking pleasure, and physical activities' (p. 543).

As a way of assessing the extent to which a client is receiving person-centred help
from a dementia-focused treatment environment, Kitwood developed dementia care
mapping (DCM). In addition to assessing the person-centeredness of the treatment
milieu, DCM is also a heuristic method of helping staff become more person-centred by
recognizing ways in which they can adhere to a person-centred approach to care
(Brooker, 2005). People using DCM collect data in two ways (Kuhn et al., 2000). The

first is the behaviour category code that consists of 24 domains (activities). In addition, staff interactions with people with dementia are footnoted and coded as being beneficial interactions or personal detractors.

Kitwood's approach to dementia care provides evidence for how person-centred care can be modified to help meet the needs of clients. While not denying the important use of state-of-the-art therapies, Kitwood's approach acknowledges the importance of the person receiving care. His approach also recognizes that interactions are opportunities to enable people to live to their full potential.

Case example: applying the person-centred approach to practice

Nicki, a 22-year-old, African-Caribbean female, recently lost her mother to cancer and is struggling with what to do with her future. She describes her mother as 'the most important person in my life'. Nicki is an only child and her father died when she was 2; he was a firefighter and died in a house fire. In order to help her daughter have a better life, Nicki's mother moved them both from Jamaica to London when Nicki was 5 years old. Her mother encouraged her daughter to do well in school, which she did (especially in mathematics and science) and hoped her daughter would one day be a physician. After Nicki had completed her schooling, her mother became sick with pancreatic cancer. For the past three years, Nicki has been her mother's primary carer and, when she was not working at the local supermarket, she would spend all her time with her mother. Now that her mother is gone, Nicki feels lost. She does not want to work at the store, but does not feel she can do anything else.

You are a social worker who utilizes the person-centred approach. You attempt to be congruent in your relationships with clients where what you are thinking and feeling on the inside is what is being displayed on the outside. In your work with Nicki, you seek to empathetically understand her and her situation and experiences and hold a positive regard towards her. You begin your process of work with Nicki by listening to her story and reflecting back to her both feelings and the content of what you hear in her story. At one point in the conversation, Nicki states that she feels so numb she is unsure that she will ever feel normal. To show congruence in the relationship you reply, 'I hear that you are feeling numb, and maybe a little lost. But, you came here for help so that we can work on these issues together during this hard time'.

At another point during treatment, Nicki begins to weep and states she disappointed her mother because she did not become a doctor. She continues, 'I don't feel as if there is anything left for me. My life is in shambles and I know that where I am right now is where I will stay'. You recognize the need to provide unconditional positive regard and state, 'I know that you are feeling as though your future will not get better and you will be stuck feeling and living as you are now. I just want you to know that I care about you and your future'. Nicki continues to weep and states how lost and hopeless she feels. As a way of showing empathy, you meet each of Nicki's statements with a reflection of both the content and emotions of what you hear.

Through the course of your meetings with Nicki, she discusses how the last three years were hard on her, particularly as she saw her mother become progressively ill. She felt powerless to help her mother. By the third session, however, she moves from stating that she was powerless to discussing how rewarding it was to be there for her mother, who had moved her to England for a better life. The conversation moves to Nicki's future. She states, 'My mum always wanted me to become a doctor. I never shared this desire. I don't know what I want to be. But, I know that I don't want to be stuck working as a cashier forever.' You continue to let Nicki know you are listening to what she is saying. At the end of the sessions together, Nicki decides that she will explore occupations and universities, and possibly enrol in an access course to assist in moving towards obtaining a degree. Nicki states, 'I think that this is the best way for me to honour my mother's memory'. You disclose that you admire Nicki's hard work over the past couple of months and state that you hope Nicki will enjoy her time at university.

Strengths and limitations

There are several strengths and limitations of the person-centred approach that are worth exploring before incorporating this approach into social work practice. Some of the strengths of this approach are as follows:

- Rogers' work has had an impact on the helping profession. Farber (2007) argues that Rogers' necessary and sufficient conditions, while not generally accepted as sole means to therapeutic change, have had a pervasive, and sometimes unnoticed, impact on psychotherapy. He lists four influences of Rogers' work: (1) a shift from understanding clinical material in terms of a one-person model to understanding these issues with a two-person model or field; (2) a similar shift from attributing therapeutic gain to accurate therapist interpretations to attributing improvement to the provision of a collaborative therapeutic relationship; (3) a shift from therapeutic neutrality and detachment towards acceptance of usefulness of overt expressions of the therapist's caring; and (4) a similar shift away from analytic anonymity towards acceptance of the usefulness of therapist disclosure to clients (Farber, 2007, p. 292). So while not sufficient, a strength of Rogers' conditions are their necessity.
- All or aspects of the person-centred approach can be used in combination with other theories and methods. For example, motivational interviewing is based on the basic principles of the person-centred approach of empathy, congruence and unconditional positive regard (see Chapter 8).
- The person-centred approach is empowering and anti-oppressive in nature. This approach seeks to work with clients and not on clients, and stresses the importance of the client directing the course of work together. Clients are not labelled, but rather are accepted for who they are and where they want to go.

Some of the limitations of the person-centred approach are as follows:

- Some theorists and practitioners question whether the six necessary and sufficient conditions are in fact sufficient for all cases. As Silberschatz (2007,

p. 266) states, 'I am in full agreement with Rogers that his proposed conditions are necessary for therapeutic change to occur, but I do question whether they are entirely sufficient in all cases'. While the conditions provide a base from which the work of practice can begin, therapeutic techniques (such as home-work assignments or breathing techniques) are often required for true thera-peutic progress to occur.

- Implementing the person-centred approach in the purest sense may not be possible in all situations. Practitioners may come under time or agency constraints when working with clients that prohibit them from implementing the person-centred approach in the purest sense. The practitioner may begin the work with the client by showing unconditional positive regard, empathy and congruence, yet have to be more directive in the work together due to time or agency constraints, thereby deviating from the non-directive nature of the person-centred approach.
- Practitioners may argue that it is not possible to be truly empathic, congruent or have unconditional positive regard for all clients. Some practitioners may find being empathic, congruent or showing unconditional positive regard diffi-cult with some clients, particularly where the client has been the perpetrator of abuse or neglect or other antisocial behaviours. Practitioners are encouraged to be honest with themselves and with clients, and should seek supervision when experiencing difficulty in establishing a relationship with a client.
- As noted by Rowe (2011), Rogers took a non-authoritative stance towards working with clients that may be uncomfortable for some social workers. While social work values collaborative relationships, power differentials do exist and should not be ignored; and some situations demand that the social worker play an active role in treatment. During times of acute crises, social workers may need to actively lead clients because times of crisis often leave clients overtaxed and unable to make concrete decisions.
- A fundamental reality of social work treatment is to provide clients with the best treatment available, including evidence-based practices (EBP) and emerging best practices (National Association of Social Workers, 2008). Ardent adherents of a person-centred approach solely use the relationship between the social worker and client as the agent of change, which is in conflict with social work's professional obligation to provide clients the option of the best treatment.

Ethical and cultural considerations

Rogers' non-directive approach to practice represents one of the few practice theories that truly start where the client is and stay with the client throughout the change process. Rogers (1957, p. 200) articulated a positive view of a person as he wrote, 'In my experience I have discovered man to have characteristics which seem inherent in his species, and the terms which have at different times seemed to me descriptive of these characteristics are such terms as positive, forward-moving, constructive, realistic, trustworthy'. Indeed, Rogers (1977; 1989a) argued that his view of a person and approach to practice were universal, cutting across different cultures. He applied his approach to resolving intercultural tensions within a community where poverty and wealth collide and between nations. In fact, one of his projects was dedicated to resolving tensions between Protestants and Catholics in Northern Ireland. Rogers believed that using the core conditions could open up communication between groups of persons who traditionally have been opposed to one another, by allowing each side to genuinely express their concerns and hearing the concerns of the other side in an open and non-judgemental way. However, Sharf (2012, p. 238) argues that necessary and sufficient conditions represent 'a set of cultural values' that may not be as universal to all cultures as Rogers articulated.

Person-centred approach and anti-oppressive practice

Rogers' person-centred approach to practice represented a significant departure from the then mainstream approaches to clinical practice. Rogers (1977; 1989b) argued that his approach was revolutionary. His approach de-emphasized the power of the professional, placing power back in the hands of clients. As he wrote:

> A person-centred approach, when utilized to encourage the growth and development of the psychotic, the troubled, or the normal individual, revolutionizes the customary behaviours of members of the helping professions. It illustrates many things: (1) A sensitive person, to be of help, becomes more person-centred, no matter what orientation she starts from, because she finds the approach more effective; (2) When you are focused on the person, diagnostic labels become largely irrelevant; (3) The traditional medical model in psychotherapy is discovered to be largely in opposition to person-centeredness; (4) It is found that those who can create an effective person-centred relationship do not necessarily come from the professionally trained group; (5) The more this person-centred approach is implemented and put into practice, the more it is found to challenge hierarchical models of 'treatment' and hierarchical methods of organization; and (6) The very effectiveness of this unified person-centred approach constitutes a threat to professionals, administrators, and others, and steps are taken – consciously or unconsciously – to destroy it.
>
> (Rogers, 1989b, p. 396)

As this quote by Rogers makes clear, the person-centred approach represents a revolutionary departure from other practice approaches that focus on pathology and differentness, and encourages practitioners to partner with their clients rather than taking a power position over their clients. Rather than seeking to separate clients from the rest of society by a label or from the practitioner by power, the approach seeks to re-humanize practice.

Research on the person-centred approach

According to Sharf (2012), research on the person-centred approach has been scant and sporadic. One such study involved Rogers et al. (1967) examining the effects of the person-centred approach on persons with schizophrenia and found that with this approach, compared with a control group, they did not have fewer days hospitalized. In a nine-year follow-up of the same persons with schizophrenia, Truax (1970) did not find a difference in amount of time hospitalized between persons who received the person-centred therapy and the control group. Farber (2007, p. 292) summarized research on the effectiveness of congruence in helping relationships by stating, 'In short, the empirical evidence tends to be moderately supportive of Rogers' ideas'. Weisz et al. (1995) conducted a meta-analysis of different approaches to child/adolescent psychotherapy and found that behavioural approaches compared to other approaches, including a person-centred approach were superior. Cottraux et al. (2008) conducted a randomized controlled study that compared person-centred therapy with cognitive behavioural therapy among persons with post-traumatic stress disorder. They found that persons receiving person-centred therapy were more likely to drop out of treatment. However, there was no difference found between the two treatment groups in relation to symptom reduction.

Research into Kitwood's person-centred approach has shown promise. For example, Terada et al. (2013) found that when the approach was provided in hospital settings, clients had better cognitive and activities of daily living functioning. In addition, researchers are exploring the use of person-centred therapy for people with post-traumatic stress disorder (Payne et al., 2007).

However, when considering a broader view of the impact of Rogers' person-centred approach, namely, the importance of the therapeutic relationship (Elliott and Freire, 2007), a different picture emerges. Research that has looked at the impact of the therapeutic relationship, or working alliance, that is developed between clients and their treatment providers shows that the relationship is an important vehicle of therapeutic change. Martin et al. (2000) conducted a meta-analysis of 79 studies that measured working alliance and found that measures of working alliance were moderately related to various client outcomes. In a broader sense, the therapeutic relationship, while not the only necessary component of the helping process, is one of the factors that make the work with clients successful.

Summary

Rogers' person-centred approach, or therapy, was a significant departure from the then dominant models of practice, behaviourism and psychodynamic theories (DeCarvalho, 1990). Rogers (1957; 1959) saw humans as growth oriented and good, and argued that persons who come to therapy are often in a state of incongruence between their self and their experiences. In order to become fully functioning, individuals need to be open to experiences, develop trust in themselves, develop a sense of self that is rooted in the person's own perceptions of self and experiences, and engage in the process of becoming (Rogers, 1961).

Rogers' view of the helping process was one that started where the client was and followed the client throughout the whole helping process. He articulated six necessary and sufficient conditions of treatment, which stipulated that in order for the helping process to work, the practitioner and client need to be in personal and physical contact, the client needs to be in a state of incongruence, the practitioner must be congruent in the treatment relationship, express unconditional positive regard towards the client and provide accurate empathetic understanding of the client's experiences, and the client must perceive the practitioner as offering empathetic understanding and unconditional positive regard. While there is some contention over the sufficiency of Rogers' necessary and sufficient conditions (Silberschatz, 2007), his legacy of the therapeutic relationship is still felt and used in clinical practice (Elliott and Friere, 2007; Farber, 2007).

Case study

James is a white British, 74-year-old widower living in an assisted living facility. When he first arrived at the facility, James was lucid, only having slight memory problems. In fact, he fondly remembered his life and enjoyed telling his three grandchildren, Evan (3), Tim (7), and Olivia (10) about his 'adventures'. Recently, James' son, Derrick, has reported that his father has not been 'himself', that he seems withdrawn and often talks negatively about his diagnosis and future life. He knows that his dementia will get worse and he will become a 'vegetable'. When Derrick asks his father the reason, James replies that he sees how people with dementia are treated. He hears staff and other residents talk in stigmatizing ways about 'those people'. He has watched as staff turn from benevolent caretakers to 'going through the motions' as a client's dementia worsens. He dreads the day that he is taken to the back wing of the facility because he knows that this means he is no longer fit to take care of himself. What has particularly worried Derrick is that his father seems to have given up on happiness and is just waiting for the worst. Describe how you would work with James and the treatment facility from a person-centred approach.

Further reading

Cooper, M., O'Hara, M., Schmid, P.F. and Wyatt, G. (eds) (2007) *The Handbook of Person-centred Psychotherapy and Counselling*. Basingstoke: Palgrave Macmillan.
    A collection of chapters addressing the six necessary and sufficient conditions and how to utilize the person-centred approach within different settings and client groups.
Rogers, C.R. (1961) *On Becoming a Person*. Boston, MA: Houghton Mifflin.
    Provides an in-depth look at Roger's theory of human development and person-centred counselling.

Rogers, C.R. (2007) The necessary and sufficient conditions of therapeutic personality change, *Psychotherapy: Theory, Research, Practice, Training*, 44(3): 240–8.

Rogers' (1957) original piece of work on the six necessary and sufficient conditions, republished from the *Journal of Counseling Psychology*.

References

Brooker, D. (2003) What is person-centred care in dementia?, *Reviews in Clinical Gerontology*, 13(3): 215–22.

Brooker, D. (2005) Dementia care mapping: a review of the research literature, *The Gerontologist*, 45(1): 11–18.

Cottraux, J., Note, I., Yao, S.N., de Mey-Guillard, C., Bonasse, F., Djamoussian, D., Mollard, E., Note, B. and Chen, Y. (2008) Randomized controlled comparison of cognitive behavior therapy with Rogerian supportive therapy in chronic post-traumatic stress disorder: a 2-year follow-up, *Psychotherapy and Psychosomatics*, 77(2): 101–10.

Crain, W.C. (2011) Conclusion: humanistic psychology and development theory, in *Theories of Development: Concepts and Applications*, 6th edn. New York: Pearson.

DeCarvalho, R.J. (1990) A history of the 'third force' in psychology, *Journal of Humanistic Psychology*, 30(4): 22–44.

Dewing, J. (2008) Personhood and dementia: revisiting Tom Kitwood's ideas, *International Journal of Older People Nursing*, 3(1): 3–13.

Elliott, R. and Friere, B. (2007) Classical person-centered and experiential perspectives on Rogers (1957), *Psychotherapy: Theory, Research, Practice, Training*, 44(3): 285–8.

Farber, B.A. (2007) On the enduring and substantial influence of Carl Rogers' not-quite necessary nor sufficient conditions, *Psychotherapy: Theory, Research, Practice, Training*, 44(3): 289–94.

Kirschenbaum, H. and Henderson, V.L. (1984) Introduction, in H. Krischenbaum and V.L. Henderson (eds), *The Carl Rogers Reader*. Boston, MA: Houghton Mifflin.

Kitwood, T. (1993) Person and process in dementia, *International Journal of Geriatric Psychiatry*, 8(7): 541–5.

Kuhn, D., Ortigara, A. and Kasayka, R.E. (2000) Dementia care mapping: an innovative tool to measure person-centred care, *Alzheimer's Care Quarterly*, 1(3): 7–15.

Martin, D.J., Garske, J.P. and Davis, M.K. (2000) Relation of the therapeutic alliance with outcome and other variables: a meta-analytic review, *Journal of Consulting and Clinical Psychology*, 68(3): 438–50.

National Association of Social Workers (2008) *Code of Ethics of the National Association of Social Workers*, http://www.socialworkers.org/pubs/code/code.asp (accessed 21 August 2013).

Payne, A., Liebling-Kalifani, H. and Joseph, S. (2007) Client-centred group therapy for survivors of interpersonal trauma: a pilot investigation, *Counseling and Psychotherapy Research: Linking Research with Practice*, 7(2): 100–5.

Rogers, C.R. (1957) The necessary and sufficient conditions of therapeutic personality change, *Journal of Counseling Psychology*, 21(2): 95–103.

Rogers, C.R. (1959) A theory of therapy, personality, and interpersonal relationships as developed in the client-centered framework, in S. Koch (ed.), *Psychology: A Study of Science: Formulations of the Person and the Social Context*. New York: McGraw-Hill.

Rogers, C.R. (1961) *On Becoming a Person*. Boston, MA: Houghton Mifflin.

Rogers, C.R. (1969) *Freedom to Learn*. Columbus, OH: Charles E. Merrill.

Rogers, C.R. (1977) *Carl Rogers on Personal Power*. New York: Delacorte Press.

Rogers, C.R. (1989a) Resolving intercultural tensions, in H. Krischenbaum and V.L. Henderson (eds), *The Carl Rogers Reader*. Boston, MA: Houghton Mifflin. (Reprinted from *Carl Rogers on Personal Power*, pp. 115–40, 1977, New York: Delacorte.)

Rogers, C.R. (1989b) The politics of the helping professions, in H. Krischenbaum and V.L. Henderson (eds), *The Carl Rogers Reader*. Boston, MA, Houghton Mifflin. (Reprinted from *Carl Rogers on Personal Power*, pp. 3–28, 1977, New York: Delacorte.)

Rogers, C.R. (1995) *On Becoming a Person: A Therapist's View of Psychotherapy*. Boston, MA: Houghton Mifflin Harcourt. (Original work published 1961.)

Rogers, C.R., Gendlin, G.T., Kiesler, D.V. and Truax, C. (1967) *The Therapeutic Relationship and its Impact: A Study of Psychotherapy with Schizophrenics*. Madison, WI: University of Wisconsin Press.

Rowe, W. (2011) Client-centered theory: the enduring principles of a person-centered approach, in F.J. Turner (ed.), *Social Work Treatment: Interlocking Theoretical Approaches*, 5th edn. New York: Oxford University Press.

Schmid, P.F. (2007) The anthropological and ethical foundations of person-centred therapy, in M. Cooper, M. O'Hara, P.F. Schmid and G. Wyatt (eds), *The Handbook of Person-Centred Psychotherapy and Counselling*. Basingstoke: Palgrave Macmillan.

Sharf, R. (2012) *Theories of Psychotherapy and Counseling: Concepts and Cases*, 5th edn. Belmont, CA: Brooks Cole.

Silberschatz, G. (2007) Comments on the 'necessary and sufficient conditions of therapeutic personality change', *Psychotherapy: Theory, Research, Practice, Training*, 44(3): 265–7.

Terada, S., Oshima, E., Yokota, O., Ikeda, C., Nagao, S., Takeda, N., Sasaki, K. and Uchitomi, Y. (2013) Person-centered care and quality of life of patients with dementia in long-term care facilities, *Psychiatry Research*, 205(1/2): 103–8.

Truax, C.B. (1970) Effects of client-centered psychotherapy with schizophrenic patients: nine years pre-therapy and nine years post-therapy hospitalization, *Journal of Consulting and Clinical Psychology*, 35(3): 417–22.

Watson, J.C. (2001) Re-visioning empathy: theory, research and practice, in D.J. Cain and J. Seeman (eds), *Humanistic Psychotherapies: Handbook of Research and Practice*. Washington, DC: American Psychological Association.

Weisz, J.R., Weiss, B., Han, S.S., Granger, D.A. and Morton, T. (1995) Effects of psychotherapy with children and adolescents revisited: a meta-analysis of treatment outcome studies, *Psychological Bulletin*, 117(3): 450–68.

Ziegler, D.J. (2002) Freud, Rogers, and Ellis: a comparative theoretical analysis, *Journal of Rational-Emotive and Cognitive-Behavior Therapy*, 20(2): 75–90.

8 Motivational interviewing

Introduction

Motivational interviewing is a method of working with clients to resolve ambivalence in favour of making a change. The method is a client-centred, yet guided, approach with a specific goal of helping clients make positive change. Motivational interviewing is 'about arranging conversations so that people talk themselves into change, based on their own values and interests' (Miller and Rollnick, 2013, p. 23). Through four broad processes of engaging, focusing, evoking and planning, motivational interviewing seeks to evoke clients' intrinsic motivation for making a change and resolving their ambivalence by increasing the positives over the negatives to changing. The role of the social worker is to listen for clients' ambivalence expressed through 'change talk' and 'sustain talk', and reflect their desires, abilities, reasons and needs back to them so they can hear and process their own reasons for change. Motivational interviewing can be used in a variety of social work settings where the aim is to create change, and where clients are ambivalent about the change. This chapter will discuss motivational interviewing by exploring its spirit, its basic processes, the stages of change, the necessary communication skills and the specific techniques that can be employed to increase clients' motivation to change.

The origins of motivational interviewing

Motivational interviewing was developed by two clinical psychologists, Dr William Miller from the University of New Mexico, and Dr Stephen Rollnick from Cardiff University. The first discussion on motivational interviewing evolved from Miller's (1983) work with clients who were experiencing problems with alcohol, which was published in *Behavioral Psychotherapy*. Since this seminal work on motivational interviewing, Miller and Rollnick (1991) established themselves as the founders and experts in developing the approach and have since been the leaders in further refining the method. Motivational interviewing was not based on one specific theory, but rather was linked to various aspects of social psychology, such as cognitive dissonance and self-efficacy, and Rogers' basic principles to therapeutic change as outlined in client-centred therapy (Britt et al., 2004). Motivational interviewing was developed to be focused on the client and to employ the principles of empathy, unconditional positive regard and congruence (Rogers, 1959), yet to encompass a more guided approach in helping the client to resolve ambivalence in the direction of positive change.

Motivational interviewing is compatible to Prochaska and DiClemente's (1983; 1984; 1992) transtheoretical model (TTM) and particularly the stages of change, which describes a five-stage process that individuals move through in making a change (Prochaska et al., 1992). The stage of change model complements motivational interviewing by providing a framework that describes the process or stages of making a change, whereas motivational interviewing provides the communication styles and interpersonal skills to assist the client in progressing through the stages towards making a change. The stage of change model is a useful tool when using motivational interviewing in the sense of assessing where the client is currently positioned and initiating work with clients that meet them in their current stage, yet with a goal of assisting the client to move through the stages of change. Motivational interviewing was developed to work specifically with clients who are in the earlier stages of change (precontemplation, contemplation) versus other types of methods (e.g. cognitive behavioural therapy), which assumes clients are already in the action stage and ready to make a change.

Motivational interviewing explained

Miller and Rollnick (2013, p. 78, original emphasis) are specific in stating that 'motivational interviewing is not a "technique" [but is a] *style* of being with people, an integration of particular clinical skills to foster motivation for change'. Motivational interviewing is a focused and goal-directed approach that seeks to resolve clients' ambivalence towards making a positive change. The social worker is intent on pursuing the goal of positive change and works with clients to elicit the intrinsic motivation, expressed through change talk, that will assist in resolving the ambivalence. Although therapeutic techniques and tools are used in the work together, the social worker should focus more on the communication style and interpersonal skills to assist in this process and should steer away from techniques that are manipulative in nature (Miller, 1994).

In understanding motivational interviewing, one must first understand the meaning and the components of motivation, particularly as it is viewed as vital to change. Motivation is conceptualized as consisting of three distinct components: (1) importance – the extent to which a client wants, desires or wills to make a change; (2) confidence – the extent to which a client believes they have an ability to make a change; and (3) readiness – whether the client is ready to make a change (Miller and Rollnick, 2002). All three components need to be present in order for clients to have motivation to change, although clients may vary in the degrees to which they view a change as important, feel confident in making a change or their readiness to make a change in the present or the near future. Importance, confidence and readiness can be assessed separately by the social worker in order to determine the extent to which the client is motivated to make a change and the specific focus of the work together. For example, a client may believe that quitting smoking is extremely important, due to health reasons, but is not confident in making the change. In this type of situation, the social worker would not need to focus on the importance of quitting smoking, but would need to focus on increasing the client's confidence in her or his ability to make the change. Therefore, in order for clients to be motivated to make a change they need to believe the importance, feel the confidence and be ready. Techniques to assess the components of motivation with a client are discussed later in this chapter.

Box 8.1   What is motivation?

Importance + Confidence + Readiness = Motivation

Source: Prochaska and DiClemente (1992)

In understanding motivation, one must also acknowledge that it is not static, but fluctuates with time and across different situations. For example, a client who uses tobacco may leave the doctor's office and immediately rate high on importance and confidence in quitting smoking, but later in the week the client's confidence, and thus readiness, lessens when playing cards with friends who use tobacco. Therefore, a social worker needs to realize that there are advantages and disadvantages to the client making a change, and the social worker's role is to help the client resolve this ambivalence in quitting smoking and support the client in making their own argument for change. Ambivalence is a normal part of making a change and is often the place where clients get stuck. Using motivational interviewing, the social worker can guide the client through the ambivalence to the point where the pros of changing outweigh the pros of the status quo and, thus, positive change occurs.

In working *with* clients, motivational interviewing focuses on the social worker's communication style and interpersonal skills and how this can impact the client in making a change (Miller and Rollnick, 2013). The social worker takes a position of *guiding* the work together versus *directing* the work or *following* the client. There are five key communication skills that aid the guiding process: open-ended questions; affirmations; reflective statements; summaries; and information and advice. The use of the five communication skills will enable the social worker to avoid the 'righting reflex' of persuading the client to do the 'right' thing as this would only increase the chances that a client will resist the change process (Miller and Rollnick, 2013). Motivational interviewing is not effective when relying on the use of the communication skills alone, but rather the social worker needs to embrace the 'spirit' that underpins motivational interviewing.

The 'spirit' of motivational interviewing

Miller and Rollnick (2013) are clear in that there is a 'spirit' or way of being with people that is intrinsic in motivational interviewing. This spirit is the true essence of motivational interviewing and is comprised of partnership, acceptance, compassion and evocation (Miller and Rollnick, 2013). Partnership consists of an active collaboration between the client and social worker that honours the client's experiences and perspectives and results in joint decision-making. The client is not viewed as someone to work *on*, but rather someone who the social worker works *with*. Acceptance comprises the following four person-centred conditions: (1) believing in the *absolute worth* and potential of every human being, which is akin to Rogers' (1959) unconditional positive regard; (2) having *accurate empathy*, where the social worker aims to see the world through the client's eyes and from their perspective; (3) *autonomy support*, where the social worker values and respects the choices clients make for their lives; and (4) *affirmation*, where the social worker looks for and acknowledges the client's strengths and weaknesses. Compassion involves the social worker promoting the welfare and well-being of the client and giving priority to their needs. Finally, evocation holds that clients are the experts in their situations and experiences, and they hold the motivation, strengths and resources to make a change. The social worker is not viewed as an expert or one who holds wisdom or the answers to clients' problems, but rather clients hold the answers and motivation to create change. The responsibility for change resides with the clients and not the social worker and the way(s) in which the clients make changes should ultimately be their decision. In possessing this spirit of motivational interviewing (partnership, acceptance, compassion and evocation), the social worker is encouraging clients to make a change that is based on their arguments and their own intrinsic motivation.

Just as there are traits that a social worker should possess when utilizing motivational interviewing, there are also traits that should not be present. Miller and Rollnick (2013) stress that although the method is guiding in the sense of trying to help the client resolve ambivalence in favour of making a change, the method is not synonymous with confrontation or other aggressive styles of intervention. Rollnick and Miller (1995) specify that motivational interviewing is not being offered if a social worker argues for change or attempts to persuade or coerce the client to change, offers direct advice or attempts to solve problems for the client, takes an expert or authoritative stance with the client or attempts to diagnosis a client. This does not mean that a social worker would not inform or advise a client but, rather, the social worker provides advice when asked, offers advice with permission ('I wonder if I might tell you something . . .'), or provides information and advice based on an understanding of the client's needs (Miller and Rollnick, 2013).

Processes of motivational interviewing

Motivational interviewing encompasses four overlapping processes of (1) engaging; (2) focusing; (3) evoking; and (4) planning. Although the processes are viewed as stair steps, where the social worker and client must touch on one in order to proceed to the next, there are times when the work together might involve going back and forth between the different processes, or up and down the stairs. It is important to remember that the 'spirit' of motivational interviewing underpins all of the work together. Miller and Rollnick (2013, p. 66) provide the following 'technical' definition of motivational interviewing that will be useful in explaining the purposes of the four processes: 'Motivational interviewing is a collaborative, goal-oriented style of communication with particular attention to the language of change. It is designed to strengthen personal motivation for, and commitment to, a specific goal by eliciting and exploring the person's own reasons for change within an atmosphere of acceptance and compassion.' The four processes described by Miller and Rollnick (2013) are:

1   *Engaging.* The process of engagement involves establishing a connection and building a trusting and respectful helping relationship. The extent to which a connection and relationship is built is determined by the interaction between the social worker and client, as well as external influences of 'the service system within which client and practitioner work, the clinician's emotional state, [and] the client's circumstances and state of mind on entering the room' (Miller and Rollnick, 2013, p. 61). Engagement is a necessary process before any other work can begin and should consider both the client's and social worker's feeling of being comfortable. It is particularly important during the engagement process to adhere to the 'spirit' of motivational interviewing.

2   *Focusing.* Focusing involves the process whereby the social worker and client decide the direction of the work. Specific questions can be asked during this process such as: 'What will be the focus of the work together?'; 'What is the client's agenda?'; 'What is the social worker's agenda?'; and 'What are the goals of the social worker and the client?' The social worker will need to be sure that she/he is working forward together with the client versus pushing or pulling the client forward (Miller and Rollnick, 2013).

3   *Evoking.* Evoking involves 'eliciting the client's own motivations for change' (Miller and Rollnick, 2013, p. 64). This occurs in conversation with the client about a change, and her/his feelings and ideas about making the change. This process can only occur after the client has identified a change goal (e.g. quit smoking; eat more healthily). The social worker listens to the change talk, or the client's reasons for making a change, and aims to help resolve ambivalence in favour of change.

4   *Planning.* The planning phase occurs when the client expresses a commitment to change and is ready to develop a plan of action. Social workers should listen for clients' own solutions to their problems as clients often hold the answers to how best to create change. The planning process might need to be revisited several times throughout the work together.

People and change

We have already discussed that motivation is fundamental to change and is comprised of three components – importance, confidence and readiness – but we still need to understand how people change. According to Miller and Rollnick (2002, p. 12), change arises 'when the person connects it with something of intrinsic value, something important, something cherished'. What we do know is that people experience and make

changes throughout their life and often without formal treatment from helping professionals. Change is a natural process and, therefore, formal treatment from helping
professionals is just one way to assist in facilitating this process by helping clients to
resolve ambivalence in favour of change (Miller and Rollnick, 2013).

In order to help facilitate change, one must understand the change process which
is best described by Prochaska and DiClemente's stages of change model, which
explains how people intentionally make a change. Stages of change is encompassed in
the transtheoretical model (TTM) (Norcross et al., 2011; Prochaska and DiClemente,
1983; 1984; 1992) along with other aspects such as the decisional-balance (Janis and
Mann, 1977), which explores the pros and cons of making a change, self-efficacy, which
represents the perception and belief of the individual in her or his ability to make a
change, and process of change, which consists of explicit and implicit activities to
which people engage in order to assist in making a change (that is, consciousness-
raising, social and self liberation, helping relationship or self re-evaluation) (Velicer et
al., 1998). Stage of change is the key component of the TTM and consists of five stages
that people pass through when progressing towards making a change regardless of
receiving treatment or making the change alone (Norcross et al., 2011). The five stages
consist of precontemplation, contemplation, preparation, action and maintenance
(Norcross et al., 2011; Prochaska et al., 1992), each described in detail here:

1   *Precontemplation.* Precontemplation represents the stage where individuals do
    not see that there is a problem to address at all. They have no intention of
    addressing their behaviour now or in the foreseeable future, specifically because
    they do not see a problem. Social workers will usually see clients in this stage if
    they have been mandated or coerced to seek treatment for a behavioural
    problem as defined by a third party (that is, courts, parents, partners). Sometimes
    clients in this stage may quickly respond to work with the social worker, due to
    the pressure from outside sources, but once the work together subsides, clients
    will resume their original behaviour. In order to assess if the client is in this
    stage, the social worker can ask: 'Are you ready to change (this behaviour)
    within the next six months?' If they say no, then they are precontemplative.

2   *Contemplation.* In this stage, people acknowledge that there is a problem to
    address and are considering how to address it, but are not yet ready to make the
    change. Individuals can stay at this stage for an extended period of time as they
    want to make a change, but always view the change as occurring in the future.
    For example, a client can state that they would like to quit smoking, but not now.
    According to Prochaska et al. (1992, p. 1103) this stage represents, 'knowing
    where you want to go, but not quite ready yet'. In order to assess if the client is
    in this stage, the social worker can ask: 'Are you ready to change (this behav-
    iour) within the next six months?' If they say yes, then they are contemplative.

3   *Preparation.* Preparation represents a stage where people are intending to
    take action in the near future (usually within one month). The individual has
    started to make a commitment to the change by changing some aspects of the
    behaviour (that is, reducing smoking from 20 cigarettes a day to 10). In order
    to assess if the client is in this stage, the social worker can ask: 'Are you ready

to change (this behaviour) within the next 30 days?' If they say yes, then they are in the preparation stage.

4   *Action.* The action stage involves individuals actually making the behavioural change. Instead of cutting down on the number of cigarettes smoked, the client actually quits smoking altogether. Clients stay in the action stage as long as they maintain the behavioural change for a period of one day to six months.

5   *Maintenance.* The maintenance stage represents the period where the individuals make the behavioural change and maintain the change for over six months. In the case of the client who smokes, the client will work on relapse prevention techniques and continue to acknowledge the benefits of making the change (Prochaska et al., 1992).

The model has historically been viewed as a linear progression from precontemplation through to maintenance, but this is not always the case with clients and is actually quite a rare occurrence. Clients may begin in the precontemplation stage, move through contemplation and preparation to action, yet relapse and start the process over again. The relapse can push the client back to the contemplation or preparation stages or the client may immediately go back to the action stage. Prochaska et al. (1992) have found that clients tend to repeat the stages several times before they remain in the maintenance stage. Figure 8.1 illustrates the five stages in the stage of change model and the various progressions that a client can take in making a change.

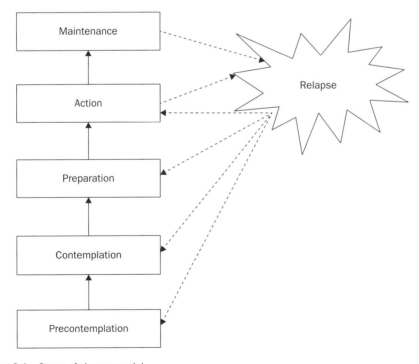

Figure 8.1   Stage of change model.

The stages of change can be useful when using motivational interviewing as the two approaches are seen as compatible and complementary. Motivational interviewing was specifically designed for those clients who are in the 'less ready' stages of precontemplation and contemplation. Motivational interviewing seeks to assist clients in moving through the stages of change from precontemplation, contemplation and/or preparation to action and then maintenance. The key is that the social worker should assess the stage of change for the client from the beginning and throughout the work together to ensure that the social worker is not jumping ahead of the client.

Individuals are often reluctant to make changes because they are ambivalent about the situation (Miller and Rollnick, 2013). Ambivalence is a normal process where people feel two ways about a situation; they view the pros and cons of both maintaining the status quo and of making a change. For example, a client who misuses alcohol may see the advantages of stopping drinking, such as better health, more disposable income or less involvement with the courts, but on the other hand may see the advantages of continuing to drink, such as feeling calm, being able to deal with uncomfortable situations or spending time with friends in the pub. Ambivalence is seen as normal and good in the sense that individuals are considering whether to make a change based on an examination of both the advantages and disadvantages to the change, but this is often where clients can become stuck. The goal of motivational interviewing is to help the client resolve the ambivalence in favour of making change.

Increasing motivation to change

Motivational interviewing values clients in voicing their own arguments for change, but the social worker can assist in facilitating this discovery and subsequent change. As discussed, client ambivalence to change is good in motivational interviewing and the goal is for the social worker to help the client resolve the ambivalence in favour of change. Often the resolution of ambivalence is initiated by developing discrepancies in clients' current behaviour and their values or future goals. According to Miller and Rollnick (2013) if there is no discrepancy there is no motivation to change, and the larger the discrepancy the more important the change can become for the client. Therefore, ambivalence and discrepancy are critical for increasing a client's motivation to change and are the key areas to explore when utilizing motivational interviewing with a client.

Intrinsic motivation is another important concept in motivational interviewing, which explains the source of motivation to change for a particular client. Intrinsic motivation is unique to each individual. For example, showing pictures of a lung overtaken by cancer may act as a source of motivation for one client to quit smoking, but for another this image may have no effect; instead the source of motivation to quit smoking for this client comes from the disapproving comments about smoking from her or his children. Showing pictures of a cancerous lung will have no effect on this client and instead of quickly labelling them as unmotivated or resistant to change, the helping professional should elicit the client's own intrinsic motivation. Therefore, the task for the social worker is to elicit from each client their intrinsic motivation and then use this as the source of motivation to fuel the actions towards change.

Miller and Rollnick (2013) explore how to get started in this process of facilitating behavioural change. They specify four core communication skills that social workers should use in the work with clients: (1) open-ended question; (2) affirmations; (3) reflective statements; and (4) summaries (OARS). Each is described in detail here:

1   *Open-ended questions.* Social workers should use primarily open-ended questions versus closed-ended questions when in dialogue with a client, particularly during the engaging process. The use of open-ended questions enables clients to tell their story and allows the social worker to gather more in-depth information. Closed-ended questions often lead to closed, short and quick conversations that are limited in information and cause the social worker to be stuck in what to ask next. The example conversation describes this experience.

Social worker:	Do you use alcohol?
Client:	Yes.
Social worker:	How long have you been drinking?
Client:	About 15 years.
Social worker:	Do you think you have a problem with your drinking?
Client:	No.
Social worker:	Have you ever tried to quit?
Client:	No.

This example illustrates how closed-ended questions can get the social worker in a question-answer trap very quickly and without much information about the client's alcohol use or her or his perception of drinking (Miller and Rollnick, 2013). The use of open-ended questions, such as 'Tell me about your alcohol use'; 'Tell me about when you first started using alcohol'; or 'What is it like for you when you use alcohol?' encourages the client to describe situations and give information and more details about the behaviour.

2   *Affirmation.* The social worker should encourage and affirm the client in this often difficult process of change. Affirmations can be given in the form of compliments or statements of encouragement that will help value the client and boost the client's self-efficacy and confidence in making a change. Such examples could include, 'I appreciate your honesty'; 'This must be very difficult for you to talk about. Thank you for sharing with me today'; 'That [action] must have taken a lot of courage'. Affirmations do not have to come solely from the social worker but, rather, the social worker could ask the client to describe their strengths and successes in an effort to self-affirm (Miller and Rollnick, 2013).

3   *Reflections.* Reflections are a vital element of staying with the client and moving with them through the stages of change. Reflective statements allow social workers to validate that they have understood the client and also encourage the client to continue the dialogue. The important point to remember is that reflections should be statements and not questions, particularly as

questions require answers and can make a client feel defensive or attacked. Simple reflections can include one or more of the following basic counselling communication tools: (1) repeating, which literally repeats back all or an element of what the client said; (2) rephrasing, which involves stating in slightly different words, yet with the same meaning back to the client; (3) para-phrasing, which involves elaborating on what the client had said by using slightly different words and inferring some meaning; or (4) reflection of feeling, which involves rephrasing or paraphrasing, yet attaching a feeling or emotion to the statement. The following is an example of using each of the four types of reflections.

Client:	I don't know what the big deal is, I don't have a problem with drinking.

(Repeating)

Social worker:	You don't know what the big deal is.

(Rephrasing)

Social worker:	Drinking isn't a problem for you.

(Paraphrasing)

Social worker:	Everyone is making a bigger deal out of your drinking than is necessary.

(Reflection of feeling)

Social worker:	You feel annoyed that people are making a bigger deal out of this than is necessary.

When using reflections with a client, the social worker should try not to focus on solving the problem, but rather stay with the client and listen to what he or she is saying.

Exercise box 8.1 Practising reflective statements

1 Smoking is not a big deal. My grandfather smoked all his life and never had a problem.
2 My friends drink loads more than I do.
3 I smoke to deal with stress. If I didn't have my cigarettes I think the stress would kill me.
4 I only use cocaine on the weekends.
5 Why does my doctor care if I drink? I'm not hurting her.

---

4   *Summaries.* Social workers can use summaries at various points in the work with clients. Summaries can be used at the end of a session to reflect back to the client what has been discussed and to highlight the main points in the conversation. Summaries can also be used throughout the conversation to highlight several statements that the client has made in an attempt to ensure the social worker understands correctly and also for the client to hear what she or he has conveyed. Summaries are often used to enable clients to hear

their change talk or sustain talk, or the desires, abilities, reasons or need to make a change or to maintain the status quo that they had expressed either explicitly or implicitly in conversation. An example of a summary that includes ambivalence (change talk and sustain talk) is as follows: 'On the one hand you really like drinking as it relaxes you and helps you to deal with stress in your life, but on the other you state you spend too much money on alcohol and it makes you feel bad in the mornings.'

Change talk and sustain talk

'Contemplating change involves self-talk, thinking about the pros and cons of available alternatives.' (Miller and Rollnick, 2013, p. 297). The pros and cons of making a change is defined as ambivalence, which is made up of change talk and sustain talk ('Yes, I want to change, but . . .'). Change talk can consist of preparatory change talk and mobilizing change talk. Preparatory change talk is often implicit in conversations and can consist of clients expressing the advantages of making a change, or their concerns about it, with maintaining current behaviours. DARN is the acronym for client language, or preparatory change talk, that communicates desires, ability, reasons and/or need to make a change. Preparatory change talk can lead to mobilizing change talk where a client begins to commit to making a change, and begins to activate a change or take steps towards a change. Mobilizing change talk is expressed through the acronym CATs – for commitment, activation or taking steps language. Moving from preparatory change talk to mobilizing change talk is synonymous with moving from precontemplation/contemplation to preparation, and then the action stages of change. Sustain talk is the clients' language that expresses their reasons for maintaining the status quo (the cons of changing). Just as change talk can be expressed though DARN and CATs, sustain talk can be expressed in the same way, with a focus on the reasons for staying the same and not making the change. The aim of the social worker using motivational interviewing (in the focusing and evoking processes) is to evoke change talk and sustain talk (ambivalence) from clients in order to gather their reasons for making a change. There is a specific focus on change talk and increasing the presence and use of change talk over sustain talk, as this language represents clients' reasons for changing: their intrinsic motivation. The social worker then reflects back the change talk to clients in order for them to hear their self-expressed arguments for change. Table 8.1 illustrates examples of preparatory and mobilizing change talk and sustain talk through DARN and CATs.

The use of DARN and CATs can assist in the social worker asking the right kind of questions to evoke change talk or the client's reasons for making a change. Social workers need to ensure they stay with clients during this process of focusing and evoking and don't start asking mobilizing questions (preparation/action stages) before the client is ready. Some useful questions to ask could include 'How would you like for things to be different?' or 'What do you wish for your future?' (Miller and Rollnick, 2013). Over the course of working together, the ratio of change talk (pros) to sustain talk (cons) should increase.

Table 8.1   Change talk and sustain talk

Preparatory change talk and sustain talk

Darn	wants, hopes, wishes, likes	CT: 'I wish I could quit smoking.'
		ST: 'I really like smoking.'
Abilities	able, can, could, possible	CT: 'I've quit smoking before.'
		ST: 'I've tried quitting, but failed.'
Reasons	specific argument for change	CT: 'My kids hate it when I smoke.'
		ST: 'I smoke to deal with my kids.'
Need	important, have to, should, must	CT: 'I'm having trouble breathing.'
		ST: 'It gets me through the day.'

Mobilizing change talk and sustain talk

Commitment	will, swear, guarantee, give word	CT: 'I'll be a non-smoker soon.'
		ST: 'I'll still be smoking in ten years.'
Activation	willing to, ready to, prepared to	CT: 'I'm ready to say goodbye.'
		ST: 'I'm not ready to say goodbye.'
Taking steps	taking steps towards change	CT: 'I cut down to two cigarettes.'
		ST: 'I went back to my usual amount.'

Source: Miller and Rollnick (2013)

Responding to discord

In some circumstances social workers may find themselves struggling in conversation with a client who is believed to be exhibiting 'resistance'. Miller and Rollnick (2013) believe that 'resistance' is actually just an expression of the other side of ambivalence (sustain talk) and discord. Discord occurs when the social worker and client are in disagreement, are not on the same wavelength, are talking at cross-purposes, or there is a disturbance in the relationship, which can be evidenced by a client arguing, interrupting, ignoring or discounting the social worker (Miller and Rollnick, 2013, p. 369). Whereas sustain talk is the argument for not changing, discord is a problem within the social worker–client relationship. Discord can be a reflection of the social worker jumping ahead of the client, inaccurately assessing the client's position in the stages of change, misjudging importance, confidence or readiness, or taking the control away from the client. Social workers utilizing motivational interviewing are not to confront a client, argue or persuade the client to make a change, but are to maintain the 'spirit' of motivational interviewing and are to collaborate with the client and move with them through the process of changing at the client's pace. Therefore, strategies to lessen the discord include giving the power and control back to the clients and encouraging them to make decisions for themselves, reassessing importance, confidence and readiness of clients and using reflective statements, such as a simple reflective response, amplified

Table 8.2 Reflective statements to respond to discord

'My wife is on at me about my drinking, but I don't drink more than anyone else. I wouldn't be here if it wasn't for my wife nagging me all the time'	
Simple reflection	'You're here because of your wife'
Amplified reflection	'Your wife should be here instead of you'
Double-sided reflection	'You don't drink more than anyone else, but you also don't like your wife nagging you about your drinking'
Emphasizing autonomy	'It's your choice whether to drink or not'
Reframing	'Your wife must really care about you'

reflection, double-sided reflection, emphasizing autonomy, or reframing. Table 8.2 illustrates examples of reflective statements that can be used to respond to discord.

Techniques to increase motivation to change

There are several techniques that can be used in motivational interviewing that can assist clients in exploring and determining their reasons for change as well as provide the social worker with an idea of specific areas that could be addressed in the work together. The techniques enable the client and social worker to explore ambivalence, develop discrepancy, evoke change talk and bring to the forefront the client's intrinsic motivation to change. The social worker can begin by asking simple open-ended questions, such as 'How would you like things to be different?'; 'What would be the good things about making a change?'; or 'What would be the not so good things about making a change?' Additional tools to help explore ambivalence, develop discrepancy, evoke change talk and intrinsic motivation are scaling, decisional-balance and looking forward/looking back questions.

Scaling

Scaling is a useful first step to help explore clients' motivation to make a change by examining the three components of motivation: importance, confidence and readiness (Miller and Rollnick, 2013). Scaling importance and confidence separately is necessary as a client may see the importance of making a change, but may not feel confident in her or his ability to make the change. Scaling involves the use of specific questions to enable a client to say how they feel about making a particular change. The scaling technique should be introduced to the client and the social worker should gain the client's permission to use the scale to reinforce the principle of collaboration. For example, the social worker could state: 'If it's okay with you, I'd like to ask you a couple of questions to see if we can better understand where you're at in quitting/starting (behaviour)?'

0	1	2	3	4	5	6	7	8	9	10
Not at all			Somewhat				Very			Extremely

Figure 8.2   Motivational interviewing: scaling exercise.

Once the client has agreed, the social worker can begin to ask the specific set of questions in combination with the scale in Figure 8.2.

Importance and confidence should be scaled separately and the social worker should ask the following questions (Miller and Rollnick, 2013):

1   On a scale of 0 to 10, with 0 being not important at all and 10 being extremely important, how important is making this change to you at the moment? *The client is to circle or state the number.*

2   What does [this number] mean to you? *This allows the client to express her or his meaning behind the number.*

3   Why have you selected a [chosen number] and not a [number below]? *This allows clients to express why they selected a specific number and not one that is lower on the scale. This also affirms the client's position by condoning the number they had selected versus asking 'why did you select a [chosen number] and not a [higher number]?'*

4   What would need to happen for you to go from a [chosen number] to a [higher number]? *This enables clients to begin to define their desires, abilities, reasons and needs for making a change and explore their intrinsic motivation.*

5   What can I do to help you move from a [chosen number] to a [higher number]? *This reinforces the partnership between the social worker and client.*

The social worker should repeat the process again to scale confidence with the client. Scaling can be completed with the client at the beginning of the work together and then periodically throughout, or it can be completed at the beginning of each session together. The scaling can be done either on a piece of paper or a flip chart and should be kept for reference in future sessions.

The scaling exercise enables the social worker to see which aspects of motivation need to be enhanced. For example, if a client scales the importance as a 9, but confidence at a 3, the social worker knows that the focus of the work together should not be on the importance of making a change but rather on enhancing the client's confidence to make the change. To enhance confidence the social worker and client can explore the past success of the client and try to build on what has worked in the past as well as explore and build on the client's strengths, resources and supports. If the client scores low on importance then the work between the social worker and client should focus on developing discrepancy between current behaviour and the client's values and goals.

Decisional balance

The use of the decisional balance is another technique that can assist the social worker and client to explore ambivalence and the client's intrinsic motivation to change. Within motivational interviewing, the decisional balance is used when the social worker maintains a neutral stance in regard to the change, versus guiding the client towards a specific change goal (Miller and Rollnick, 2013). The decisional balance was devised from Janis and Mann's (1977) decision-making or conflict model where decision-making involves the assessment of both the advantages and disadvantages to making a decision. The use of a decisional balance sheet allows the client to explore both the pros and cons of changing and of staying the same. By creating a decisional balance worksheet, such as the one displayed in Figure 8.3, the social worker and client would explore each box by asking the client the following questions: (1) What are the good things about (staying the same)?; (2) What are the not so good things about (staying the same)?; (3) What are the not so good things about (changing)?; and (4) What are the good things about (changing)?

The clients are asked to fill in the boxes for each question, or the social worker can fill in the boxes if necessary. The social worker then summarizes the two sides of the boxes, which represents the client's ambivalence. The left-hand column represents the reasons for staying the same and the right-hand column represents the reasons for changing. The social worker and client can also see the client's intrinsic motivation to make the change, which would be displayed in the right-hand column. Therefore, in helping the client to resolve the ambivalence in favour of change the social worker should focus on the reasons given by the client in the right-hand column as they represent the client's intrinsic motivation.

Good things about (staying the same)	Not so good things about (staying the same)
Not so good things about (changing)	Good things about (changing)

Figure 8.3 Motivational interviewing: decisional balance worksheet.

Looking back/looking forward

A social worker can also use exploratory questions with a client to help evoke change talk and reasons for making a change. The looking forward and looking back questions attempt to solicit the client's future goals and ambitions and also explore the potential positives in the client's life before taking on the behaviour in discussion. In looking back the social worker explores what the client's life was like before the current behaviour. The social worker can ask the following questions: (1) What were things like in your life before the (current behaviour)?; (2) Do you remember a time when things were going well for you? Tell me what was different about that time (Miller and Rollnick, 2013). Looking back can potentially help clients see the positives in their life before the problem or current behaviour emerged. This can act as a source of hope or motivation for the client in alleviating the problem to return to the more positive state.

In looking forward, the social worker can ask the following questions: (1) How would you like for your life to be different? or (2) How do you envisage your life in five years? After asking one or both of these initial questions, the social worker then asks: how has your (current behaviour) helped or hindered you in reaching this goal? The use of language is extremely important in keeping with the basic principles of motivational interviewing. The social worker is to ask how the behaviour 'helps or hinders', which acknowledges that the current behaviour has both costs and benefits for the client and the use of 'hinder' carries less of a negative meaning than words such as 'hurt or harm'.

Develop a change plan

The goal of motivational interviewing is to explore and resolve ambivalence in favour of making a change. A change plan will occur in the planning process when the change talk has moved from preparatory to mobilizing, thus indicating that the client has progressed through the stages of change to the preparation stage. The plan should address the end goal(s), some specific tasks to be completed in order to reach the goal, and some tips and techniques that others have found useful in making a similar behavioural change. The social worker needs to verify with the clients what tips and techniques they believe would be beneficial to them. The plan should also address a relapse, such as strategies to prevent a relapse and steps a client will take if a relapse does occur.

Case example: applying motivational interviewing to practice

Andrew is a 45-year-old, white British male who has been referred to a drug and alcohol treatment agency by his probation officer to address his alcohol use. You are a social worker at the agency who has been assigned to work with Andrew and you use a motivational interviewing approach with your clients. Andrew's referral provided you with limited information on him or his alcohol use. Therefore, you anticipate gathering more information about Andrew and his current situation from him in the initial session together (*engaging process*).

At the first meeting together, you begin the conversation by asking Andrew, 'Tell me why you have decided to come in today?' (*open-ended questions*). Andrew discloses that his probation officer has informed him that she believes him to have a drinking problem and needs to seek counselling to 'overcome his addiction'. In staying with Andrew with an aim of exploring more about his views (*spirit*), you reflect back, 'Your probation officer thinks you have an alcohol addiction' (*reflection*). This reflection encourages Andrew to continue in the conversation and provide more information around the perceived alcohol addiction. Andrew explains that he has recently been arrested for drinking and driving and he is ordered to attend counselling as part of his probation requirement. You reflect back, 'You're here because of drinking and driving' (*reflection*). Andrew then discloses the details of the drinking and driving incident and explains that drinking and diving is a rare occurrence for him and he was in the 'wrong place at the wrong time'. He states that he did not ever think that he had a problem with alcohol, but the drinking and driving incident was a real wake-up call; 'I have to do something about my drinking' (*preparatory change talk – need*).

You want to explore more about Andrew's alcohol use (*focusing process*) but do not want to push Andrew or jump ahead of him (*spirit*). In order to explore this subject in a less threatening manner, you ask, 'Tell me a little about your alcohol use' (*open-ended questions*). Andrew expresses having used alcohol since he was in his late teens and describes how he has progressively had to increase the intake of alcohol in order to get the same effect; it takes six to eight cans or pints of lager in order to feel anything. Andrew discusses how his alcohol use has caused problems with his work by having hangovers and calling off of work 'too many times' and his wife is always on at him about how much money he spends on lager (*preparatory change talk – reason*). She wishes that he would 'slow down' on the drinking and maybe spend more time with the family and less with his friends. Despite the problems with work and his wife, Andrew feels the pressure from friends to continue drinking and alcohol allows him to deal with the stress in this life (*ambivalence*). He states, 'Quitting may not be a bad thing for me, but I'd have to find something else to help me deal with the stress' (*sustain talk – need*). You affirm Andrew's position, 'This must be very difficult for you. Thank you for being honest with me' (*affirmation*). You notice the ambivalence that Andrew is expressing in regard to his alcohol use and begin to assess Andrew as being in the contemplative stage of change, seeing both the pros and cons of staying the same and of quitting his alcohol use. You can identify that the change goal is to quit, or reduce, Andrew's alcohol use.

To further explore Andrew's ambivalence towards quitting drinking (*evoking process*), you propose working through a decisional-balance worksheet. You ask: 'I'd like to explore the good and not-so-good things about your drinking. Is it OK to work through a decisional balance worksheet together?' (*gaining permission*). Andrew agrees, and he fills out the sheet in Figure 8.4. Although Miller and Rollnick (2013) propose the use of the decisional balance when the social worker is in a neutral stance, you believe that looking at the pros and cons for changing and staying the same may be a helpful tool in tipping the ambivalence in favour of change.

Good things about drinking	Not so good things about drinking
• Helps with stress • I drink with my friends • I like the way it makes me feel • It's fun	• Spend too much money • Wife hates it • Too many hangovers • I have too high a tolerance
Not so good things about quitting	Good things about quitting
• What will I do with my friends? • Withdrawal symptoms • Won't be able to deal with stress • Don't know what I'll do for fun	• Go to work all the time • My wife will be happy • More time with my family • More money for the family

Figure 8.4 Example of completed decisional balance worksheet.

Based on Andrew's responses, you summarize the worksheet: 'On the one hand drinking is fun; it's what you do with your friends, and it helps you deal with stress. But on the other, you are spending too much money on alcohol, your wife doesn't like it, and it is affecting your work' (*summarize*). Based on the worksheet, you assess that Andrew's *intrinsic motivation* is the effect that drinking is having on his body, his work and his family. These are the reasons that will help motivate Andrew to make the change.

You want to assess Andrew's level of motivation to make a change and ask him to participate in the scaling exercise with you. You introduce the scaling to Andrew, 'If it's OK with you, I'd like to ask you a couple of questions to see if we can better understand where you're at in quitting drinking?' (*gaining permission*). Andrew gives his consent and you begin by assessing importance: 'On a scale of 0 to 10 with 0 being not important at all and 10 being extremely important, how important is quitting drinking to you at the moment? Andrew responds with a 7 and states that a 7 represents that he sees quitting drinking as important when he thinks about his work, wife and the fact that he is on probation, but it's not 'extremely' important at this stage. You next ask Andrew, 'Why have you selected a 7 and not a 3?' Andrew responds that the 7 was over the middle range of the scale and he does see an importance in quitting, but the 3 would mean to him that there was no importance in quitting as it was below the middle range. You then ask Andrew, 'What would need to happen for you to go from a 7 to a 8 or 9?' Andrew states that his wife would need to threaten to leave him or he would have to miss several more days of work. Finally, you ask Andrew, 'What can I do to help you move from a 7 to an 8 or 9?' Andrew states he would like to know more about the negative effects of alcohol on his body, particularly as his father has died from sclerosis of the liver. You assess that Andrew sees the importance of making a change and that this could be strengthened by providing him with information about the health effects of drinking, which you acknowledge to him that you will provide at the next session together.

You next scale confidence with Andrew where he rates himself as a 5. Andrew discloses that he would like to think that he could quit drinking, but knows that the pressure from his friends would be too great and he is not sure he has the confidence or 'willpower' to stick with a plan (*sustain talk – ability; reason*). Andrew states that you could help him move up on the scale by thinking through some techniques or strategies in how to deal with the pressure from his friends. Based on the scaling exercise, you have assessed that Andrew is beginning to see the importance in making a change, but is struggling in his confidence to make the change. You realize that your work together should focus on his confidence and some strategies to deal with some of his fears.

In subsequent weeks of work with Andrew, you focus on providing Andrew with information on the health effects of drinking and work through some techniques and strategies on how Andrew can deal with the stress in his life without alcohol and how to cope with not drinking around his friends (*planning process*). You reassess Andrew's importance and confidence at each session and find that he is gradually moving up on both scales towards a 10. After several weeks of work together, Andrew moves into the preparation stage and begins to cut down on the units of alcohol he drinks and the number of days that he drinks per week (*mobilizing change talk – taking steps*). You and Andrew begin to develop a quit plan which addresses his goal of quitting drinking, some techniques to deal with stress, such as taking walks and spending quiet time alone with his wife, and strategies to be with his friends without drinking, such as switching to non-alcoholic beer and changing the venue to that of his house. Andrew continues to meet with you several weeks after his quit date in order to address and monitor relapse and work through relapse prevention techniques.

Strengths and limitations

There are several identified strengths and limitations to utilizing motivational interviewing in social work practice. The strengths include the following:

- Motivational interviewing is versatile and can be used in combination with other theories and methods. For example, the approach can be used at the beginning of work together with a client in order to help the client move through the stages of change and then the social worker may switch to a cognitive behavioural approach or task-centred approach to further the change process.
- Research on the effectiveness of motivational interviewing has expanded beyond the addictions field and has been shown to work with eating disorders, medication and treatment compliance, health risk behaviours, gambling, water purification and diet and exercise. Research into the effectiveness of this method is ongoing.
- Motivational interviewing is an empowerment-based approach in the sense that the client is valued, viewed as the expert and holds the motivation,

strengths and resources to change. The social worker is not to confront or persuade the client to change, but rather stay with the client and help them resolve ambivalence in favour of making a positive change.

- The approach can be viewed as 'realistic' in the sense that the social worker will stay with the client at the moment and not push them to explore areas or topics that the client does not want to explore.

The limitations include the following:

- Motivational interviewing is a relatively new approach and is still undergoing extensive evaluations, particularly with regard to whom the approach is not appropriate and when the approach is the most or least effective. Despite this, the evidence is building, and Miller and Rollnick (2013) encourage practitioners to implement motivational interviewing in new settings where it is deemed appropriate.
- Motivational interviewing may not be appropriate for all situations or populations as it requires a particular level of understanding on the part of the client. For example, the approach may not work if clients are not in a position to make connections between their current behaviour and values or future goals.
- Motivational interviewing may be less successful when working with involuntary clients who do not see that they have a problem, but rather a third party is forcing them to work on their problems. Involuntary clients may make a change relatively quickly due to the external pressures, but will most likely resume their behaviours once the third party has removed themselves from the client.
- The techniques of motivational interviewing may be difficult to strictly adhere to if clients stress a need for specific direction from the social worker or if the social worker is used to playing an 'expert' role. The social worker and client are to collaborate and participate in joint decision-making and the social worker is not to get into the trap of providing suggestions or strong guidance to the client; the motivation, strengths and resources lie with the client.

Ethical and cultural considerations

Motivational interviewing views clients as the expert in their situations, and values their experiences and perspective, yet the social worker is focused and goal driven in guiding the client to resolve ambivalence in favour of change. In maintaining this focus, the social worker should be considerate to the different social and cultural factors that affect people's behaviours, experiences and perceptions about their behaviour (Miller and Rollnick, 2013). For example, a social worker from the United States may have a different view of the use of alcohol than a social worker from the UK and, more simply, the view of alcohol use can vary among different communities and neighbourhoods within the same country. Therefore, social workers should be cautious not to allow their social and cultural influences to intervene in the work with the client, rather the client's social and cultural influences should be elicited from the client and should drive the work together; a client will only change if she or he sees the change as personally relevant (Miller and Rollnick, 2013).

Motivational interviewing seeks to stay with the client and help her or him resolve ambivalence in favour of making a change. This approach does not fully support situations where clients have been mandated to seek help for behaviour(s) that someone else has identified as a problem. In addressing these power-differential situations, Miller and Rollnick (2013, pp. 245–6) have developed the following guidelines for ethical practice that seeks to maintain the spirit of motivational interviewing:

1   Motivational interviewing should not be used if the scientific evidence indicates that doing so would cause harm to the client.
2   If you detect dissonance in the client–social worker relationship or an area of ethical concern, clarify the client's aspirations as well as your own.
3   If your idea of best interest for the client is different from the client's, reconsider and negotiate your agenda, making clear your own concerns and aspirations for the person.
4   The greater your personal investment in a particular client outcome, the more inappropriate it is to use this approach.
5   If your role includes coercive power to influence the person's behaviour and outcomes, then the use of strategic evoking is inappropriate.

Anti-oppressive practice and motivational interviewing

Motivational interviewing is an empowerment-based approach and is anti-oppressive in nature as it is based on communication skills and an interpersonal style that values and respects the client and views the client as the expert. The 'spirit' of motivational interviewing holds that clients and social workers collaborate and work in partnership through the process of change, that social workers acknowledge that the client is the expert and the strengths, resources and motivation lie with them, and the social worker acknowledges that the choice and responsibility to change lie with the client. The approach is clear in moving with clients and not pushing, pulling or persuading them to make choices or decisions that they do not feel ready to pursue.

The language used in motivational interviewing is anti-oppressive, for example, the use of 'interview' versus therapy, treatment or counselling stresses the importance of a collaborative relationship and doesn't imply who holds the power in the situation (Miller and Rollnick, 2002). Additionally, the use of help or hinder and good and not so good are used to explore the pros and cons of staying the same and changing without placing blame or stressing to clients that they are participating in a behaviour that is bad. In supporting autonomy and providing affirmations, the approach seeks to value clients and point out their strengths, resources and accomplishments to provide an environment that is safe to make a change.

Research on motivational interviewing

Since motivational interviewing was first discussed over 30 years ago, the approach has undergone numerous evaluations to examine its effectiveness across different situations and populations. The number of writings since 1983 is over 1,200, with more than 200 clinical control trials examining the effectiveness of motivational interviewing when working with alcohol and other drug use, cigarette and smokeless tobacco use, health risk behaviours, medication and treatment compliance, water purification, diet and exercise, eating disorders and gambling (see www.motivationalinterviewing.org for a full bibliography). Despite the growing evidence-base of this method, some studies demonstrate that it might not be the actual use of motivational interviewing 'treatment techniques' that are the key component of effectiveness, but rather that the 'client response to motivational interviewing is significantly influenced by clinician and contextual aspects of delivery – factors that are not adequately standardized by following a treatment manual' (Miller and Rollnick, 2013, p. 696). Reasons for this have been hypothesized to be based on the clinical skill of the practitioner, a lack of measuring the fidelity of motivational interviewing in studies, but, more specifically, the therapeutic relationship where the 'spirit' of motivational interviewing enhances the relationship and, thus, increases the chance of change occurring (Miller and Rollnick, 2013).

A meta-analysis conducted by Lundahl et al. (2010) examined the effectiveness of motivational interviewing in terms of helping clients with change by looking at 25 years of empirical studies. A total of 119 studies were included, which examined the use of motivational interviewing with substance use (alcohol, tobacco, drugs), diet, exercise, safe sex, gambling and engagement in treatment variables. The results revealed the following:

- The overall effect of motivational interviewing interventions was small but significant across a wide range of problem domains. Seventy-five per cent of participants gained some improvement from motivational interviewing (p. 151).
- 'When compared to other active treatments such as 12-step and cognitive behavioural therapy (CBT), the MI interventions took over 100 fewer minutes of treatment on average, yet produced equal effects' (p. 152).
- Motivational interviewing is useful when addressing addictive behaviours as well as enhancing general health-promoting behaviours, and is useful with clients who experience both high and low levels of distress (p. 152).
- Motivational interviewing is useful in increasing clients' intention to change and boosts their confidence in their ability to change (p. 152).
- Motivational interviewing is portable 'across many different treatment formats or roles' (p. 153).

Summary

Motivational interviewing is 'a collaborative, goal-oriented style of communication with particular attention to the language of change. It is designed to strengthen personal motivation for, and commitment to, a specific goal by eliciting the person's own reasons for change within an atmosphere of acceptance and compassion' (Miller and Rollnick, 2013, p. 66). The social worker works from a client-centred approach, yet is focused and goal directed in resolving ambivalence in favour of change. The social worker should continually assess the client's position in the stages of change model as well as where she or he rates on importance, confidence and readiness. The 'spirit' of motivational interviewing provides the foundation for work between the social worker and client and consists of partnership, acceptance, compassion and evocation. The social worker moves through the four processes of motivational interviewing (engaging, focusing, evoking and planning) while utilizing the key communication skills of open-ended questions, affirmations, reflections and summaries (OARS) that reflect back the client's ambivalence, which is comprised of change talk and sustain talk. Open-ended questions, scaling, decisional balance and looking back/looking forward questions are useful techniques to assess a client's motivation to make a change, explore ambivalence, evoke change talk and uncover the intrinsic motivation for change. The social worker adheres to the 'spirit' of motivational interviewing and seeks to help the client resolve ambivalence in favour of positive change.

Case study

Anna is a 16-year-old, white British female who has been referred to child and adolescent mental health services (CAMHS) by her general practitioner (GP) due to an eating disorder. On your first meeting with Anna, she discloses that she has been struggling with bulimia nervosa for the past four years and would like to quit binging and purging and using laxatives. Anna reports that she binges and purges at least once a day and uses up to eight laxatives a day in order to control her weight. Anna expresses feelings of guilt and shame about her behaviour, but also reports receiving feelings of accomplishment and control when she purges. Anna discloses that she is beginning to see some changes to her teeth and mouth, which she knows is a direct result of purging. Social activities have been scarce for Anna as she refuses invitations to go out with friends or family if food is involved. Anna describes wanting to make a change as she knows that her actions are affecting her health and social life, but does not want to gain weight or lose control of her eating habits. Describe how you would utilize the motivational interviewing approach with Anna.

Further reading and web resources

http://www.motivationalinterviewing.org
> Provides information on motivational interviewing as well as a complete bibliography.

Arkowitz, H., Westra, H.A., Miller, W.R. and Rollnick, S. (eds) (2008) *Motivational Interviewing in the Treatment of Psychological Problems*. New York: Guilford Press.
 Applies motivational interviewing to the treatment of a variety of psychological problems (that is, anxiety, depression, PTSD, eating disorders).
Levounis, P. and Arnaout, B. (2010) *Handbook of Motivation and Change: A Practical Guide for Practitioners*. Arlington, VA: American Psychiatric.
 A beginner's guide to motivational interviewing.
Miller, W.R. and Rollnick, S. (2013) *Motivational Interviewing: Preparing People for Change*, 3rd edn. New York: Guilford Press.
 The third edition of Miller and Rollnick's introductory book on motivational interviewing. Discusses all the basic processes and characteristics, and presents research on utilizing motivational interviewing with various populations in various settings.

References

Britt, E., Hudson, S.M. and Blampied, N.M. (2004) Motivational interviewing in health settings: a review, *Patient Education and Counseling*, 53(2): 147–55.
Janis, I.L. and Mann, L. (1977) *Decision-making: A Psychological Analysis of Conflict, Choice, and Commitment*. New York: Free Press.
Lundahl, B.W., Kunz, C., Brownell, C., Tollefson, D. and Burke, B.L. (2010) A meta-analysis of motivational interviewing: twenty-five years of empirical studies, *Research on Social Work Practice*, 20(2): 137–60.
Miller, W.R. (1983) Motivational interviewing with problem drinkers, *Behavioral Psychotherapy*, 11(2): 147–72.
Miller, W.R. (1994) Motivational interviewing: III. On the ethics of motivational intervention, *Behavioural and Cognitive Psychotherapy*, 22(2): 111–23.
Miller, W.R. and Rollnick, S. (1991) *Motivational Interviewing: Preparing People for Change*. New York: Guilford Press.
Miller, W.R. and Rollnick, S. (2002) *Motivational Interviewing: Preparing People for Change*, 2nd edn. New York: Guilford Press.
Miller, W.R. and Rollnick, S. (2013) *Motivational Interviewing: Preparing People for Change*, 3rd edn. New York: Guilford Press.
Norcross, J.C., Krebs, P.M. and Prochaska, J.O. (2011) Stages of change, *Journal of Clinical Psychology*, 67(2): 143–54.
Prochaska, J.O. and DiClemente, C.C. (1983) Stages and processes of self-change of smoking: toward an integrative model of change, *Journal of Consulting and Clinical Psychology*, 51(3): 390–5.
Prochaska, J.O. and DiClemente, C.C. (1984) *The Transtheoretical Approach: Crossing Traditional Boundaries of Therapy*. Homewood, IL: Dow Jones-Irwin.
Prochaska, J.O. and DiClemente, C.C. (1992) Stages of change in the modification of problem behaviors, in M. Hersen, R.M. Eisler and P.M. Miller (eds), *Progress in Behaviour Modification*. Newbury Park, CA: Sage.
Prochaska, J.O., DiClemente, C.C. and Norcross, J.C. (1992) In search of how people change: applications to addictive behaviors, *American Psychologist*, 47(9): 1102–14.

Rogers, C.R. (1959) A theory of therapy, personality, and interpersonal relationships as developed in the client-centered framework, in S. Koch (ed.), *Psychology: The Study of Science: Vol. 3, Formulations of the Person and the Social Contexts*. New York: McGraw-Hill.

Rollnick, S. and Miller, W.R. (1995) What is motivational interviewing? *Behavioural and Cognitive Psychotherapy*, 23(4): 325–34.

Velicer, W.F., Prochaska, J.O., Fava, J.L., Norman, G.J. and Redding, C.A. (1998) Smoking cessation and stress management: applications of the transtheoretical model of behavior change, *Homeostasis*, 38(5/6): 216–33.

9   Cognitive behavioural therapy

Introduction

Cognitive behavioural therapy (CBT) is a well-researched psychological approach that is based on theories of behavioural conditioning, learning theory and cognitive theory (Thomlison and Thomlison, 2011). CBT is actually a combination of two therapies, behavioural therapy and cognitive therapy, which when combined focus on the impact of thoughts and feelings (cognitions) and behaviours in causing psychological distress and dysfunction. Behavioural and cognitive therapies were incorporated into social work due to the criticism of the use of non-scientific psychoanalytic casework that was prominent within social work and the lack of interventions established as effective in bringing about change (Howe, 2009). Whereas behavioural therapy focuses on the cause and formulation of behaviours and how these learned behaviours contribute to current problems, cognitive therapy focuses on the development of cognitions, or thoughts and feelings, and how faulty beliefs or faulty information processing can lead to difficulties in clients' personal and social systems. CBT combines both the behavioural and cognitive aspect in creating psychological distress and dysfunction. CBT aims to 'seek to help clients to analyse and "reality test" existing patterns of thinking, emotional reactions and behaviour identified via an assessment of current difficulties, and to try out new approaches in a stepwise fashion, monitoring and evaluating effects in all three areas' (Sheldon, 2011, p. 3).

CBT postulates that thoughts, feelings and beliefs are intertwined and should be assessed in combination when attempting to alleviate or diminish clients' problems and difficulties. The role of the social worker in utilizing CBT is to assess the client's behaviours, thoughts and feelings and how these are contributing to the client's presenting problem, and then provide interventions that will assist the client in altering behaviours or thought processes to produce a more positive and acceptable outcome. This chapter will discuss CBT by exploring the origins of the method, which consist of the development of behavioural and cognitive therapies; the basic assumptions of the approach; and specific assessment, intervention and evaluation techniques that can be employed to diminish or alleviate client distress or dysfunction.

The origins of cognitive behavioural therapy

During the 1970s social work was under criticism for the lack of scientific interventions that could be tested and shown to be effective when working with clients (Howe, 2009). Due to this criticism, social work began to explore behavioural and cognitive therapies and later incorporated CBT in social work practice. As CBT is a combination of behavioural and cognitive therapies, the origins of each will be discussed in turn before focusing solely on CBT.

Behavioural therapy

The origins of behavioural therapy can be traced back to the 1950s, when it was predominately based on the theoretical ideas of classical conditioning and operant conditioning developed through the work of experimental psychologists who conducted research on humans and animals in the early 1900s (Sharf, 2012). The most widely cited study of influence on the development of behavioural therapy was the work of Ivan Pavlov who conducted a study on the conditioning of dogs. Pavlov's classic study involved observing that dogs would salivate before food was placed on their tongues. Pavlov experimented with presenting a sound or light one to two seconds before the dogs were to be fed, which led them to associate the sound or light with food, and, thus, to begin to salivate when the sound or light was presented before the food. The association between the sound or light and food became so strong that the dogs began to salivate when the sound or light was presented alone. In this experiment, Pavlov found that the dogs were conditioned to salivate by providing an antecedent to a consequence and, thus, they had leant a new behaviour.

Building on Pavlov's research, John Watson initiated an experiment with 11-month-old Little Albert with a hypothesis that an emotional reaction could be conditioned (Watson and Rayner, 1920). Little Albert was observed playing comfortably with tame rats and rabbits, but was startled by loud noises. Watson began to present a loud noise immediately before introducing the tame rat over a one week period. After this period of time, Little Albert became frightened and scared when the rat or rabbit alone was presented.

These two studies were testing the *classical or respondent conditioning* model that later served as one part of the foundation to behavioural therapy. The classical or respondent conditioning model holds that behaviours are a result of prior learning. Behaviours are learned, therefore behaviours can be unlearned. Classical conditioning specifically focuses on the antecedents to behaviours (Sharf, 2012). For example, in learning to drive a car we are informed that if the brake lights of the car in front of us come on, we are to initiate a stop as well in order to avoid a collision. Over time and in future driving situations we begin to initiate a stop without much thought prior to the action. We have been conditioned to initiate a stop when we see brake lights in front of us.

Operant or instrumental conditioning equally served as a part of the foundation of behavioural therapy and is based on the works of Edward Lee Thorndike and B.F.

Skinner. Thorndike initiated experiments to test the learning of new behaviours. One such experiment (Thorndike, 1911) involved observing the actions and behaviours of caged cats who were attempting to get to food that was placed outside the cage. The cats attempted many actions to free themselves and eventually were able to un-cage themselves by releasing the latch on the cage. Over time, the cats began to free themselves from the cage more quickly by doing actions that led them to the reward (that is, food) versus actions that did not lead them to the reward, such as biting at the cage. Thorndike developed the *law of effect* based on this experiment where he found that providing consequences or rewards for behaviours led to learning (Kazdin, 2008; Sharf, 2012). Positive consequences would increase the likelihood of performing the behaviour in the future and negative consequences would decrease the likelihood of performing the behaviour in the future (Howe, 2009).

B.F. Skinner built on the principles of operant conditioning, which stressed the importance of the antecedents and consequences of behaviours (Sharf, 2012). Skinner theorized that behaviours can be changed based on the consequences that are presented, which he termed positive and negative reinforcers, where positive consequences or reinforcers will lead to an increase in the behaviour and negative consequences or reinforcers will lead to a decrease in the behaviour.

As the models of classical and operant conditioning illustrate, behaviours can be learned, unlearned and adjusted based on the consequences received from the behaviour. These two models serve as the theoretical framework from which behavioural therapy was developed. Behavioural therapists were particularly interested in assessing how behaviours are learned or acquired, how they are maintained and how they can fluctuate based on the consequences or reinforcers for the behaviour (Howe, 2009). Behavioural therapists focus on the problems of the present and attempt to modify or correct behaviours that are contributing to the presenting problem, particularly through a process of unlearning faulty, undesirable behaviours and providing opportunities to learn new behaviours with positive or more acceptable consequences.

Cognitive therapy

While the use of behavioural therapy was widening during the 1960s, cognitive therapy was beginning to form based on the work of Albert Ellis who was a psychoanalyst and later a psychology professor, and Aaron Beck who was trained as a psychiatrist and psychoanalyst. Ellis developed rational emotive behaviour therapy (REBT), a form of cognitive therapy, during the 1950s, due to his dissatisfaction with his work as a psychoanalyst. Ellis believed that therapy with clients would be more effective if he addressed the behavioural and emotive aspects that were contributing to the client's problems versus merely encouraging clients to talk freely about experiences and problems (that is, free associate) (Sharf, 2012). Ellis developed the A–B–C model, which examined how activating events (A) did not automatically produce a behavioural or emotional consequence (C), but rather the individual's belief system (B) mediated the behavioural consequence (C). The A–B–C model will be discussed in more detail later, particularly as it relates to CBT.

Beck's early research focused on depression (for example, Beck Depression Inventory) and the importance of one's cognition in contributing to and treating the depression. Through his work as a psychoanalyst and researcher, Beck realized the importance that cognition – particularly faulty, negative thoughts of the client – played in contributing to psychological distress and dysfunction. Beck found that individuals who were depressed or presented with other psychological difficulties often over-magnified and overgeneralized their faulty behaviours or personal deficiencies, which were often based on set beliefs, or schemas, that they had developed and for which they held themselves accountable. Beck theorized that early childhood experiences contribute to the development of basic beliefs and schemas, or automatic thought processes, which contributes to how an individual thinks, feels and behaves. These basic beliefs and schemas are activated in future situations, which trigger the automatic thoughts, which are expressed through emotions, behaviours and physiological responses (Liese, 1994). For example, a student was raised by a mother who told her that 'Satisfactory is not good enough. Don't ever settle for anything less than excellent'. The student proceeded through school with the basic belief that anything less than excellent meant she would be a failure, worthless and unlovable by her mother. The student comes to study social work at a university where her first mark in the programme is a 'satisfactory'. The student makes an appointment with her tutor to discuss withdrawing from the programme. When the student arrives she appears unclean and disorganized and the tutor suspects the student is experiencing some depressive symptoms. This example illustrates how the basic beliefs and schemas instilled in the student were activated when she received a satisfactory mark and resulted in negative beliefs and distressing emotions.

Cognitive theorists acknowledged that the way we think impacts on the way we feel (Thomlison and Thomlison, 2011). Therefore, treatment in cognitive therapy aims to identify the client's distorted beliefs or faulty thinking that are sustaining the presenting problem, provide interventions that will challenge these beliefs and thoughts, and work with the client to create new beliefs and thoughts that are more positive and acceptable to the client and that will reduce or alleviate the presenting problem.

Whereas behavioural therapy focused on the behaviours and cognitive therapy focused on the cognitions, cognitive behavioural therapy (CBT) formed as a combination of the two by focusing on the interaction of behaviours and cognitions of clients who are experiencing psychological distress and dysfunction. CBT is predominately influenced by the *social learning theory* of Albert Bandura (1977), which stresses the importance of considering observable behaviours of the individual and her or his environment and unobservable behaviours of the individual, such as thoughts and emotions. Social learning theory holds that individuals learn by observing and modelling others within their environment, which includes modelling behaviours, thoughts and feelings. Individuals are more likely to model and exhibit behaviours, thoughts and feelings that are reinforced by their environments regardless of whether the behaviours, thoughts and feelings are positive or negative in nature (Sharf, 2012).

Cognitive behavioural therapy (CBT) explained

CBT is an approach that involves assessing and changing behaviours, thoughts and feelings in combination when working with clients to alleviate psychological distress and dysfunction. CBT involves a focus on presenting problems and the contemporary causes of the problems and stresses the equal involvement of the social worker and client in changing faulty learning processes or behaviours. CBT holds that clients' problems and difficulties are a result of thoughts, feelings and behaviours being integrally bound up in one another and, therefore, how clients view themselves or situations impacts on how they respond to such situations both behaviourally and emotionally (Vonk and Early, 2009). When utilizing CBT with clients, the goal is to change the clients' existing faulty or negative thoughts, feelings and behaviours with more acceptable and positive thoughts, feelings and behaviours that will diminish or alleviate the presenting problem.

To further illustrate how thoughts, feelings and behaviours are intertwined, we will revisit Ellis's A–B–C model, which is based on social learning theory. As Figure 9.1a illustrates, situations are often viewed as activating events (A) leading to behavioural and emotional consequences (C). For example, a student received a satisfactory on her university essay (A) and she feels worthless and schedules a meeting with her tutor to withdraw from the programme (C). What we are leaving out in this scenario is how event A is filtered through our cognitive processes (B) as illustrated in Figure 9.1b. For example, a student received a satisfactory on her university essay (A). The student thinks she is worthless as she remembers the message instilled by her mother: 'Satisfactory is not good enough. Don't settle for anything less than excellent' (B). Therefore, the student feels worthless, unable to continue and schedules a meeting with the tutor to withdraw from the programme (C). This example illustrates how cognitive processes (B), with regard to an activating event (A), mediate the behavioural and emotional consequences (C). These basic beliefs and schemas, as instilled in the student, could continue to cause problems for her when she enters the workforce. For example, the student's boss gives her a satisfactory on her annual review (A). The student thinks she is a failure and remembers the rule as told to her by her mother that satisfactory is

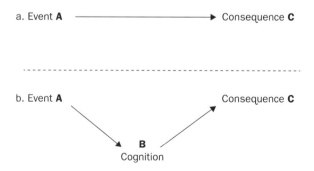

Figure 9.1   Thoughts and feelings mediate consequences.

not good enough (B). The student feels she is a failure and quits her job (C). Without the student changing or modifying her faulty thought processes, she will continue to view herself as a failure and worthless and remove herself from situations where she is told she is satisfactory.

Utilizing CBT in practice means that the social worker would have a belief that 'problem behaviours can be identified and changed, cognitions shape behaviours, and that affecting behavioural change requires a systematic approach' (Thomlison and Thomlison, 2011, p. 84–5). There are three basic assumptions of CBT, each of which are described in detail here:

1   *Individuals' cognitions (thinking) mediate emotions and behaviours* (Trower et al., 1988; Vonk and Early, 2009). Individuals do not merely respond to situations or stimuli, but rather filter the situation or stimuli through their cognitive processes. This filtering process is shaped by the basic beliefs and schemas that have been developed through past experiences and by modelling behaviours and emotions as observed within individuals' environments. The emotions and behaviours that result from the individuals experiencing a situation or stimuli will vary based on their cognitive processes.

2   *Faulty or distorted cognitions lead to psychological distress and dysfunction* (Trower et al., 1988). Individuals who have developed basic beliefs and schemas that are faulty, distorted or unrealistic will process situations and stimuli through this faulty system and produce consequences (emotions or behaviours) that are negative or problematic in nature.

3   *Diminishing or alleviating psychological distress and dysfunction requires modification and change to the faulty or distorted cognitions and behaviours* (Trower et al., 1988; Vonk and Early, 2009). As cognitive processes mediate the consequences (emotional and behavioural), the interventions to alleviate negative consequences require a change in the cognitive processes and/or behaviours. Interventions require a challenge to the existing cognitive processes, and a replacement of these faulty or distorted beliefs and schemas with positive, more accurate, ones that will produce responses to situations and stimuli (that is, consequences) that are free of psychological distress and dysfunction.

Applying cognitive behavioural therapy (CBT) to practice

The goal of CBT is to replace maladaptive thoughts and/or behaviours with more positive, acceptable ones in an attempt to resolve problems and difficulties in clients' lives. This approach requires social workers and clients to work collaboratively and Vonk and Early (2009) specify roles for each in this process. The role of the social worker is of a supportive teacher or guide who takes a more directive stance with the client in pointing out how the presenting problem is a result of the interaction of the client's thoughts, feelings and behaviours. The social worker facilitates the assessment process by guiding the client through exercises that illustrate the connection of thoughts, feelings and behaviours as contributing to the presenting problem. As the social worker is more directive in this approach, she or he specifies intervention techniques that will attempt to modify the client's cognitive processes or behaviours, which often include assigned work for the client to complete outside the session. The social worker may offer concrete suggestions that the client should try in attempting to change thoughts or behaviours (Macdonald, 2007).

The role of the client is to take responsibility for discussing thoughts, feelings and behaviours, and for sharing how these may be contributing to her or his presenting problem. The client participates in the therapeutic process by informing the social worker of her or his problems, completing assignments and tasks, and taking more control of the sessions as the work together proceeds. Whereas the social worker is viewed as having expertise in CBT techniques and strategies, the client is viewed as the expert on her or his experiences and situations (Vonk and Early, 2009). The collaborative relationship should continue from assessment, where the problem is discussed and goals selected by the client, to the evaluation of the work together.

The process of applying CBT to practice involves three stages: (1) assessment; (2) intervention; and (3) evaluation. Each is discussed in detail here:

1   *Assessment*: The assessment serves as the most significant stage as this is where the client and social worker explore how the client's thoughts, feelings and behaviours are contributing to the presenting problem. Every assessment should begin with the client's definition of the presenting problem with specific detail in terms of frequency, intensity and duration. The presenting problem(s) is then directly related to the treatment or care plan. The use of the A–B–C model at this stage enables clients to understand the patterns of their thought, feelings and behaviours, particularly as they relate to the presenting problem. As described earlier, the A–B–C model consists of: (A) activating event – what occurs just before the feeling or behaviour? – (B) belief system or attitude (cognitive processes) – how did you think or feel about this? – and (C) behavioural and emotional consequences – what were the emotional and behavioural reactions? During the assessment stage, the social worker discusses the A–B–C model with the client and then applies the model to the client's presenting problem. For example, our student who receives a satisfactory on her essay reports her presenting problem as feeling worthless and incapable of continuing with the social work programme. You explain the A–B–C model to the student by discussing how her thoughts and feelings may be contributing to her presenting problem (that is, negative emotional consequences). You ask the student to keep a record on a sheet of paper consisting of three columns of when she feels worthless and incapable of continuing with a task over the next week. In the first column, the student states the activating events (A) where she reports what happened immediately before she had feelings of being worthless and incapable of continuing with a task, the second column consists of her thoughts and feelings immediately following this activating event (B), and the third column consists of the emotional and behavioural consequences (C), where she reports how she feels and what she does in response to

the activating event. This exercise will assist the social worker and client in understanding the pattern of thoughts, feelings and behaviours of the client and will assist in determining the most appropriate intervention to address the presenting problem. Interventions can be tailored to address what happens immediately before the behaviours by changing the activating event, or what happens immediately after the activating event by changing the thoughts, feelings or behaviours (Howe, 2009).

Another critical aspect of CBT is the ability to evaluate the effectiveness of the intervention with the client. The evaluation process begins in the assessment stage where the client reports the intensity, frequency and duration of the presenting problem *before* the intervention occurs. This information is often collected through either standardized assessment instruments, such as the Beck Depression Inventory, the Achenbach Child Behaviour Checklist (Achenbach, 1991) or through self-report of the client as gathered by the social worker. A quick and convenient way to collect the intensity, frequency and duration of the problem pre-intervention, often called baseline data, is to ask the client 'How many times have you [*felt, or behaved*] over the past [*day, 3 days, week, month*]?' (Granvold, 1996). This information can be recorded on a chart where the behaviour or feeling is recorded on the horizontal line and the frequency of the behaviour or feeling is recorded on the vertical line. Figure 9.2 illustrates an example of charting the frequency of the presenting problem; this client reports experiencing the problem seven or eight times per day. The dashed vertical line represents when the intervention was initiated. Recording of the frequency of the problem after the intervention should continue in order to assist with evaluation.

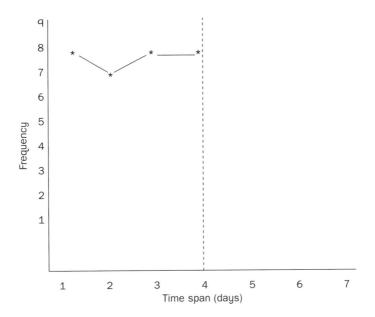

Figure 9.2   Assessment: collecting baseline data.

2   *Intervention*: CBT pulls together a range of techniques and strategies from behavioural, cognitive and rational emotive behaviour therapy that all seek to reach the goal of alleviating presenting problems by modifying maladaptive or faulty cognitions and/or behaviours. Once the presenting problem is identified by the client and the contribution of thoughts, feelings and behaviours to the problem has been assessed, the social worker can select the most appropriate intervention to alleviate the problem. Below is a list of a sample of techniques or strategies that a social worker could utilize in the work with a client. Additional intervention techniques can be found through the further reading section at the end of this chapter.

(a) Cognitive restructuring – the social worker works with the client to change the faulty or irrational cognitions with more acceptable and accurate ones that reduce the presenting problem. The intervention may simply be a discussion of the evidence for or against the existing cognitions. The social worker could begin this process by asking such questions as: 'What is the evidence that you are worthless [or other belief]?', 'How could this situation be described or interpreted differently?' or 'What are the consequences if this belief is in fact correct?' (DeRubeis et al., 2009; Sharf, 2012).

(b) Relaxation techniques – the social worker teaches the client skills for relaxing, particularly for use during stressful or anxiety-evoking situations. The process typically involves tensing and relaxing muscles groups from the head to the toes. The social worker may suggest the client practises the relaxation techniques outside the office for 10–15 minutes once or twice a day in order for the client to feel comfortable utilizing the technique during stressful or uncomfortable situations (Sheldon, 2011).

(c) Social skills training – the social worker and client identify a situation where the client's behaviour is problematic and seek to modify the behaviour to be more acceptable in such situations. In learning this new behaviour, the social worker and client identify small tasks or stages in order to achieve the new behaviour and will begin by practising these new skills in the session together. The social worker may demonstrate the behaviour and then have the client practise with the social worker. The social worker and client identify situations where certain behaviours are appropriate and inappropriate. The social worker may assign homework tasks to the client to practise these new skills outside the session and report back to the social worker as to how the client experienced the developed skill (Sheldon, 2011).

(d) Assertion training – this process is similar to social skills training in that the social worker and client identify situations that are problematic for the client, which usually consist of situations where clients are not able to meet their needs, are shy, are being taken advantage of or are being discriminated against. The aim of assertion training is for the client to learn appropriate self-expression. The social worker and client should practise these skills together before the client transfers them to the real-life settings (Sheldon, 2011).

(e) Problem-solving skills – the social worker and client identify a problem and work through potential solutions to the problem together. The process often involves identifying a goal, or solution to the problem, establishing tasks to reach the goal, accomplishing the tasks and then reporting on the progress to reaching the goal. The skills learned through the work together are to be transferable to other situations where the client encounters a problem.

(f) Aversion therapy – clients are exposed to a behaviour or situation (usually the problematic behaviour) while simultaneously being exposed to unpleasant or uncomfortable behaviours or sensations. The goal is for the client to associate the problematic behaviour with the unpleasant or uncomfortable behaviours or sensations and thus cease the problematic behaviour. For example, a client who has a problem with swearing may wear a rubber band around her or his wrist and snap the band every time she or he uses a swear word.

(g) Systematic desensitization – clients are exposed to anxiety-evoking situations, either in live practice or through imaginary form, while simultaneously being exposed to behaviours that compete with anxiety, such as relaxation (Sharf, 2012). Clients may first learn relaxation skills and then gradually expose themselves to anxiety-evoking situations while incorporating their new relaxation skills. Wolpe (1958) developed three steps to incorporating this approach in practice: (1) the client learns relaxation skills; (2) the social worker and client discuss anxiety-evoking events and arrange them by level of anxiety; and (3) the client images these events while simultaneously utilizing the relaxation skills. The goal is for the client to associate the problematic, anxiety-evoking situation with more pleasant and comfortable behaviours.

(h) Reinforcement – this technique has also been referred to as token economies, often used with children. Based on the model of operant conditioning, positive reinforcements are given for good behaviour, and negative reinforcements are given for not so good behaviour. For example, if Susan would like to stop swearing, she may put a pound in a jar each day that she does not swear and treat herself to a reward at the end of the week with the money in the jar. Additionally, if Susan does swear during the day, she has to remove a pound from the jar. The goal is for clients to be encouraged to modify problematic behaviours.

(i) Modelling and role-plays – modelling, based on the work of Bandura (1977) involves teaching, motivating and encouraging positive behaviours while discouraging negative behaviours. Modelling can take place in the therapeutic setting where the social worker models a particular behaviour or action and then works with the client to model the behaviour. Other forms of modelling can be seen through the use of films or videos, participating in groups or through visualization (Sharf, 2012). Role-plays often coincide with modelling where the social worker and client practise demonstrating specific behaviours and actions in a simulated situation.

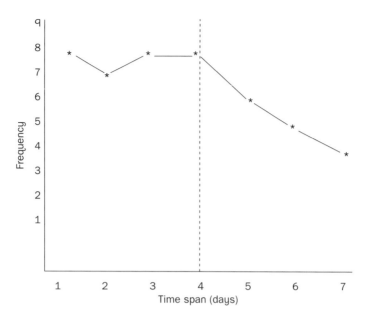

Figure 9.3   Evaluating: monitoring frequency of behaviours post-intervention.

3   *Evaluation*: A significant component of CBT is the ability to examine the effectiveness of the intervention. As discussed under the assessment stage above, the social worker gathers information around the problem in terms of intensity, duration and frequency. This information serves as the baseline data, which illustrates the extent of the problem before an intervention is implemented. The social worker is advised to continue collecting the intensity, duration and frequency of the problem throughout the work together in order to determine whether the intervention is working or when to incorporate a new intervention if the existing one is not working. Keeping track of the intensity, duration and frequency of the problem can also serve as a useful tool for clients by demonstrating the progress they have made or the work still to be achieved. Figure 9.3 illustrates how the frequency of the behaviour for this client had decreased after the intervention was implemented (as indicated by the dashed vertical line).

Exercise box 9.1   Exploring CBT

In pairs or small groups discuss the following:

1   Think of a social work situation in which CBT would be appropriate.
2   Describe the role of the social worker and the client in this situation.
3   Discuss how you would assess, intervene and evaluate in this situation.

Case example: applying the cognitive behavioural approach (CBT) to practice

Dan is a 33-year-old, white British, single father who comes to the parent–toddler play group at the local family centre. Dan has two children: Alex, aged 4, and Samantha, aged 2. The mother of Dan's children, Lacy, has misused drugs for several years and left Dan and the children approximately one year ago; she has had no contact with Dan or the children since she left. Dan works part-time in construction, when work is available, and is taking full responsibilty for the care of the children. Dan has asked to speak to you as the social worker at the family centre and reports becoming more concerned about his ability to parent and manage his children. Dan states that over the past year he has started to feel increasingly anxious and overwhelmed and believes that he has had several panic attacks, particularly when the children are acting up. During these anxious times, Dan finds himself yelling at the children and then feeling guilty afterwards. You agree to work with Dan and believe, with Dan's permission, that CBT is the most appropriate approach.

You begin your session with Dan by asking him to describe the presenting problem. During this assessment stage, Dan reports that he feels overwhelmed and anxious when the kids are acting up, and feels unable to control the children or his feelings and actions. Dan describes a situation where he found the children in the bathroom where they had unrolled all the toilet roll and had it all over the bathroom and hallway. When he discovered this, he felt his chest tighten and his heart pound and responded to the children by yelling at them until they cried and appeared frightened. Dan reports that he felt horrible after he yelled at the children and guilty for making his children appear fearful of him. You seek to gather as much information from Dan about the presenting problem and particularly its intensity, frequency and duration. Dan reports that his feelings of anxiety and his yelling at the children began after Lacy left, about one year ago and have got progressively worse. You ask Dan to self-report on how many times he believes he felt anxious or overwhelmed and how many times he has yelled at the children over the past three days. Dan discloses that he has felt anxious and yelled at the children at least twice a day over the past three days. (*Note: If you were to suspect any potential abuse or neglect, you would contact Children and Young People Services immediately.*)

You next want to explore with Dan how his thoughts, feelings and behaviours are interconnected and how his cognitive processes are mediating his behaviours and emotions. You ask Dan for permission to work through the A–B–C model with him. Dan agrees and you begin by asking him to think about the times when he feels anxious and overwhelmed. On a piece of paper with three columns, you ask him to list the activating event (A) in the first column by asking questions such as, 'What happened just before you felt anxious and overwhelmed and yelled at the children?' or 'Where were you and what was going on just before you felt anxious and overwhelmed and you yelled at the children?' You then ask Dan to list in the second column what he thought and felt when he experienced the activating event (B). Lastly, you ask Dan to report in the third column the emotional and behavioural consequences (C) by asking such questions as,

Table 9.1 Example of A–B–C assessment exercise

Activating event (A)	Belief system/attitudes (B)	Consequences (C)
I walked into the bathroom and saw the toilet paper all over the room	My chest tightened, heart pounded. I thought, 'I can't handle this!' 'I can't be a single dad!'	I yelled at my kids. I felt guilty and sad that I had yelled. I felt like a horrible parent and anxious that I can't take care of my children

'How did you respond to this activating event?' or 'What were the consequences – both positive and negative – on your thoughts, feelings and behaviours?' Dan completes the A–B–C model of assessment as in Table 9.1.

You and Dan discuss how his thoughts, feelings and behaviours in regard to the activating event are causing him to feel sad and guilty and are causing him to yell at his children and believe that he cannot take care of them. You both agree that you will work together to modify the way in which Dan thinks and responds to activating events, such as this situation, in the future. Dan's first homework assignment is to keep a record of events over the next few days that cause him to feel anxious, sad and/or guilty in regard to how he responds to his children. Dan is to bring the record to the next session to assist in understanding together how his thoughts, feelings and behaviours are contributing to the presenting problem of feeling overwhelmed, anxious and unable to control his feelings and actions in regard to his children.

At the next session together, you first review with Dan the frequency of the presenting problem since you last were together. Dan reports that although he has not yelled at the children as often over the past few days, there has still been at least one time a day where he felt anxious, overwhelmed and unable to control his feelings and actions. You and Dan enter into the intervention stage and begin to work towards modifying his thoughts, feelings and behaviours in regard to activating events. You first initiate *cognitive restructuring* where you ask Dan for evidence in regard to his thought of 'I can't handle this! I can't be a single dad!' You ask Dan to provide you with evidence that he cannot handle his children. Dan states that if he could handle his children then they would not act up and he would not feel the need to yell at them. You ask Dan if this situation could be described or interpreted differently. Dan reports that he understands all children will act up from time to time and that they are not perfect. He knows that all parents will have to discipline their children when they misbehave or do something they should not. You also ask Dan to describe the consequences if it were true that he could not handle his children. Dan states the consequences would have to include him not being able to look after his children and that they may have to live with someone else. Through this process of questioning, Dan begins to provide an argument for all children misbehaving on occasion and all parents having to provide consequences for children's behaviours. Dan also begins to provide evidence of times when he does handle situations with his children and how he has been able to take over the role of a single father during the past year. You and Dan begin to point out the times when Dan is in control of his children and how he is able to provide for them. You and Dan then participate in a *role-play* where you describe a situation where the children are acting up and ask Dan to think of the times where he has demonstrated control and care for his children. You task Dan with replacing his thought of 'I can't handle this!' with thoughts of 'I can handle this. I love my children and provide for them every day'.

You and Dan also work through practising *relaxation techniques* that Dan can use when faced with anxiety-evoking situations. You ask Dan to close his eyes and work through tensing and relaxing each muscle group from the head to the toes. You task Dan with participating in this exercise twice a day for 10–15 minutes when he is able to be alone and to refer to this exercise when he begins to feel anxious and overwhelmed.

In subsequent sessions with Dan, you evaluate your work together. You assess that Dan has greatly reduced the number of times when he feels anxious and overwhelmed and the number of times that he has yelled at his children. Dan reports giving himself more credit for taking care of his children and has practised the relaxation techniques, which have greatly reduced his anxiety. He also continues to attend the parent–toddler group, which helps him to learn strategies from other parents on how to respond and react to his children (*modelling*).

Strengths and limitations

There are several identified strengths and limitations to utilizing CBT in social work practice. The strengths include the following:

- CBT is highly structured and can be relatively easy to use by following valid treatment manuals (Thomlison and Thomlison, 2011). Social workers may find this approach easy to learn and implement as it has a specific method of assessment, through the use of the A–B–C model, and a variety of interventions that are accompanied with detailed instructions on how to implement them into practice. (See *Cognitive-Behavioral Methods for Social Workers: A Workbook* (Corcoran, 2006) for a review of treatment manuals).
- There is a widening body of evidence for the effectiveness of CBT in teaching skills or modifying maladaptive cognitions and behaviours of clients with a variety of problems (see Sheldon, 2011).
- CBT is a brief intervention that provides clients with tools that they can utilize in real-life situations. As this approach seeks to be brief in nature, the goal of the work between social worker and client is to teach clients new skills or ways of thinking and feeling that they can transfer to other situations or to future problems that occur once the work together has ceased.
- Although directive, CBT stresses the importance of a collaborative relationship and views the client as the expert in her or his own experiences and situations.

The limitations include the following:

- The individual is the focus of work in CBT, therefore, social and political factors contributing to the presenting problem can often be ignored (Enns, 2004). CBT in its purest psychologically based sense is focused on the individual and her or his thoughts, feelings and behaviours. In focusing on the individual only, other factors, such as oppression, discrimination, racism, poverty and/or cultural expectations that may be contributing to the presenting problem are not addressed. As the profession of social work seeks to view persons within their environment, social workers should consider the impact of the client's culture and environment when conducting an assessment and addressing the presenting problem.
- CBT requires the client to be committed to the process. As this approach seeks to modify maladaptive cognitive and problematic behaviours, the client must be engaged and willing to participate in this process. This could prove difficult when social workers are working with involuntary clients or with clients who do not view themselves as having any problems to address. In such situations, social workers may have to incorporate other methods with the client to begin with, such as the person-centred approach or motivational interviewing, and then move on to CBT once the client is ready to participate. Social workers cannot force clients to change thoughts, feelings and/or behaviours that they do not recognize as problematic.
- CBT focuses on the here and now and contemporary causes of behaviour and does not provide attention to underlying problems that may be contributing to the presenting problem. Social workers may need to move beyond the boundaries of CBT in particular situations where attention to underlying or past problems is crucial to alleviating current symptoms. This could be seen in such situations where clients have experienced past traumatic events, such as abuse or neglect. As a general rule, CBT is not appropriate for those who prefer or desire talking therapy.
- The social worker is to be directive when implementing this approach, which could be viewed as disempowering. Social workers should be mindful of the necessity to collaborate with clients, particularly in an attempt to provide an empowering environment. Making the roles of the social worker and client explicit in the beginning can assist in avoiding a disempowering environment.

Ethical and cultural considerations

Although CBT focuses on the individual and her or his thoughts, feelings and behaviours that need to be modified, the approach cannot be fully utilized without considering the multicultural issues that could affect the presenting problem or the individual's view of the problem. There is evidence that CBT works across cultural groups (Butler et al., 2006), but the approach will need to be modified based on the individual's culture and environment. Social workers are encouraged to examine the impact that culture plays in defining the presenting problem, particularly as the extent to which thoughts, feelings and behaviours are appropriate and acceptable will vary by culture. Social workers must not assume thoughts, feelings and/or behaviours are maladaptive or problematic without considering the cultural and environmental context of the individual. Social workers should also seek to implement interventions that are congruent with the client's culture. For example, the social worker may want to consider the influence of family, community healers, spiritual leaders and/or culturally specific practices and rituals in assisting the client to modify thoughts and behaviours. In this process, the social worker and client may have to incorporate empowerment and advocacy skills in attempting to reduce the stigma or oppression that the individual's culture and/or environment is placing on the individual and contributing to the presenting problem. When utilizing CBT with clients and particularly when assessing appropriate antecedents and consequences of behaviours, social workers should become knowledgeable about what are seen as appropriate and inappropriate roles and behaviours within the client's culture and environment (Tanaka-Matsumi et al., 2005), yet be willing to challenge those roles that discriminate and/or oppress and contribute to the presenting problem.

Cognitive behavioural therapy (CBT) and anti-oppressive practice

CBT was developed to address the faulty cognitions and behaviours of individuals. In implementing this approach, the helping professional (that is, psychologist, psychiatrist, social worker, counsellor) is seen as having the expertise to assess, and provide interventions. Embedded in this expertise is the expectation that the helping professional will incorporate an element of teaching in the sessions by highlighting the connections that the client's thoughts, feelings and behaviours contribute to the presenting problem as well as an element of direction as to how the sessions and interventions are structured. The approach does stress that the client is to take more responsibility in directing the sessions and intervention activities over time. When considering these initial premises of CBT, social workers may find anti-oppressive practice less implicit in this approach and will therefore need to make modifications in order to ensure the approach is aligned with the principles and values of social work.

Social workers utilizing CBT while adhering to anti-oppressive practice will need to consider the following, which are not necessarily core components of this approach. First, the social worker and client relationship should be collaborative and egalitarian in nature. In establishing this type of relationship, the social worker may need to incorporate aspects of Rogers' (1957) person-centred approach (see Chapter 7), particularly expressions of empathy, congruence and unconditional positive regard by the social worker. Secondly, although the social worker may have knowledge and expertise in implementing this approach, any agendas and assessments should be transparent to the client and should be mutually agreed (Miller, 2006). Thirdly, as mentioned above under ethical and cultural considerations, social workers must assess the cultural (that is, roles, norms, stereotypes) and environmental (that is, poverty, oppression) factors that are defining and contributing to the presenting problem versus assessing the problem as strictly the responsibility of the individual. Social workers may need to combine CBT with other anti-oppressive methods, such as empowerment, the strengths perspective and advocacy in order to appropriately and fully tackle the presenting problem. Additionally, interpersonal relationships should be considered and assessed to determine whether these interactions and relationships are sustaining unwanted behaviours or emotions (Miller, 2006). Finally, social workers must consider the capabilities of the clients to participate in the assessment and intervention processes, particularly their ability to make the connections between events, cognitions and consequences, and tailor the work together that best builds on clients' strengths (that is, use of visual aids, work with carers, friends and/or family members).

Research on cognitive behavioural therapy (CBT)

CBT values evaluations of the approach in various situations and with various populations in order to determine its effectiveness. Butler et al. (2006) have examined meta-analyses that reviewed the effectiveness of CBT across different problem areas. They found that there were large effect sizes for the use of CBT with unipolar depression, generalized anxiety disorder, panic disorder, post-traumatic stress disorder, and childhood depression/anxiety, and moderate effect sizes with problems of marital distress, anger, childhood somatic disorders, and chronic pain. They also found that the positive results of CBT across different problem areas were sustained beyond the end of treatment. Thomlison and Thomlison (2011) reviewed the literature to identify the empirical support of CBT with different problems. They found that CBT is effective in addressing problems such as addictions, anxiety disorders, attention disorders, autism, child maltreatment, conduct disorders, couple problems, depression, developmental disabilities, eating disorders, family violence, gerontology, juvenile delinquency, obsessive-compulsive disorder, pain management, phobic disorders, post-traumatic stress, psychosis, sexual deviance, sleep disturbances, stress management and substance abuse. The research on the effectiveness of cognitive behavioural therapy has lead to clinical practice guidelines, as established by the National Institute for Health and Clinical Excellence (NICE) in the UK, for utilizing this evidence-based approach with eating disorders (NICE, 2004), obsessive compulsive disorder (NICE, 2005), generalized anxiety disorder and panic disorder (NICE, 2011), attention deficit hyperactivity disorder (NICE, 2008), anti-social personality disorder (NICE, 2009a) and depression (NICE, 2009b).

Summary

CBT is an approach that seeks to explore how thoughts, feelings and behaviours work in combination to contribute to the presenting problem. The approach relies on the classical and operant conditioning models of behavioural therapy and the social learning model of cognitive therapy. CBT is highly structured and consists of a three stage process: (1) assessment; (2) intervention; and (3) evaluation. The assessment stage is critical in exploring how thoughts, feelings and behaviours are contributing to the presenting problem and is often assessed through the A–B–C model, which explores the activating event (A), the belief system and attitudes (B) in response to that event, and the positive and negative consequences on emotions and behaviours (C) as a result. There are a number of interventions that social workers can utilize in modifying thoughts and behaviours in an attempt to alleviate the problem. Evaluating the effectiveness of the intervention is a critical element of CBT and begins in assessment when the intensity, duration and frequency of the problem are recorded and continually reviewed throughout the work together. CBT is a highly researched method that has been shown to be effective with clients with various problems.

Case study

Tanya is a 20-year-old, white British female who is referred to adult mental health services due to self-harming behaviours. Tanya is employed as a retail clerk and is attending university to work towards a management degree. Tanya's family lives over an hour away from the university and she lives with two other students from her degree programme during term times. Tanya's room-mates have grown increasingly concerned for her mental health and safety as they have noticed numerous cut marks on her forearms and have found razor blades in the bathroom rubbish bin. Tanya's room-mates have confronted her with their concerns and encouraged Tanya to seek help to address her self-harming behaviours. Tanya comes to see you and reports that she does participate in self-harm by cutting herself whenever she feels stressed, overworked or unable to accomplish all the tasks she has to do between work and school. In your discussion with Tanya, you uncover that Tanya comes from a very 'successful' family where her father is a general practitioner and her mother is a prominent business executive. Tanya discloses that she feels unable to live up to her parents' expectation of her and is ultimately unhappy because she is the 'failure of the family'. Tanya reports her last self-harming experience was two days ago when her boss relayed to her that she will be fired if she is late to work in the future. Describe how you would utilize the cognitive behavioural approach with Tanya, particularly in regard to assessment, intervention and evaluation.

Further reading

Fuggle, P., Dunsmuir, S. and Curry, V. (2013) *CBT with Children, Young People and Families.* London: SAGE Publications.
  Provides an overview of the different stages of CBT when working with children, young people and families.
Sheldon, B. (2011) *Cognitive-behavioural Therapy: Research and Practice in Health and Social Care*, 2nd edn. Abingdon: Routledge.
  Explores the history, theory, practice and research of CBT.
Wills, F. and Sanders, D.J. (2013) *Cognitive Behaviour Therapy: Foundations for Practice.* London: SAGE Publications.
  Provides an overview of CBT while adhering to social work values and practices.

References

Achenbach, T.M. (1991) *Manual for the Child Behaviour Checklist/4–18 and 1991 profile.* Burlington, VT: Department of Psychiatry, University of Vermont.

Bandura, A. (1977) *Social Learning Theory.* Englewood Cliffs, NJ: Prentice-Hall.

Butler, A.C., Chapman, J.E., Forman, E.M. and Beck, A.T. (2006) The empirical status of cognitive-behavioural therapy: a review of meta-analyses, *Clinical Psychology Review,* 26(1): 17–31.

Corcoran, J. (2006) *Cognitive-Behavioral Methods for Social Workers: A Workbook.* Boston, MA: Pearson.

DeRubeis, R.J., Webb, C.A., Tang, T.Z. and Beck, A.T. (2009) Cognitive therapy, in K.S. Dobson (ed.), *Handbook of Cognitive-behavioral Therapies,* 3rd edn. New York: Guilford.

Enns, C.Z. (2004) *Feminist Theories and Feminist Psychotherapies: Origins, Themes, and Diversity,* 2nd edn. New York: Haworth.

Granvold, D.K. (1996) Constructivist psychotherapy, *Families in Society: The Journal of Contemporary Human Services,* 77(6): 345–59.

Howe, D. (2009) *A Brief Introduction to Social Work Theory.* Basingstoke: Palgrave Macmillan.

Kazdin, A.E. (2008) *Behavior Modification in Applied Settings,* 6th edn. Long Grove, IL: Waveland Press.

Liese, B.S. (1994) Brief therapy, crisis intervention and cognitive therapy of substance abuse, *Crisis Intervention,* 1(1): 11–29.

Macdonald, G. (2007) Cognitive behavioural social work, in J. Lishman (ed.), *Handbook for Practice Learning in Social Work and Social Care: Knowledge and Theory,* 2nd edn. London: Jessica Kingsley.

Miller, L. (2006) *Counselling Skills for Social Work.* London: Sage Publications.

National Institute for Health and Clinical Excellence (NICE) (2004) *Eating Disorders: Core Interventions in the Treatment and Management of Anorexia Nervosa, Bulimia Nervosa and Related Eating Disorders.* http://www.nice.org.uk/cg009 (accessed 17 July 2013).

National Institute for Health and Clinical Excellence (NICE) (2005) *Obsessive Compulsive Disorder: Core Interventions in the Treatment of Obsessive-compulsive Disorder and Body Dysmorphic Disorder.* http://www.nice.org.uk/cg31 (accessed 17 July 2013).

National Institute for Health and Clinical Excellence (NICE) (2008) *Attention Deficit Hyperactivity Disorder: Diagnosis and Management of ADHD in Children, Young People and Adults.* http://www.nice.org.uk/cg72 (accessed 17 July 2013).

National Institute for Health and Clinical Excellence (NICE) (2009a) *Antisocial Personality Disorder: Treatment, Management and Prevention.* http://www.nice.org.uk/cg77 (accessed 17 July 2013).

National Institute for Health and Clinical Excellence (NICE) (2009b) *Depression: The Treatment and Management of Depression in Adults (update).* www.nice.org.uk/cg90 (accessed 17 July 2013).

National Institute for Health and Clinical Excellence (NICE) (2011) *Generalised Anxiety Disorder and Panic Disorder (With and Without Agoraphobia) in Adults.* http://www.nice.org.uk/cg113 (accessed 17 July 2014).

Rogers, C.R. (1957) The necessary and sufficient conditions of therapeutic personality change, *Journal of Counseling Psychology*, 21(2): 95–103.

Sharf, R.S. (2012) *Theories of Psychotherapy and Counseling: Concepts and Cases*, 5th edn. Belmont, CA: Brooks Cole.

Sheldon, B. (2011) *Cognitive-behavioural Therapy: Research and Practice in Health and Social Care*, 2nd edn. Abingdon: Routledge.

Tanaka-Matsumi, J., Higgenbotham, H.N. and Chang, R. (2005) Cognitive behavioral approaches to counseling across cultures: a functional analytic approach for clinical applications, in P.B. Pedersen, J.G. Draguns, W.J. Lonner and J.E. Trimble (eds), *Counseling across Cultures*, 5th edn. Thousand Oaks, CA: Sage.

Thomlison, R.J. and Thomlison, B. (2011) Cognitive behavior theory and social work treatment, in F.J. Turner (ed.), *Social Work Treatment: Interlocking Theoretical Approaches*, 5th edn. New York: Oxford University Press.

Thorndike, E.L. (1911) *Animal Intelligence: Experimental Studies*. New York: Macmillan.

Trower, P., Casey, A. and Dryden, W. (1988) *Cognitive-behavioural Counselling in Action*. London: Sage.

Vonk, M.E. and Early, T.J. (2009) Cognitive-behavioral therapy, in A.R. Roberts (ed.), *Social Workers' Desk Reference*, 2nd edn. New York: Oxford University Press.

Watson, J.B. and Rayner, R. (1920) Conditioned emotional reactions, *Journal of Experimental Psychology*, 3(1): 1–14.

Wolpe, J. (1958) *Psychotherapy by Reciprocal Inhibition*. Stanford, CA: Stanford University Press.

10 Solution-focused practice

David C. Kondrat

Introduction

Solution-focused practice is a short-term model of practice that seeks to amplify what clients are already doing well and help them realize a future where the problem is no longer a problem. Solution-focused practice is built on the belief that concentrating on solutions to problems and times when client problems do not occur (that is, exceptions) matters more than focusing on the problems themselves (De Jong and Berg, 2008). As a constructivist form of therapy, solution-focused practice holds that individuals create their own sense of reality through the use of language and, therefore, this reality is changed through the use of language in the treatment milieu (de Shazer and Berg, 1988; Miller, 1997). As with the strengths perspective (Chapter 3), solution-focused practice represents a radical shift away from problem-based interventions towards interventions that utilize clients' strengths and resources to move clients towards a preferred future. This chapter provides an overview of solution-focused practice, a discussion on the principles and assumptions of solution-focused practice and an illustration of how to apply solution-focused practice to social work situations.

The origins of solution-focused practice

Solution-focused practice was developed at the Brief Family Therapy Centre in Milwaukee, Wisconsin, by Steve de Shazer and colleagues who were greatly influenced by the Mental Research Institute (MRI) in Palo Alto, California (Hoyt, 2002). The therapeutic approach used at the MRI was based on the interactional processes of individuals and families and an analysis of how attempts to solve problems actually contributed to a continuation of the problem where the problem often became worse (Shoham and Rohrbaugh, 2002). The therapeutic goal was to interrupt this cyclical process of failed attempts to solve problems by thinking outside of the box (that is, introducing second-order change). In addition, de Shazer (1997) was influenced by Ludwig Wittgenstein's philosophy of language, which underscored the problematic ways in which language confounds philosophical problems and everyday life.

The inception of the solution-building process came out of the work at the Brief Family Therapy centre. The therapists at the centre operated from a system in which one therapist worked directly with the client system and the other therapists observed the session from behind a one-way mirror enabling them to provide advice to the primary therapist. The initiation of solution building is described by De Jong and Berg (2008) based on the specific work of de Shazer and a family who reported 27 unclearly defined problems for which de Shazer or the therapeutic group were unable to come up with a suggested intervention:

> Still, wishing to encourage the family members to focus on something different from their problems, de Shazer and his colleagues told them to pay careful attention to 'what is happening in your lives that you want to continue to have happen?' When the family returned two weeks later, they said that things were going very well, and they felt their problems were solved.
>
> (De Jong and Berg, 2008, p. 12)

Rather than pushing the family to focus on what was wrong and develop an intervention to interrupt these patterns of behaviour, the question opened the family to the idea that things were not always problematic. Since that seminal event, solution-focused practice has developed into a systematic approach to treatment that has been applied to a number of different client situations (Kim, 2008) and solution-focused techniques have been applied in clinical supervision (Selekman and Todd, 1995).

Solution-focused practice explained

Solution-focused practice emerged from a number of different theoretical orientations and can be viewed as both a perspective, or a world view or way of understanding reality, and as a method (Lipchik, 1994). As a perspective, solution-focused practice encompasses basic rules and assumptions about change, interaction and goal setting (Walter and Peller, 1992). Solution-focused practice represents a move away from social work's traditional problem-solving approach to practice towards one that seeks to use clients' own lived experiences and strengths in finding a path towards desired futures (De Jong and Berg, 2008). Commenting on the problem-focused paradigm, Miller (1997, pp. 13–14) writes:

> Solution focused therapists state that trouble-focused stories worsen clients' troubles when they are treated as master narratives that define the most important aspects of clients' lives and selves. They become self-fulfilling prophecies which both predict that clients' lives will be troubled and encourage clients to interpret their lives as filled with signs of trouble.

Concentrating on clients' problems or what they do wrong has the potential of causing an iatrogenic effect. In order to limit any negative effects by focusing on problems, solution-focused social workers attempt to remedy problems through the interaction with the client and the thoughtful and solution based use of language (de Shazer, 1997).

This perspective of solution-focused practice is encapsulated in a few general rules and a series of assumptions, which when followed allow the social worker to work with clients towards meeting their goals. Hoyt (1996) lists the rules of solution-focused practice that he learned from his conversations with de Shazer:

1   If it ain't broke, don't fix it.
2   Once you know what works, do more of it.
3   If it doesn't work, don't do it again; do something different.

Based on these three general rules, the goal of solution-focused practice is to have clients continue to do what is working for them, and to try new things instead of doing something they feel is not working.

Walter and Peller (1992) articulate assumptions of solution-focused practice. While much of the work of solution-focused practice involves specific questioning strategies to help clients search for what they are already doing well or what they want to have happen, these assumptions guide the social worker throughout the process, especially when the social worker moves away from the usual questions. These assumptions provide a complete picture for how to be truly solution focused. The following are seven of the key assumptions of solution-focused practice provided by Walter and Peller (1992):

1   *Focusing on the positive, on the solution, and on the future facilitates change in the desired direction. Therefore, focus on solution-oriented talk rather than on problem-oriented talk* (Walter and Peller, 1992, p. 10). Solution-focused practice holds that the use of problem-saturated language and focusing on the client's problem-laden past perpetuates the client's problem. As described earlier, Miller (1997) argues that a problem focus creates a self-fulfilling prophecy that leads to an iatrogenic effect; therefore, solution-focused social workers must use positive or solution-oriented talk. Rather than talking with clients about areas in which they are deficient or focusing on the severity of their problems, the social worker should focus the conversation on what the client is doing right or what the client will be doing in the future to feel like things are going in the desired direction. Furman and Ahola (1992, p. 91) summarizes this process: '[A] positive view of the future invites hope and hope in its turn helps to cope with current hardships, to recognize signs of indicating the possibility of change, to view the past as an ordeal rather than a misery, and to provide the inspiration for generating solutions.'
2   *Exceptions to every problem can be created by social workers and clients, which can be used to build solutions* (Walter and Peller, 1992, p. 11). Clients are often unaware of times when things are going well as clients tend to become focused on their problems and their failed attempts to solve their problems. Yet, the problems are not always problematic for clients as there are times that the problems do not occur, often referred to as exceptions

to the problem. The social worker collaborates with clients to help them become aware of the times when the problems are not present, to amplify the importance of these times, and to encourage clients to do more of what is working.

3   *Change is occurring all the time* (Walter and Peller, 1992, p. 15). In line with the assumption that there are exceptions to every problem, nothing in a client's life is ever the same. Each day, minute or second brings different experiences that affect clients and how they live their lives. Each experience a client has is different, even if the experience appears to be the same from the client's vantage point. Change is the one constant. In applying this assumption to a person with depression, Walter and Peller (1992, p. 17) write:

> If we put the assumption that change is occurring all the time together with the precious assumption that exceptions can be created to a problem, we can then begin to search out for those times when someone acts in non-depressed ways. If someone is acting in non-depressed ways sometimes, there may be something different about those contexts or about what the person does or thinks at such times that enable acting differently from the problem.

By viewing the client's world as ever changing, the social worker is able to search for and find times in the client's life that are exceptions to the problem, and help the client build solutions to the problem utilizing these important times.

4   *Small changing leads to larger changing* (Walter and Peller, 1992, p. 18). This assumption can be understood in four ways. First, clients often use the same solutions to solve problems, even if the solution does not work; this process is often referred to as first order change (Watzlawick et al., 1974). Making one change in how clients attempt to solve a single problem can affect how they try to solve different problems; this process is referred to as second-order change (Watzlawick et al., 1974). Second, success in solving problems is generative. Being successful in one small area can lead clients to be successful at trying new solutions to even larger and more complex problems. Third, the way in which a client experiences and defines a problem determines the problem's size and severity. Making a change in how clients view their problem can go a long way in creating larger change. Finally, problems are often complex, thus, solutions to problems often require many little steps. Clients are able to move towards their preferred life by moving small step by small step.

5   *Clients are always cooperating* (Walter and Peller, 1992, p. 21). Traditionally, clients who do not follow what social workers suggest have been labelled resistant or uncooperative. Solution-focused practice takes a different stand. When clients do not do what social workers suggest, they are communicating that what was suggested by the social worker will not work for them. When they do something else, they are providing the social worker with clues as to how clients think and how best to guide clients towards workable solutions.

6   *People have all they need to solve their problems* (Walter and Peller, 1992, p. 23). In line with the strengths perspective (Chapter 3), solution-focused practice holds that clients have all the resources they need to build their solutions, and the role of the social worker is to help clients find their strengths and put them to use in the solution building process.

7   *Therapy is a goal- or solution-focused endeavour, with the client as expert* (Walter and Peller, 1992, p. 28). Traditional views of practice often hold that the social worker is the expert, yet solution-focused practice does not hold to this idea. Clients have the responsibility for creating change in their lives as they determine what they want to work on and what goals they want to set. As social workers, 'we do not view ourselves as expert at scientifically assessing client problems and then intervening. Instead, we strive to be expert at clients' frame of reference and identifying those perceptions that clients can use to create more satisfying lives' (De Jong and Berg, 2008, p. 19).

Exercise box 10.1 Thinking about solutions

In pairs or a small group, take turns answering the following questions:

1   Think about a time in your life when you felt you could not overcome a life obstacle. Were you able to overcome the obstacle? Think about a time when you felt confident that you could overcome an obstacle. Were you able to overcome the obstacle?
2   Solution-focused practice social workers hold that change is always occurring. What does this mean for searching for the root cause of a client's problem?
3   Do you believe that clients are always cooperating? Why or why not?
4   What steps would you need to take to become a solution-focused practitioner? How would you integrate the rules and assumptions of solution-focused practice into your practice?
5   Are there times when focusing on problems are more important to helping a client than searching for solutions?

A solution-focused approach to practice

While the rules and assumptions of solution-focused practice provide a way to view and approach working with clients, the innovators of solution-focused practice developed a regimented process for actually implementing this method. De Jong and Berg (2008, pp. 17–18) identify five stages in the solution-building process, which are described in detail below:

1   *Stage 1: Describe the problem.* Clients talk to the social worker about the problem that brought them to seek help. The social worker asks questions about the problem, but is careful to not ask about a root cause of the problem; solution-focused practice holds that what created the problem is not what

continues to sustain the problem. While listening to clients describing their problem, the social worker moves the client towards solution-oriented talk.

2   *Stage 2: Develop well-formulated goals.* During this stage the social worker works with the client to develop a picture of a preferred future. As will be discussed shortly, the miracle question or one of its derivatives is often used to help clients articulate this preferred future. De Shazer (1991, p. 112) argues that a well-formulated goal is: '(1) small rather than large; (2) salient to clients; (3) described in specific, concrete behavioural terms; (4) achievable within the practical contexts of clients' lives; (5) perceived by the clients as involving their "hard work"; (6) described as the "start of something" and not the "end of something"; and (7) treated as involving new behaviour(s) rather than the absence or cessation of existing behaviours'.

3   *Stage 3: Explore exceptions.* During this stage the social worker seeks out times in the client's life when the client's goals are already happening and when the problem is perceived to be lessened or non-existent. In addition, the social worker helps the client see her or his role in creating these exceptions.

4   *Stage 4: End-of-session feedback.* At the end of each session, the social worker provides the client with feedback, which includes a compliment, a bridging statement and suggestion for what the client might do outside of treatment. The compliment is based on what the client is already doing well and the bridge links the compliment to the suggestion. The suggestion 'always focuses on what the clients, given their frames of reference, need to do more of and differently in order to enhance their chances of success in meeting their goals' (De Jong and Berg, 2008, p. 18). Depending on the situation, different forms of suggestions are recommended. For example, for clients who have a clearly stated goal (or miracle) and no exceptions, social workers can ask clients to pretend the miracle has happened and to pay attention to what is different. For motivated clients with no goal, clients can be asked to do something different or to try something new. For clients who have a goal and have times that are exceptions to the problem, the social worker can ask clients to keep trying what works and to pay attention to what is helpful.

5   *Stage 5: Evaluate client progress.* Solution-focused practice social workers use a 0 to 10 scale to evaluate clients' progress towards meeting their goals. The use of these scaling questions will be described later in this chapter.

Solution-focused practice questioning strategies

This section will describe three general types of questioning strategies that are typical of solution-focused practice: goal questions, exception questions and scaling questions. Each is discussed in detail below:

1   *Goal questions.* Goal questions are used to help develop well-formulated goals (stage 2). The most common goal question is the miracle question, which asks: 'Suppose that one night there is a miracle and while you are sleeping the

problem that brought you into therapy is solved: How would you know? What would be different?' (de Shazer and Berg, 1988, p. 5). The miracle question provides an opportunity for clients to consider a time when they are not plagued by their problems. They are asked to consider the possibility that their future may be different. The miracle question does not stand alone; follow-up (satellite) questions are important for helping clients develop well-formulated goals. De Jong and Miller (1995, p. 731) provide a few of these questions:

(a) What is the very first thing you will notice after the miracle happens?
(b) What might your husband (child, friend) notice about you that would give him the idea that things are better for you?
(c) When he notices that, what might he do differently?
(d) When he does that, what would you do?
(e) And when you do that, what will be different around the house?

These satellite questions help the client to move from very large ideas about their future to smaller more manageable goals. Again, solution-focused practice social workers hold that only small changes are necessary to create larger change. Walter and Peller (1992) argue that the miracle question may be inappropriate for some clients and provide some alternatives. For example, for little children, social workers might ask: 'If we had a magic wand and the problem went away, what would you be doing differently?' (Walter and Peller, 1992, p. 79). For clients who do not like the use of the word 'miracle': 'If this were the last session and you were walking out of here with the problem solved, or you were at least on track to solving it, what would you be doing differently?' (Walter and Peller, 1992, p. 80). For clients who blame social workers: 'If coming here were useful, what would you be doing differently?' (Walter and Peller, 1992, p. 80). Greene et al. (1998, p. 397) also provide a variant of the miracle question, the dream question, which they argue increases client empowerment:

> Suppose that tonight while you are sleeping you have a dream. In this dream you discover the answers and resources you need to solve the problem that you are concerned about right now. When you wake up tomorrow, you may or may not remember your dream, but you do notice you are different. As you go about starting your day, how will you know that you discovered or developed the skills necessary to solve your problem? What will be the first small bit of evidence that you did this?

As with the miracle question, each of these strategies require the use of follow-up or satellite questions to help clients develop well defined goals.

There are times when clients find it hard to answer the miracle question or one of its derivations. Outcome questions provide another alternative to the miracle question for these situations (Greene et al., 2006). For example the social worker may ask:

Let's say that in six weeks from now you and I are having coffee together at McDonald's and at that time you have made the changes you want to make. What will I notice that is different about you that will tell me you have made these changes? What will you be telling me about yourself that will indicate you have made these changes? (Greene et al., 2006, p. 349).

2   *Exception questions.* Exception questions 'are used by the worker to discover a client's present and past successes in relation to the client's goal' (De Jong and Miller, 1995, pp. 731–2). An example of an exception question might be: 'You mentioned that if your miracle happened, you and your daughter would have better communication and that you would be able to talk openly with each other. Are there times when this is already happening?' Follow-up questions are used to determine the client's role in making these exceptions happen. By amplifying these exceptions, clients are made to feel a personal sense of agency and that they have power over their lives. However, sometimes clients are unable to identify current exceptions to their problems and during these times social workers can probe for past successes by asking if the event had occurred at some time in the past.

Sometimes clients are unable to identify any current or past successes, which is often the case with clients who are in crisis situations or feel hopeless. At such times, the social worker can use coping questions, which explore how clients have been able to cope with overwhelming experiences (De Jong and Miller, 1995). For example, a suicidal client who presents to an emergency room may not be able to identify any past or present successes. The social worker may ask the client: 'It sounds like things are really tough right now. But you were able to make it into the ER. Given such trying circumstances, how were you able to make it in here today?' These questions help the client to feel a sense of personal power and highlight the client's ability to cope in the face of trying conditions (Greene et al., 2006).

3   *Scaling questions.* Clients are asked to rate some aspect of their life from 0 to 10, with 0 representing the problem or situation at its worst and 10 representing the absence of the problem. Almost any aspect of a client's life can be scaled, including progress towards finding a solution, motivation to work on a solution, severity of a problem, the likelihood of hurting self or another person, self-esteem, and so on (De Jong and Miller, 1995, p. 732). For example, a client may be asked: 'On a scale from 0 to 10, where 0 represents the problem at its worst and 10 represents the absence of the problem, where do you find yourself today?' Follow-up questions can be used to elicit goals by asking clients what life would look like if they moved up one point on the scale. Similarly, the follow-up questions can be used to amplify client strengths. For example, in a subsequent meeting with a social worker, the client may report that she or he has moved up one point on the scale. The social worker can follow up by asking the client what the client did to move up one point. As might be obvious, scaling questions provide a way for the client and the social worker to track the client's progress towards meeting her or his goals.

Case example: applying solution-focused practice

Gretchen, a white British, single mother of one, came in to the local community centre requesting to meet with a social worker. You are the centre's social worker who utilizes solution-focused practice with clients. You begin the session by asking Gretchen what she would like to be called. She responds 'G is fine, that is what all my friends call me.' You then ask G what she likes to do during her spare time. After a few minutes of polite conversation, you explain to G that the session today will consist of talking for about 45 minutes after which time you both will take a short break and you will leave the room for a few minutes and come back with some suggestions for G. G agrees to the proposed plan for the session.

You begin by asking G, 'What are you hoping to accomplish by coming to see me today?' (*Stage 1: Describe the problem*) G responds by telling how her daughter, Krista, and her are having problems. Krista has recently turned 16 and has been staying out late at night with John who is 21. G says the troubles started when Krista came home one day with a love bite on her neck. G tried to confront Krista, but Krista yelled at her mother saying she was old enough to date and her mother just did not understand her anymore. G had forbidden her daughter to see John. You ask G if this has worked to which G responds 'no'. Krista is secretly seeing John behind her back. G had grounded Krista, but caught her sneaking back into their apartment at two in the morning about a week ago. G states that she is at her wits end.

You state, 'I can see that things are really rough between you and your daughter and that you really want to help her and protect her. Now I would like to ask you a little bit of a weird question. Suppose that one night there is a miracle and while you are sleeping the problem that brought you in to see me is solved: How would you know? What would be different?' (*Stage 2: Develop well-formulated goal; goal questions*) G states, 'I guess my daughter would listen to me. She would stop seeing the boy and would spend more time at home or with friends her own age'. You respond, 'That's a great! Tell me what would you be doing if she were to act the way you want her to act?' G responds, 'I would be spending more time with Krista and we would be having long conversations'. You then ask G to describe what this would look like if this were to happen. G responds:

> Well, I guess I would be a bigger part of my daughter's life. We would have breakfast together in the morning and we would have dinner together a couple of times a week. Maybe we would go out to the movies or go watch cricket from time to time. Krista really loves watching cricket. [*Laughing*] I am more of a football fan myself. I love Manchester United. You never know, maybe she would come to a Manchester United match with me. [*Pause*] I think we would just be doing more stuff together. I really want to just be with my daughter.

You respond, 'It sounds like there are a lot of things that would be different. But the biggest thing is that you and your daughter would be talking and doing stuff together?'

G confirms, 'That sounds right'. You then inquire, 'Are there times now that you two have pleasant conversations or just hang out together?' (*Stage 3: Explore exceptions; exception questions*) G replies, 'About two weeks ago, we had a pleasant breakfast. I took Krista to her favourite restaurant. We talked about how things were going for her at school. She is a successful student. She asked about my job. Then we just talked about life. We did not argue at all. I really liked that'. To further explore exceptions to the problem, you ask, 'Have there been other times like this?' G describes going shopping with Krista and being able to laugh and joke with one another. You then ask G, 'Tell me, during these two times, what were you doing differently?' G paused and then answered, 'Well I think that I did not start out by yelling at her. I asked her questions and listened to her. She did the same'. You respond, 'So you took a real interest in what she was doing and she did the same. Is that what you would like to accomplish by coming to see me?' G replies, 'Yes. I would be taking more of an interest in her life and learning about her'.

In order to further explore G's goals, you ask, 'OK. This sounds like a good goal. So on a scale from 0 to 10, where 0 is the goal not happening and 10 is this goal absolutely happening, where would you rate yourself now?' (*Scaling questions*) G responds with a 3 and you ask her what she would need to happen to move from a 3 to a 4 on the scale. G replies, 'I guess we would be having breakfast together more often'. You affirm G's position and response and state that you are going to take a few minutes and then come back with some feedback. (*Stage 4: End-of-session feedback*) Upon your return, you state to G:

> It sounds to me like you really care about your daughter. You want her to be happy and you want to spend more time with her, getting to know her. I also heard you say that there are times when this is already happening. You two have had pleasant conversations and got to know each other better. You really enjoy these times with your daughter. So between now and the next time we meet, I would like you to do two things. First, I would like you to try and have more of these talks with your daughter. Maybe breakfast or dinner would be a naturally good time to do this. Also, I would like you to notice other times that you and your daughter are getting along and report these times back to me.

You and G meet a week later and you start the session by asking, 'So what has been different since the last time we met?' G responds:

> Actually, a lot of things. Well, for starters Krista and I agreed to have dinner together four nights a week. We devised a rule. We would spend the time talking about our lives and not argue. We actually did it five times! I learned that she was not happy with John and that they were no longer seeing each other. I told her about heartbreaks in my life and how hard they were. We listened to each other's stories. I am not saying that everything has been perfect, but things are going much better.

You affirm G's current position and positive experience by stating, 'Wow. That is wonderful. Let me ask, what do you think you did to help make this happen?' G answered:

> After I left our meeting together, I started thinking about when I was 16. I real-
> ized that I wanted to just spend time with my mother. I know that she was my
> parent, but I also wanted her to be a friend. She was always so busy with work
> and keeping the house clean. So, when I got home I asked Krista to have dinner
> with me. Together, we devised our rule. While I know that I am her mother and
> have to play that role, I decided that I could also be her friend.

You affirm G's accomplishments and readdress the scaling of G's goal: 'So it sounds like
things are going well. Do you remember the 0 to 10 scale we used at our meeting?'
G remembers the scale and is willing to revisit her position on the scale. You remind G
that she rated her goal a 3 at the last session and ask her where she is now on the scale.
G responds with a 6. You respond to G, 'That is a lot of progress. Tell me what else has
been different?'

You and G meet four more times and by the end of your time together, G reports
that things are going much better. She and Krista are being more open with each other
and G found a pleasant balance between being a mother and a friend of Krista. During
their last session, G reported being a 9 on the scale.

Strengths and limitations

There are several identified strengths and limitations to utilizing solution-focused practice in social work. The strengths include the following:

- Solution-focused practice focuses on clients' strengths (Greene and Lee, 2011).
  The method seeks to identify clients' strengths and past successes at overcoming and/or coping with the presenting problem. The goal of the work together
  is to utilize the client's strengths and resources to move them towards her or
  his preferred future. While the strengths perspective and solution-focused
  practice developed separately, many from a strengths-perspective use
  solution-focused questions to elicit strengths. In fact, Saleebey (2013) provides
  examples for how solution-focused interviewing can be used within the context of strengths-based practice.
- Solution-focused practice is an empowerment-based approach. The client is
  viewed as the expert of her or his experiences and the social worker is to work
  collaboratively with the client in overcoming the presenting problem. The
  client defines the problem and the client is responsible for identifying goals
  that are personally meaningful.
- Solution-focused practice can be implemented with a variety of clients and in
  a variety of settings (see research section below). There is a growing body of
  evidence to support the use of solution-focused practice across client problems (Gingerich and Eisengart, 2000; Walsh, 2010).
- Solution-focused practice techniques and questions can be used in combination with other methods. For example, the miracle question and exception
  questions are often found to be used in crisis intervention, and scaling

questions are often found to be used in motivational interviewing. Therefore, this approach can be used alone, or aspects of the approach can be combined with other approaches.

The limitations include the following:

- Solution-focused practice focuses more on solutions rather than the problem(s) (Walsh, 2010). Critics of solution-focused practice argue that by not focusing on clients' problems, social workers miss important information that may be useful in helping clients move towards their goals. In addition, some clients expect to talk with social workers about their problems. As a result, some clients may not make progress or leave the practice of a solution-focused social worker. Although solutions are the focus and problems are not to be dwelt upon, social workers should listen to clients if they want to discuss their problems. In listening to problems, social workers should attempt to move clients into looking at solutions versus dwelling on failed attempts to solve the problem.
- Solution-focused (SF) practice fails to recognize power differences that exist within society. Dermer et al. (1998) argue that overlooking the effects of society draws away from potential solutions to clients' problems. While agreeing that early writings on solution-focused practice were remiss in discussing inequality and power imbalances, Lethem (2002, p. 191) argues, 'When finding a non-blaming, non-pathological way of describing a client's predicament, it is not unusual to hear a SF therapist refer to social disadvantages that may have contributed to distress and difficulties'. Within the assumptions of solution-focused practice is a clear understanding that clients possess the necessary agency to overcome many obstacles in their battle to find solutions.

Ethical and cultural considerations

According to Lee (2003), solution-focused practice represents an approach to practice that respects and honours cultural differences and cultural values. While other practice approaches can be hierarchical, with the social worker being the expert, solution-focused practice views clients as the expert and their life experiences as potential solutions. Solution-focused social workers are interested in the context of a client's situations as the client describes her or his life in her or his own language. Solution-focused social workers seek out clients' strengths and resources in helping clients search for solutions. If important to the client, cultural practices may be used in the formation of goals and solutions. As Lee (2003, p. 393) summarizes:

> By emphasizing contextual knowledge and taking a not-knowing stance, a solution-focused approach requires clinicians not to rely on prior experiences or theoretically formulated truths and knowledge to understand and interpret

therapeutic needs. Instead, understanding is to be continuously informed by the client who is the 'expert' of the situation and who holds the key to its solutions. By emphasizing strengths and positives, such an approach fully utilized the indigenous, culturally based resources and strengths available within the client's socio-cultural milieu.

Social workers work collaboratively with clients to identify preferred futures and client-defined goals. Social workers must be open to the goals that the clients establish for themselves and not attempt to persuade or push clients to select goals that they do not find to be personally meaningful. In keeping an open mind to the client-defined goals, social workers must also adhere to the professional code of ethics and code of practice to ensure clients are not going to harm themselves or others.

Anti-oppressive practice and solution-focused practice

Solution-focused practice honours clients and their lived experiences. Rather than focusing on clients' problems, solution-focused social workers see clients and their situations as full of resources. No assumptions are made about the client's abilities or disabilities. Unlike some therapies which view clients as passively affected by their environment, such as behaviourism, and require a skilled social worker to resolve their problems, solution-focused practice assumes that clients have the agency necessary to solve their problems. In addition, Walsh (2010, p. 240) argues that solution-focused practice is a form of social justice practice as he states, 'The therapy has applicability for a broad range of presenting issues that could include poverty, unemployment, discrimination, and other forms of injustice'. In developing solutions, clients can tackle these injustices as they affect their lives, which will often involve the use of solution-focused practice with other anti-oppressive methods and may involve interventions into the outside community, organization or political system by the social worker or other activists groups.

Research on solution-focused practice

There is a growing base of research evidence to support the use of solution-focused practice across a range of client problems. Gingerich and Eisengart (2000) conducted a literature review of 15 controlled outcome studies of solution-focused practice. Client populations included depressed college students, persons in need of parenting skills, orthopaedic patients, prisoners at risk of recidivism, antisocial adolescent offenders, high school students, couples in therapy, persons with problem drinking, families, persons using public social services and persons receiving outpatient mental health services. Five of these studies were well controlled of which four showed significantly positive effects compared with no treatment or treatment as usual. One study found no differences between solution-focused practice and interpersonal therapy for depression.

Kim (2008) conducted a more recent and rigorous review of the solution-focused practice research literature. He conducted a meta-analysis of 22 published and unpublished studies of solution-focused practice. Half of these studies used true experimental designs and the rest employed quasi-experimental designs. Nine studies explored the effect of solution-focused practice on externalizing behaviour outcomes and found a non-statistically significant small and positive effect for solution-focused practice compared to control groups. Twelve studies explored the effects of solution-focused practice on internalizing behaviour outcomes. Results from this analysis showed a small statistically significant positive effect for solution-focused practice compared to the control group. Finally, eight studies explored the effect of solution-focused practice on family and relationship outcomes. Kim found a small but positive non-statistically significant effect for solution-focused practice compared to the control group. One problem with this study was the small sample size. While two of the three results showed a non-statistically significant effect, in all cases the effect size favoured solution-focused practice. Both Gingerich and Eisengart (2000) and Kim (2008) argue for more well-controlled research to determine the true effectiveness of solution-focused practice.

Since the publication of Kim's (2008) meta-analysis, more research on solution-focused practice has shown promising results, including well-controlled studies. Knekt et al. (2008) conducted a randomized clinical trial, comparing solution-focused practice to long-term and brief psychodynamic therapy. The researchers followed the participants for three years and assessed depression and anxiety symptoms. Significant differences in depression and anxiety were noted in all three groups over the three years of the study, with both the short-term psychodynamic and solution-focused groups showing treatment gains earlier than the long-term psychodynamic group. Smock et al. (2008) conducted a randomized clinical trial in which they compared problem-oriented group treatment to solution-focused group treatment for persons with an active substance abuse problem. At follow-up, participants in the solution-focused group showed significantly better results than participants in the problem-oriented group on measures of both depression and symptom distress. No between-group differences in substance use were noted. Finally, Panayotov et al. (2012) adapted solution-focused practice for work with persons with severe mental illness and medication adherence. Using a single case design, improvements in medication adherence were noted over the course of the study. The more recent studies of solution-focused practice show that this model of therapy is comparable or better than other models of care and that solution-focused practice can be taken out of traditional psychotherapy practice and be applied in groups, or for specific purposes.

Summary

Solution-focused practice is one approach to working with clients that is future and solution focused. While most theories and models of practice focus intervention efforts on what clients are doing wrong, solution-focused practice, as with the strengths perspective, focus on what clients are doing right. Solution-focused practice is a pragmatic model of practice that encourages clients to do more of what works (exceptions to the problem). Relying on a group of underlying rules and assumptions and using a series of structured steps and questions, solution-focused practitioners work with clients on developing a picture of a preferred future. They help clients develop well-formulated goals, determine when the goal is already happening, encourage clients to do more of the goal, and help clients track their progress through the use of a ten-point scale. While research on solution-focused practice is still in its infancy, the literature suggests that this model of practice is suitable across multiple client groups.

Case study

Isabel, a white British female aged 32, arrives at a community mental health centre. About three months ago, she lost her job of 12 years where she had been a supervisor in a steel mill. Isabel had not attended university and has no formal qualifications. She states that she has tried to look for work, but has been unsuccessful. Recently, Isabel has found it difficult to get out of bed, eat or even leave her flat. When she does leave her flat, she gets heart palpitations and starts to sweat. She feels hopeless and does not expect to find a job. Isabel's general practitioner (GP) has referred her to the community mental health team to see a social worker. Describe how you would use solution-focused practice with Isabel.

Further reading and web resources

De Jong, P. and Berg, I.K. (2008) *Interviewing for Solutions*, 3rd edn. Belmont, CA: Thomson.
Provides an overview of solution-focused practice and specific techniques in interviewing.

De Shazer, S. (1988) *Clues: Investigating Solutions in Brief Therapy*. New York: W.W. Norton.
Provides an overview of solution-focused practice by the founder of the approach.

Franklin, C., Trepper, T.S., Gingerich, W.J. and McCollum, E.E. (eds) (2012) *Solution-Focused Brief Therapy: A Handbook of Evidence-Based Practice*.
New York: Oxford University Press.
Provides an overview of the evidence for the use of solution-focused practice.

Greene, G.J. and Lee, M.Y. (2011) *Solution-Oriented Social Work Practice: An Integrative Approach to Working with Client Strengths*. New York: Oxford University Press.
Provides a collection of chapters on different applications of solution-focused practice.

Macdonald, A. (2007) *Solution-focused Therapy: Theory, Research and Practice*. London: Sage Publications.
Provides an overview of solution-focused therapy, explores the research around the effectiveness of this approach and explores how to apply it to practice.

Solution-Focused Brief Therapy Association: http://www.sfbta.org
Provides up-to-date information on SFT including current research and clinical tools.

References

De Jong, P. and Berg, I.K. (2008) *Interviewing for Solutions*, 3rd edn. Belmont, CA: Thomson.

De Jong, P. and Miller, S.D. (1995) How to interview for client strengths, *Social Work*, 40(6): 729–36.

De Shazer, S. (1988) *Clues: Investigating Solutions in Brief Therapy*. New York: W.W. Norton.

De Shazer, S. (1991) *Putting Differences to Work*. New York: W.W. Norton.

De Shazer, S. (1997) Some thoughts on language use in therapy, *Contemporary Family Therapy*, 19(1): 133–41.

De Shazer, S. and Berg, I.K. (1988) Constructing solutions, *Family Therapy Networker*, 12: 42–3.

Dermer, S.B., Hemesath, C.W. and Russell, C.S. (1998) A feminist critique of solution-focused therapy, *The American Journal of Family Therapy*, 26(3): 239–50.

Furman, B. and Ahola, T. (1992) *Solution Talk: Hosting Therapeutic Conversations*. New York: Norton.

Gingerich, W.A. and Eisengart, S. (2000) Solution-focused brief therapy: a review of the outcome research, *Family Process*, 39(4): 477–98.

Greene, G.J., Kondrat, D.C., Lee, M.Y., Clement, J., Siebert, H., Mentzer, R.A. and Pinnell, S.R. (2006) A solution-focused approach to case management and recovery with consumers who have severe mental disability, *Families in Society*, 87(3): 339–50.

Greene, G.J. and Lee, M.Y. (2011) *Solution-oriented Social Work Practice: An Integrative Approach to Working with Client Strengths*. New York: Oxford University Press.

Greene, G.J., Lee, M.Y., Mentzer, R.A., Pinnell, S.R. and Niles, D. (1998) Miracles, dreams, and empowerment: a brief therapy practice note, *Families in Society*, 79: 395–9.

Hoyt, M.F. (1996) Solution building and language games: a conversation with Steve de Shazer (and some after words with Insoo Kim Berg), in M.F. Hoyt (ed.), *Constructive Therapies*, vol. 2. New York: Guilford Press.

Hoyt, M.F. (2002) Solution-focused couple therapy, in A.S. Gurman and N.S. Jacobson (eds), *Clinical Handbook of Couple Therapy*, 3rd edn. New York: Guilford Press.

Kim, J.S. (2008) Examining the effectiveness of solution-focused brief therapy: a meta-analysis, *Research on Social Work Practice*, 18(2): 107–16.

Knekt, P., Lindfors, O., Härkänen, T., Välikoski, M., Virtala, E., Laaksonen, M.A., Marttunen, M., Kaipainen, M. and Renlund, C. (2008) Randomized trial on the effectiveness of long- and short-term psychodynamic psychotherapy and solution-focused therapy on psychiatric symptoms during a 3-year follow-up, *Psychological Medicine*, 38(5): 689–703.

Lee, M.Y. (2003) A solution-focused approach to cross-cultural clinical social work practice: utilizing cultural strengths, *Families in Society*, 84(3): 385–97.

Lethem, J. (2002) Brief solution focused therapy, *Child and Adolescent Mental Health*, 7(4): 189–92.

Lipchik, E. (1994) The rush to be brief, *Family Therapy Networker*, 5: 88–9.

Miller, G. (1997) *Becoming Miracle Workers: Language and Meaning in Brief Therapy.* Hawthorn, NY: Aldine de Gruyter.

Panayotov, P.A., Strahilov, B.E. and Anichkina, A.Y. (2012) Solution-focused brief therapy and medication adherence with schizophrenic patients, in S. Franklin, T.S. Trepper, W.J. Gingerich and McCollum (eds), *Solution-Focused Brief Therapy: A Handbook of Evidence-Based Practice.* New York: Oxford University Press.

Saleebey, D. (2013) Introduction: power in people, in D. Saleebey (ed.), *The Strengths Perspective in Social Work Practice*, 6th edn. Boston, MA: Pearson.

Selekman, M.D. and Todd, T.C. (1995) Co-creating a context for change in the supervisory system: the solution-focused supervision model, *Journal of Systemic Therapies*, 14(3): 21–33.

Shoham, V. and Rohrbaugh, M.J. (2002) Brief strategic couple therapy, in A.S. Gurman and N.S. Jacobson (eds), *Clinical Handbook of Couple Therapy*, 3rd edn. New York: Guilford Press.

Smock, S.A., Trepper, T.S., Wetchler, J.L., McCollum, E.E., Ray, R. and Pierce, K. (2008) Solution-focused group therapy for level 1 substance abusers, *Journal Of Marital and Family Therapy*, 34(1): 107–20.

Walsh, J. (2010) *Theories for Direct Social Work Practice*, 2nd edn. Belmont, CA: Wadsworth.

Walter, J.L. and Peller, J.E. (1992) *Becoming Solution-focused in Brief Therapy.* New York: Brunner/Mazel.

Watzlawick, P., Weakland, J.H. and Fisch, R. (1974) *Change: Principles of Problem Formation and Problem Resolution.* New York: W.W. Norton.

11 Task-centred social work

Introduction

The task-centred model is a short-term approach to social work practice that focuses on alleviating specific problems of clients (Fortune and Reid; 2011 Reid and Epstein, 1972). The approach was developed after extensive experimentation with brief interventions and work with clients that focused on identified problems and incremental steps towards reaching a specified goal (Reid and Shyne, 1969). The fundamental nature of task-centred social work is to collaborate with clients to alleviate explicit problems that are acknowledged and understood by them, establish goals that are personally meaningful and that alleviate the problems, and develop tasks to be completed in incremental stages to reach the goal. Task-centred social work holds that clients build confidence and self-esteem by experiencing small successes and completing tasks along their journey towards reaching goals (Marsh, 2007).

The focus of task-centred social work is initially on problems and goals, but the process of work with the client moves from the identification of problems through a sequence of incremental steps, called tasks, to the desired goal (Marsh, 2013). Basically, task-centred social work is a way of working with clients to achieve their goals and alleviate immediate problems. This chapter explores task-centred social work practice by exploring the origins of the approach, the basic characteristics, values and premises, and the sequences in applying the approach to social work practice.

The origins of task-centred social work

Task-centred social work practice is a model that originated within social work, primarily in North American casework practice, and was developed out of research conducted in social work practice. Task-centred social work practice began to develop and flourish after the prominent study by Reid and Shyne (1969), *Brief and Extended Casework*, which evaluated the effectiveness of short-term casework as compared to the traditional long-term work focused on psychosocial practice. For the study, Reid and Shyne explored the outcomes of work with two groups of families with relational problems who were either offered a brief service of eight interviews or the usual long-term service provided by the agency that could last up to 18 months. The goal of the study was to see how much could be accomplished in a limited amount of time. The short-term and long-term treatments were rather vague, but the short-term treatment consisted of eight interviews, which focused on identifying the familial problems and the goals related to alleviating the problems (Reid and Epstein, 1972). At the conclusion of the study, Reid and Shyne discovered that the short-term treatment group improved more than the long-term treatment group; in fact the latter group was found to have regressed. Any progress made in the long-term treatment group had occurred within the early stages. Short-term treatment was shown to be more effective, when compared to long-term treatment and, thus, the development of task-centred social work practice as a form of short-term treatment began.

Reid and Epstein (1972) began the development of task-centred social work, and the approach has continued to be developed across many countries. Their focus was to develop a method that could be applied to short-term casework, could be used alongside other theories and methods, and which would be useful to social work practitioners, teachers and students participating in casework (Reid and Epstein, 1972). In simple terms, Reid and Epstein defined task-centred casework as 'a system of time-limited treatment for problems of living' (1972, p. 1).

Reid and Epstein's (1972) book, *Task-centered casework*, was the first book to illustrate the step-by-step process of implementing the task-centred approach. Reid and Epstein formed an approach that focused on the early establishment of goals, the development of tasks, and a commitment to adhere to time limits. Time limits were important in this brief-treatment model due to the belief that when deadlines are established clients and social workers will be more motivated to take action and complete the tasks to reach the end goal. Reid and Epstein were clear in communicating that their proposed approach drew from other related and established theories, such as general systems theory, communication theory, role theory, psychoanalytic theory and learning theory. Additionally, they acknowledged that practitioners may need to use the task-centred approach in combination with other relevant theories or methods. Since Reid and Epstein's work in North America, other theorists have adapted the method to other settings or cultures, for example, Doel and Marsh (1992) are the prominent task-centred theorists in the UK.

Task-centred social work explained

Task-centred social work is a short-term, problem-solving approach and is applicable to work with individuals, families, groups and communities. Reid and Epstein (1972) specified the various problems to which the model is suitable to address, which are still applicable today. The problems can include one or more of the following: interpersonal conflict; dissatisfaction in social relations; relations in formal organizations; difficulty in role performance; problems of social transition; reactive emotional distress; and/or inadequate resources. The key to identifying problems is that the client must express a desire to work on the problem either independently or in collaboration with the social worker.

Task-centred social work consists of specific sequences that the social worker and client should progress through, which are described in more detail below. The basic process of the approach includes identifying the problem(s) as perceived by the client, exploring the problem(s) in detail, selecting the problem that is causing the client the most distress as the target for intervention, defining a goal which removes or diminishes the problem, establishing tasks for both the client and social worker that moves the client towards the goal, and evaluating the end work. Evaluation explores whether the client has reached the desired goal and whether the problem has been removed or diminished. If the social worker and client are not able to identify a target problem then there is no reason to continue work with the client (Reid and Epstein, 1972).

The task-centred approach has clear links with systems theory and encourages the social worker to focus beyond the individual as the agent of change by examining the other systems impacting the individual's life. For example, there may be identified problems such as poverty or oppression that are affecting the client with whom you are working (that is, individual, family, group, community) and your tasks may include penetrating into one or more systems (that is, social service agency, policy, policing procedures) in order to alleviate a problem.

The following values are inherent in the task-centred approach and are particularly useful for social work (Doel, 1991; Fortune and Reid, 2011; Marsh, 2007).

1   A commitment to *partnership and empowerment*. The relationship between the client and social worker is one of partnership and collaboration. The social worker and client should hold a common purpose in their work together and the client should specify problems from her or his perspective and establish goals that are personally meaningful. If there does exist any inequalities in the sense of power, roles or responsibility, these need to be made explicit in order to create a true partnership. In certain situations, the nature of the social work role and involvement of the client with social services does not lend itself to a truly collaborative or partnership relationship – for example, a child protection situation where the social worker's role is to protect the child from further abuse and neglect, but the parents do not acknowledge that there is abuse or neglect present within the family. The parents are required to work with social services to regain custody of their children and the social worker is ultimately seen as having the power and control in this relationship. The social worker's responsibility is to acknowledge and make explicit this power imbalance while seeking to work collaboratively with the parents to reach their goals (that is, to regain custody of the child) as well as those mandated by the courts (that is, ensuring a safe living environment for the child).

2   A belief that *clients are the best authority on their problems*. Clients are seen as experts on their situation and problem definitions and, therefore, are encouraged to describe their problems from their perspective and establish personally meaningful goals that they perceive will alleviate the problems. Again, in particular situations the problem may be defined by outside sources (that is,

courts, social service agencies) which are not congruent with the client's definition of the problem. This dilemma is discussed later in the chapter.

3 A commitment to *building on people's strengths rather than analysing their
deficits.* All clients are seen to possess strengths and the social worker should
identify each client's strengths and resources. Acknowledging the strengths
and accomplishments of the client enables a greater sense of confidence and
self-esteem in the client.

4 A commitment to *providing help rather than treatment.* The social worker and
client are in a partnership and should work collaboratively through the task-
centred process to alleviate problems. The social worker is there to help and
guide the client through this process, not to treat the client or alleviate the
problems for her or him.

Basic characteristics and principles

In addition to the value base of task-centred social work, there are several characteristics and principles that describe the nature of this approach. According to Fortune and
Reid (2011, pp. 514–15) the following eight characteristics and principles describe the
task-centred model:

1 *Focus on client-acknowledged problems.* The focus of the work with the client
is on the problem(s) that the client has explicitly identified as a concern in her
or his life (problems-in-living).

2 *Problem-solving actions (tasks).* The approach focuses on specific tasks,
or problems-solving actions, that will assist the client to reach an end
goal which alleviates or diminishes the identified problem. These tasks
should be discussed and agreed in the session with the social worker, and
most tasks are to be completed outside the session. The social worker and
client agree who is to take responsibility for completing the tasks as some
tasks may need to be completed by the social worker or other groups in the
client's life.

3 *Integrative stance.* The task-centred approach is a very specific model of practice that often has to be used in combination with other theories and methods.
For example, the task-centred approach may be combined with cognitive
behavioural therapy or structural family work. The task-centred approach
could be used as the primary method or could be used as secondary to other
interventions.

4 *Planned brevity.* Task-centred social work is meant to be a short-term treatment method usually lasting between six and twelve weeks during a four-
month period. Extensions beyond this time frame can be negotiated as
necessary.

5 *Collaborative relationship.* The approach values a collaborative relationship
between the social worker and client. The social worker conducts the initial
problem assessment with the client and there should be no hidden goals or

agendas on the part of the social worker. Each subsequent sequence in the approach is to be conducted in collaboration with the client and she or he is to establish goals and develop tasks.

6   *Empirical orientation.* Task-centred social work values research and evaluation, and social workers are encouraged to collect data at the assessment, process and outcome stages of the approach. The task-centred approach has been scrutinized through numerous studies which has contributed to the improvement of the approach and has demonstrated its continual success.

7   *Systems and contexts.* The focus of the work is generally on the individual, but the individual must be assessed within her/his environment. The social worker may find that problems are the result of faulty systems or merely the contexts in which the individual lives. In such situations, contextual change may need to occur in order to alleviate a problem.

8   *Structure.* The task-centred social work is a structured approach with set sequences in which to follow, which are detailed below.

Sequences in task-centred social work

Task-centred social work consists of a specific process with three main sequences. Although the process appears linear, the social worker may discover that the sequences are not always as orderly as described below. Social workers may move through the sequences in a linear fashion, yet have to revisit an earlier sequence in response to the needs of different people. The three basic sequences are (1) exploring problems, (2) establishing goal(s) and time limit(s), and (3) developing tasks. These three basic sequences are sandwiched by a period of preparation and evaluation or otherwise referred to as entry and exit (Reid and Epstein, 1972). Each sequence is described below based on the writings of Doel (1991), Doel and Marsh (1992), Fortune and Reid (2011), Marsh (2007), Reid and Epstein (1972), and begins with the preparation/entry phase and concludes with the evaluation/exit phase.

1   *Preparation or entry.* This is the beginning of the task-centred approach where the social worker asks, 'Who is the client?' and determines the mandate or reason for intervention. The social worker is tasked with determining why any work should or could be done with a client and the client is tasked with acknowledging the reason for social work involvement. The social worker should establish a clear reason as to the purpose for working together. If a reason cannot be established, then there is no basis for work together. Often the reason may be clear where the client comes voluntarily for a request to receive help or assistance. Other times the reason is less clear, for instance, when a client acknowledges that something is wrong but is unable to clearly express the problem or need for help. Additional examples include when a third party has requested the client to receive help or assistance on a problem that is either unbeknown to the client or is not identified as a problem to the client, or when clients present with problems that actually involve other

people's behaviour, such as a controlling partner. The social worker must establish a clear reason for her or his involvement with the client, determine the ability for the social worker and client to work together to alleviate an identified problem, and analyse the ability of the agency to adequately assist the client.

2   *Sequence 1: Exploring problems.* The first sequence of work to be done with the client involves an exploration of the problems. This sequence focuses specifically on what is wrong as perceived by the client, the social worker and other people in the client's life. Although the social worker and outside people contribute to this discussion, the client should take the lead on identifying the problems. The following three activities assist in exploring the problems with the client: (a) problem scanning; (b) problem details; and (c) problem priorities.

(a) *Problem scanning.* This is the first stage in exploring problems and is often compared to a brainstorming exercise. This exercise involves clients discussing their problems, difficulties and issues in a broad sense. The social worker encourages the client to freely discuss their concerns and problems and to give the social worker an overall picture of what is wrong. The client may describe problems around physical or material difficulties, such as accommodation, financial debt, employment or transportation, or emotional or relationship difficulties, such as marriage problems or problems with partners, children, employers, community members and/or feelings of anxiety or depression. Nothing should be excluded at this stage. The social worker should not solicit too many details from the clients at this stage and should not offer solutions to the problems. The social worker and/or client should make a list of the problems or difficulties identified at this stage, which could serve as a list of topics to be discussed in the next stage. If the social worker has assessed a problem or difficulty, or if a problem has been defined by a third party, those should only be mentioned at this stage and explored in more detail later.

(b) *Problem details.* This stage involves a further exploration of the identified problems or difficulties. The social worker and client more carefully explore the details of each problem area identified in the previous stage. The social worker uses open-ended questions and encourages the client to answer questions that begin with who, what, when, where, why and how (Doel, 1991). Social workers ask clients to give examples to support their position and to further explain their problem situation. This allows clients to break down a problem that might seem more general to specific examples of how it is directly affecting them.

(c) *Problem priorities.* Prioritizing the problems is the next stage after the problems have been identified and listed under general headings and the problems have been further explored giving detail to each. This stage involves the social worker and client examining the list of problems, ranking them in order of priority and then selecting one or two (three at most) to be the focus of the work together. The social worker and client must consider the feasibility of working on the problem, whether a third party has mandated a client to work on a problem, and the urgency of the problem. Doel (1991, p. 27) has identified some suggested areas to consider when prioritizing the problem:

- the urgency of the problem
- the consequences of not alleviating the problem
- the chances of success at alleviating the problem
- the ability of the worker and agency to help with the problem
- the motivation of the client to work on the problem
- the support that the client will receive from others
- the specific nature of the problem.

3 *Sequence 2: Setting goal(s) and a time limit.* The previous sequence addresses and fully explores 'what is wrong' in the client's life and this sequence explores 'what is wanted' from the client (Doel, 1991). This sequence explores what the client wants in relation to the problem(s) that were selected to be the focus of intervention. The client is to define what she or he wants in terms of a goal, which is often the reverse of the problem. For example, a mother may state that the problem is a lack of sleeping space for her children and she describes the goal as obtaining a house with enough sleeping space for her children. Doel (1991; 2002) specified three key factors for the social worker to consider when working with the client to establish goals: (1) the goal is what the client wants as clients are more motivated to work towards goals that they have defined; (2) the practicality of obtaining the goal and consideration of any likely obstacles or constraints; and (3) the desirability of the goal or analysis of whether it is right to help the client achieve the goal. Marsh and Doel (2005) state that goals should be SMART, which is an acronym standing for Specific, Measurable, Achievable, Realistic and Timely. They stress that the key to establishing goals is that the social worker is there to help not to direct.

Once a goal or goals are established, the social worker and client must decide a time limit in which to achieve the goal. Again, the time limit needs to take into account the practicality of achieving the goals and to prepare for any constraints or obstacles. The time limit enables the social worker and client to establish the framework of their work together and encourages a regular progress update to ensure that the goal will be achieved within the time frame. Not only should there be an established time frame to reach the goal, but the social worker and client should establish a time frame for their work together, which can include the number and length of meetings. For example, 'we will meet once a week for at least one hour for the next three months'. The social worker and the client should formulate a service contract which specifies the problems selected for the work together, the agreed goal(s) and the established time limit. Both social worker and client should have a copy of the written service contract as well as any other individuals actively involved in the work. Social workers should be conscious to provide the service contract to individuals based on any visual impairments or difficulties with literacy (Doel, 2002).

4   *Sequence 3: Planning and specifying tasks.* This sequence is the planning stage where the tasks required to reach a goal are established. The tasks involve pieces of work done by the client and the social worker in order to move the client closer to reaching the goal and alleviating or diminishing the problem (Doel, 1991; Marsh, 2007). The tasks can either be physical activities, such as searching the newspapers for rental houses or they can be emotional or mental activities, such as reflections of feelings, or documentations of behaviours (Doel, 2002). As with the establishment of goals, the agreed tasks should be something the client and social worker are able and willing to complete and they should be directly related to accomplishing the end goal. Some tasks are able to be completed during a session, such as filling out an employment application, and others will be completed outside of the session.

       The client and social worker should review and evaluate the tasks at each session and should participate in a discussion around what tasks were successfully completed, what obstacles were encountered and what new tasks need to be developed. This process takes place at each session until all necessary tasks have been completed and the goal has been reached.

5   *Ending the work: termination and evaluation.* The end of work between the client and social worker should have been established when the service contract was devised and agreed. A social worker may be faced with a situation where the established time frame for work with a client needs to be renegotiated and possibly extended. The end of work takes place when the goal has been achieved and the problem alleviated or diminished. This stage also serves as a time for evaluation where the social worker and client can assess whether their work together has led to the client's desired result. The social worker should acknowledge the client's strengths, progress and achievements and encourage the client to utilize these strengths when faced with future endeavours.

Table 11.1 summarizes the five steps with the three main sequences of the task-centred approach. Fortune and Reid (2011) categorize the steps and sequences into three phases: (1) the initial phase (sessions 1–2) where the reason for intervention is established, the problems are explored, the goals are developed and a service contract is formulated and agreed; (2) the middle phase (each subsequent session) where the social worker and client review the problem and tasks, resolve any obstacles identified, and develop and select new tasks to be accomplished; and (3) the terminal phase (final session) where the problem is reviewed, any successful problem-solving strategies are identified, and any further problems remaining are discussed including any potential future plans to alleviate the problems. The middle phase is where the main substance of work between the social worker and client takes place. During this phase the social worker and client are setting tasks, reviewing tasks, setting more tasks, reviewing the tasks; all in a continual process of moving the client towards goal achievement.

Table 11.1 List of the five steps with the three main sequences for task-centred practice

Steps and sequences	Purpose
1. Preparation	Establish the justification for social work involvement at this time
2. Sequence 1: Exploring problems	Explore and determine the concerns/problems
a. Problem scanning	Develop a list of all identified concerns/problems
b. Problem details	Explore each problem in more detail: who, what, when, where, why and how?
c. Problem priorities	Rank the problems and identify no more than three to be the focus of work
3. Sequence 2: Establish goal and time limit	Define a goal in relation to the problem(s) and a time limit to reach the goal
4. Sequence 3: Develop tasks	Establish the tasks that need to be completed in order to reach the goal
5. Evaluation	Evaluate the process of work: has the client achieved what he/she wanted?

Sources: Reid and Epstein (1972); Doel (1991); Doel and Marsh (1992).

Exercise box 11.1   Who defines problems and goals?

1   When working with clients what role do you think social workers should play in defining problems and goals?
2   What role should third parties (that is, courts, social service agencies, family members) play in defining clients' problems and goals?

Case example: applying task-centred social work to practice

Emma, a 32-year-old, white British female, comes to you for help with her son. She states she is completely stressed out and unable to cope because her 5-year-old son is uncontrollable. You are a social worker who utilizes the task-centred social work approach in working with your clients and you begin implementing the steps and sequences of the approach in the first session with Emma.

The first step in the task-centred approach, *preparation or entry*, involves establishing 'who is the client' and the reason for the intervention. At your first session, Emma discloses to you that she needs help with her son, Archie, as she is unable to control his behaviour and her family and friends refuse to be alone with Archie. Emma states that she believes she needs to learn new parenting skills to help her control his behaviour. Emma describes feeling very stressed and run down and states she is not sure how she will carry on in her life if she cannot get Archie under control and alleviate the stress in her life. From Emma's disclosure of frustration with Archie's behaviour, you have determined that Emma is the primary client with whom you will work, but you also acknowledge that Archie may be a target of intervention as well. You also determined that the reason for your work with Emma is to assist in learning new ways to control Archie's behaviour and, as a result, alleviate her stress and feelings of being run down.

Your next step with Emma involves the first sequence in the task-centred approach, *exploring problems*, where you participate in three activities with Emma to further explore and define the problems with which she is experiencing. You begin with a *problem scan* where you ask Emma to devise a list of all the problems. As the social worker, you do not offer advice or suggestions at this stage, but rather allow Emma to discuss the problems that she is experiencing at this time in a broad sense. You and Emma agree that she will write each problem down on a piece of paper that you both can view. Emma lists the following problems:

1 I'm stressed out.
2 Archie won't listen to me and always acts up.
3 Archie's Dad won't help me out with money.
4 No one will watch Archie for me.
5 I don't have a job.
6 I don't have a place of my own. I'm staying with my sister.

Once the exhaustive list of problems and difficulties has been compiled, you move to the next stage in this sequence, *problem details*, and encourage Emma to discuss each of the listed problems in detail. In order to support Emma in this discussion, you ask her open-ended questions around each problem area that begins with either who, what, when, where, why or how. For example in regard to Emma's stress you could ask question such as: 'Why are you feeling stressed?', 'How do you know that you are stressed?', 'When do you feel a little less stressed?' and/or 'What is happening during those times?' In regard to Archie's behaviour you could ask: 'Where or when does Archie act up?', 'What does Archie do that tells you he is acting up?', 'How do you respond?', 'When doesn't he act up?' Such questions allow you and Emma to explore each of the problems in more detail and enable you both to have an understanding of the context in which the problem is occurring.

Based on the problem details exercise, Emma has revealed that she is feeling overwhelmed and stressed because she is living at her sister's house with Archie and although her sister has never told Emma a time frame in which she needs to move out, Emma feels as though she and Archie are intruding and inconveniencing her. Emma states that money is tight at the moment as she is not working and Archie's father does not pay any support. Emma says she feels as if she has knots in her stomach on a daily basis as she realizes she is not supporting her son as she would like. Emma states she would like to live alone with Archie without depending on family, have a job to support him and have some help with watching Archie so she can work. Emma reveals that she often allows Archie to get away with things because she feels guilty for not being able to provide for him as she would like. Emma reveals that since moving into her sister's house, Archie's behaviour has got worse; he throws temper tantrums whenever he is told 'no'. Emma feels embarrassed and unable to control her situation.

The next step with Emma is to *prioritize the problems* and select the top one or two (three at most) to be the focus of intervention. Emma tells you that she thinks if she can get her own place she will be in a better position to help Archie to stop 'acting up'. She realizes that in order to get her own place, she will need to apply for housing assistance from the local authority. Emma also states she would like to get a job and believes this will help her chances of moving out of her sister's house more quickly. In helping her financial situation, Emma states she will need to petition the courts to have Archie's father pay child support. Emma believes that if she could tackle getting a job and her own place to live as well as financial support from Archie's father, her stress will be greatly reduced and she will be able to control Archie's behaviour and in turn her family and friends will be more willing to help out with him. Therefore, Emma has selected the following three problems to be the focus of intervention:

1   I don't have a job.
2   I don't have a place of my own. I'm staying with my sister.
3   Archie's Dad won't help me out with money.

You and Emma now move into the second sequence, *setting goal(s) and a time limit*. You ask Emma to define her goals in light of the problems Emma has selected as the focus of intervention. Emma defines the following three goals:

1   Get a job.
2   Move into a house of my own with Archie.
3   Get child support from Archie's father.

You and Emma decide that you will meet together once a week for at least one hour for the next eight weeks. You and Emma construct a written contract with the listed problems, the goals and the specified time frame (Figure 11.1). You make a copy for yourself and one for Emma.

You now move into sequence 3 with Emma, *planning and specifying tasks*. You and Emma discuss the tasks that need to be completed in relation to each of the goals over the next week. For example, in relation to goal 1, 'I want to get a job', you and Emma agree that Emma will make a list of her employment skills and strengths to discuss in the next session. Additionally, Emma will begin to look at some employment advertisements and make some notes of jobs that interest her. In relation to goal 2, 'I want to move into a house of my own with Archie', you and Emma agree that Emma will bring a copy of the housing benefit application to the next meeting to fill out. Lastly, in relation to goal 3, 'Get income support from Archie's father', you and Emma agree that you will inquire into this process and bring any relevant paperwork to the next meeting. These tasks are agreed to be completed for the next session at which time you and Emma will review the tasks looking at what went well and what did not go so well, and establish new tasks to be completed over the following week. This process will be continued until Emma has reached her goals.

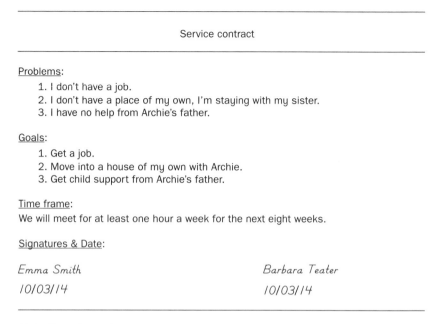

Service contract

Problems:
    1. I don't have a job.
    2. I don't have a place of my own, I'm staying with my sister.
    3. I have no help from Archie's father.

Goals:
    1. Get a job.
    2. Move into a house of my own with Archie.
    3. Get child support from Archie's father.

Time frame:
We will meet for at least one hour a week for the next eight weeks.

Signatures & Date:

Emma Smith   *Barbara Teater*
10/03/14   *10/03/14*

Figure 11.1   Example service contract between Emma and social worker.

Once Emma has reached her goals, you enter into the final step, *ending the work: termination and evaluation*, where you and Emma review the progress and accomplishments that have been made and prepare to end the work together. Emma has become employed, has moved into her own apartment with Archie and is receiving child support from Archie's father. Emma reports that her stress has been greatly reduced and she and Archie are working on a routine to help with his behaviour. You and Emma discuss any further plans or goals that she can work towards using her strengths and resources that she has developed over the past eight weeks to assist in those plans.

Strengths and limitations

There are several strengths and limitations of the task-centred approach that are worth exploring before incorporating this method into practice. The strengths include the following:

- The task-centred approach is a generic approach in the sense that it can be applied to a variety of problems and difficulties. The key is that the client must identify a goal to work towards in order for this method to be appropriate (Fortune and Reid, 2011).

- The task-centred approach can be easily used in combination with other theories and methods and across many settings. For example, a social worker may begin by utilizing motivational interviewing with a client who is ambivalent about making a change and then switch to task-centred social work when the client is ready to work towards alleviating the identified problem.
- The approach is empowering in that the social worker and client enter into a partnership where the client identifies the problem, specifies a goal and participates in small tasks that lead to reaching the goal. The social worker and client participate in this process of completing tasks and working towards goals (Fortune and Reid, 2011).
- The approach has continually been subjected to research and has been found to be a cost-effective, short-term method of working (Marsh, 2013).
- The approach incorporates aspects of systems theory and therefore, although clients define the problems and goals, they do not have to be the focus of intervention and the problem does not necessarily have to reside with them. For example, the problem of an individual may best be alleviated by intervening into a social service agency.

The limitations of the approach include the following:

- The task-centred approach may not be appropriate for all clients. For instance, the approach requires that the client make links between problems, tasks and goals (that is, actions and consequences), yet some clients may experience limitations to or difficulties with this type of thought (Fortune and Reid, 2011). If this is experienced in a social work setting, the social worker may need to consider working more directly with the carer than the client.
- The task-centred approach may be difficult to implement if the client is mandated to work with you (Doel, 1991; Marsh, 2013). Some clients may not acknowledge any problems in their life that require attention. The social worker should attempt to collaborate with the client and find mutual agreement on the reason for their work together. For example, the problem for the client may be the agency's involvement and the social worker could then ask what the client would like to do to alleviate this problem. In this sense a true collaborative partnership may not be achievable as problems are externally defined by a third party and the client is mandated to work towards alleviating this problem. The social worker should make this power imbalance explicit when working with the client and could compromise by including the problem as externally defined and a problem as defined by the client.
- The approach may be criticized by strengths-based practitioners due to the initial focus on problems. Despite the fact that problems are explored and defined, the main focus of the work is to move the client towards their stated goal through the completion of small tasks. The approach values the identification and building of client strengths along this process.
- Alternatively, the approach may be criticized for not focusing on long-term individual or social problems (Payne, 2005). The approach is short term in

nature and is focused on the client whether that is an individual, family, group or community. Social workers need to be considerate and respectful of clients who express a need to disclose the problems of their past, yet they should ultimately attempt to move the client to the present to solve the problem (Marsh and Doel, 2005).

Ethical and cultural considerations

There are ethical and cultural considerations to consider when incorporating the task-centred approach in social work practice. First, the social worker should keep in mind the principles and values of social work practice when establishing goals and tasks with the client. Although the social worker is to promote empowerment by encouraging the client to develop goals and tasks that are personally meaningful to them, the social worker will need to ensure that the goals and tasks do not cause harm to the client or anyone else and are compatible with the principles and values of social work.

Second, the task-centred social work approach was developed in North America by social work academics and later revised and adapted in the UK. The approach has since been integrated in social services in various countries within Europe, the Middle East, Africa and Asia, and has been used with people of different social classes and cultural groups (Fortune and Reid, 2011).

Finally, when implementing task-centred social work in practice with individuals from cultures that differ from the dominant culture of society, social workers should consider the following questions: should individuals be responsible for accomplishing tasks on their own, or should the focus be on group or family tasks? Are there any community rituals or routines that could be incorporated into the work together? Should the social worker allow more time to develop a relationship with the client? Such considerations should be discussed with the client from the beginning of the work together.

Task-centred social work and anti-oppressive practice

Task-centred social work's value base is in alignment with empowerment-based approaches and anti-oppressive practice (Rooney, 2010). The approach also stresses the importance of assessing systems and contexts, which might reveal that a problem is due to discrimination or oppression that is limiting an individual's ability to access needed resources (Fortune and Reid, 2011). The approach stresses a partnership between the social worker and client, and any difficulties in reaching or maintaining a true partnership should be made explicit. Additionally, any power differences or use of professional authority are to be made clear in the beginning of the work together.

In some situations, the social worker and/or client may be unclear as to the purpose of their work together. For example, a client may be court-mandated to work with a social worker to address her or his drug and/or alcohol use. In considering anti-oppressive practice, the task-centred approach would encourage the social worker and client to attempt to reach a consensus on the work together but not enforce consensus where none exists (Doel, 2002). This is based on the principle that clients are viewed as the expert on their experiences, problems and future expectations, and the social worker is there to help, not direct, clients to reach their goals.

The social worker and client should consider areas in which the client is experiencing oppression and/or discrimination and how this is contributing to the problem situation. A thorough systemic and context examination may highlight how the problems are fuelled by oppression or discrimination, which is out of the control of the client. The social worker and client can agree tasks for the social worker that attempt to confront and eliminate the oppression and/or discrimination and thus alleviate the identified problem(s).

Research on task-centred social work

Task-centred social work has been developed with a strong empirical base. For example, Reid and Epstein (1977) edited a book entitled *Task-centered Practice* which was a collection of research papers on the implementation of task-centred practice with numerous populations groups. The articles had come out of a Conference on Applications of Task-Centered Treatment held at the University of Chicago in 1975. Since this time, the evidence for the effectiveness of task-centred social work continues to grow. For example, the approach has been evaluated and slightly refined based on work with the following populations: (1) older adults (Naleppa and Reid, 1998); (2) group work settings (Bielenberg, 1991; Pomeroy et al., 1995; Scharlach, 1985); (3) children and adolescents (Caspi, 2008; Colvin et al., 2008a; 2008b; Reid and Donovan, 1990); (4) families (Bielenberg, 1991); and (5) school social work (Bailey-Dempsey and Reid, 1996; Colvin et al., 2008a; 2008b; Reid and Bailey-Dempsey, 1995). The approach stresses the importance for social work practitioners to evaluate their work with clients by collecting data at the beginning, during the process and at the end of the work together.

Summary

Task-centred social work is a short-term, problem-solving approach to working with individuals, families, groups and communities. The approach is considered a generic practice method that can be used to address many different types of problems in various types of settings and in combination with other theories or methods. Clients and social workers work together in partnership and any power inequalities are to be made explicit. The approach involves clients identifying the problems in their life, selecting one or two (three at most) to be the focus of intervention, establishing goals to alleviate or diminish the problems and the development of small tasks to assist in the achievement of the goals. Task-centred social work has been subjected to evaluation and has been established as a cost-effective method when used with various populations.

Case study

Frank is an 82-year-old, white British male who has been referred to Adult Social Care by a hospital after fracturing his hip in a recent fall in his home. Frank has been discharged home, but is living on the ground floor and is unable to use the stairs to go to his bedroom and bathroom. The referral form states that Frank lives alone and has one daughter who lives nearby and sees Frank regularly. You call Frank to make an appointment to go to his house and complete an assessment. Frank tells you that he is scared that he will have to move into a care home. He wants to stay in his home as long as possible and is willing to look at all the options in order to do so. Frank tells you he doesn't have much money. Describe how you would carry out the task-centred approach in working with Frank.

Further reading

Doel, M. and Marsh, P. (1992) *Task-centred Social Work*. Aldershot: Ashgate.
  A detailed account of the task-centred approach, with each chapter focusing on one sequence or phase. A case example is used to illustrate the approach.
Fortune, A.E. and Reid, W.J. (2011) Task-centered social work, in F.J. Turner (eds), *Social Work Treatment: Interlocking Theoretical Approaches*, 5th edn. New York: Oxford University Press.
Marsh, P. and Doel, M. (2005) *The Task-centred Book*. Abingdon: Routledge.
  Discusses the task-centred approach particularly from the viewpoints of practitioners, services users and carers.
Reid, W.J. and Epstein, L. (1972) *Task-centered Casework*. New York: Columbia University Press.
  Original book describing the method of task-centred practice.

References

Bailey-Dempsey, C. and Reid, W.J. (1996) Intervention design and development: a case study, *Research on Social Work Practice*, 6(2): 208–28.
Bielenberg, L. (1991) A task-centered preventive group approach to create cohesion in the new stepfamily: a preliminary evaluation, *Research on Social Work Practice*, 1(4): 416–33.
Caspi, J. (2008) Building a sibling aggression treatment model: design and development research in action, *Research on Social Work Practice*, 18(6): 575–85.
Colvin, J., Lee, M., Magnano, J. and Smith, V. (2008a) The partners in prevention program: further development of the task-centered case management model, *Research on Social Work Practice*, 18(6): 586–95.
Colvin, J., Lee, M., Magnano, J. and Smith, V. (2008b) The partners in prevention program: evaluation and evolution of the task-centered case management model, *Research on Social Work Practice*, 18(6): 607–15.

Doel, M. (1991) Task-centred work, in J. Lishman (ed.), *Handbook of Theory for Practice Teachers in Social Work*. London: Jessica Kingsley.

Doel, M. (2002) Task-centred work, in R. Adams, L. Dominelli and M. Payne (eds), *Social Work: Themes, Issues and Critical Debates*, 2nd edn. Basingstoke: Palgrave.

Doel, M. and Marsh, P. (1992) *Task-centred Social Work*. Aldershot: Ashgate.

Fortune, A.E. and Reid, W.J. (2011) Task-centered social work, in F.J. Turner (eds), *Social Work Treatment: Interlocking Theoretical Approaches*, 5th edn. New York: Oxford University Press.

Marsh, P. (2007) Task-centred practice, in J. Lishman (ed.), *Handbook of Theory for Practice Teachers in Social Work*, 2nd edn. London: Jessica Kingsley.

Marsh, P. (2013) Task-centred practice, in M. Davies (ed.), *The Blackwell Companion to Social Work*, 4th edn. Chichester: John Wiley & Sons.

Marsh, P. and Doel, M. (2005) *The Task-centred Book*. Abingdon: Routledge.

Naleppa, M.J. and Reid, W.J. (1998) Task-centered case management for the elderly: developing a practice model, *Research on Social Work Practice*, 8(1): 63–95.

Payne, M. (2005) *Modern Social Work Theory*, 3rd edn. Basingstoke: Palgrave Macmillan.

Pomeroy, E.C., Rubin, A. and Walker, R.J. (1995) Effectiveness of a psychoeducational and task-centered group intervention for family members of people with AIDS, *Social Work Research*, 19(3): 129–52.

Reid, W.J. and Bailey-Dempsey, C. (1995) The effects of monetary incentives on school performance, *Families in Society*, 76(6): 331–40.

Reid, W.J. and Donovan, T. (1990) Treating sibling violence, *Family Therapy*, 17: 49–59.

Reid, W.J. and Epstein, L. (1972) *Task-centered Casework*. New York: Columbia University Press.

Reid, W.J. and Epstein, L. (1977) *Task-centered Practice*. New York: Columbia University Press.

Reid, W.J. and Shyne, A.W. (1969) *Brief and Extended Casework*. New York: Columbia University Press.

Rooney, R.H. (2010) Task-centered practice in the United States, in A.E. Fortune, P. McCallion and K. Briar-Lawson (eds), *Social Work Practice Research for the 21st Century*. New York: Columbia University Press.

Scharlach, A.E. (1985) Social groupwork with institutionalized elders: a task-centered approach, *Social Work with Groups*, 8(3): 33–47.

12 Crisis intervention

Introduction

Crisis intervention is a brief intervention that focuses on mobilizing clients' strengths and resources in order to overcome a crisis situation and improve their level of coping, confidence and problem-solving. According to Eaton and Roberts (2009, p. 207) 'a crisis can be precipitated by any intensely stressful or traumatic event, as perceived by the client, in which the individual does not have the ego strengths and coping abilities to deal effectively with the presenting problem'. Crisis intervention is based on crisis theory which holds that individuals have coping mechanisms to deal with stressful events, yet in some situations, the events stretch individuals beyond their normal coping abilities and throw them into a state of disequilibrium. When individuals' normal coping strategies and mechanisms fail to address the event and their strengths and resources are not sufficient to deal with the event, individuals perceive the situation as a crisis. The goal of crisis intervention is to address the crisis with coping strategies, help individuals improve their level of coping, confidence and problem-solving, and enable individuals to draw upon newly identified strengths, resources and coping mechanisms when faced with stressors in the future. Although the crisis experience may be traumatic for individuals, this experience can serve as an opportunity for growth and development (Roberts, 2005).

Crisis intervention is appropriate for work with individuals, families and/or communities immediately following a crisis situation and is short term in nature, lasting only between one and six weeks. Professional bodies that intervene in crisis situations adhere to several different crisis intervention models, yet within the social work, mental health and counselling professions, Roberts's (1991) seven-stage model is the most widely recognized and utilized crisis intervention model. This chapter explores the definition of a crisis, reviews crisis theory and the basic assumptions of crisis intervention, and details Roberts's (1991) seven-stage crisis intervention model.

The origins of crisis intervention

Crisis intervention as a formal theory and method was primarily developed by American psychiatrists in the 1940s, particularly through the works of Erich Lindemann, followed by Gerald Caplan in the 1960s. Lindemann (1944) began to develop a crisis theory based on his research of the reactions and grieving processes of the survivors and family and friends who lost their loved ones in the Coconut Grove nightclub fire in Boston, Massachusetts, where 493 people were killed. Lindemann examined the psychological stages of grief of the survivors and relatives, which laid the foundation for future theorists to further build on crisis theory. Caplan was one of the theorists who expanded on Lindemann's work and related crisis intervention to concepts used in systems theory, such as homeostasis, steady state and disequilibrium. Caplan (1961; 1964) theorized that a crisis was the result of an individual experiencing an event where her or his normal coping mechanisms and resources are unable to deal effectively with the event, which in turn results in an upset in the individual's homeostasis and, subsequently, psychological and physiological distress. This equilibrium model would thus require intervention with individuals to return them to a steady state where they can effectively utilize their strengths, resources and coping mechanisms in order to ensure growth and development.

Lydia Rapoport (1962; 1967), as a social work practitioner, continued to build on the crisis theory work of Caplan (1961) by utilizing the systems theory terminology and acknowledging that a crisis was a disruption to an individual's homeostasis or steady state. She argued that a crisis state was precipitated by the following three interrelated factors: '(1) a hazardous event; (2) a threat to life goals; and (3) an inability to respond with adequate coping mechanisms' (Roberts, 2005, p. 17). Therefore, crisis intervention required a focus on quickly returning the individual to a steady state or homeostasis. Other theorists and practitioners within the social work and mental health professions continued to address the crisis intervention model, particularly in regard to mental health crises (Bott, 1976; Scott, 1974), ethical considerations (O'Hagan, 1986; 1991) or the incorporation of a cognitive and behavioural approach (Thompson, 2011). Current crisis intervention writings and research related to the social work profession are built on the works of Albert Roberts who was Professor of Criminal Justice at Rutgers University and who developed the crisis intervention model as discussed in this chapter. Modern-day crisis intervention theory may still utilize the terminology of systems, but acknowledges that crisis intervention is not just returning someone to a pre-existing state (that is, homeostasis), but rather involves improving the individual's coping, confidence, problem-solving, strengths and resources in order to maximize the ability of the individual to cope with stressors in the future. Crisis intervention is viewed as providing an opportunity for growth and change.

Crisis intervention explained

Crisis intervention is a brief intervention that is designed and specifically used to assist individuals, families and/or communities to overcome a perceived crisis and improve levels of coping. A crisis is a subjective term, particularly as one person's crisis would be another person's challenge. Two people faced with the same situation may view her or his ability to overcome and cope with the event very differently. One person may react with her or his coping mechanisms and overcome the event, while another person's existing coping mechanisms may not appropriately deal with the event and the person is thrown into a crisis situation. Therefore, before exploring the definition of a crisis one must understand that a crisis is subjective and varies from person to person.

Exercise box 12.1   What is a crisis?

In pairs or small groups discuss the following:

1   What is a crisis?
2   Give an example of a crisis or crisis situation from your placement or life in general.

Roberts and Yeager (2009, p. 2) define a crisis as a 'subjective response to a stressful or traumatic life event or a series of events that are perceived by the person as hazardous, threatening, or extremely upsetting, which do not resolve using traditional coping methods'. A crisis is different to a stressful situation. Although uncomfortable and often anxiety-provoking, individuals are able to utilize coping mechanisms to overcome a stressful situation, whereas in crisis situations individuals' existing coping mechanisms do not work and individuals are unable to cope with and overcome the situation (Wright, 1991). As discussed earlier, each person may view a situation or event in a different way; one may view it as a stressful situation and overcome the obstacle while another person may be unable to adapt or cope with the situation and thereby perceive it as a crisis. This differentiation is often a result of the person's personality, resources, supports, and coping skills and past experiences with stressors (Roberts and Yeager, 2009). Regehr (2011, p. 136) has identified four factors that contribute to a crisis: (1) a precipitating event; (2) the individual's crisis-meeting resources, which include both personal and social resources and support; (3) other stressors that are currently presenting challenges; and (4) the meaning attributed to the stressful event – the extent to which the person perceives the event as a threat. The four factors can vary across situations. For example, an individual may experience a loss of a family member to cancer *(precipitating event)*, attempt to use internal coping skills to lessen the emotional pain, but has no other family or external support *(individual's crisis-meeting resources)*, is experiencing a recent partner breakdown *(other currently presenting challenges)* and is feeling devastated at the loss of such a close family member *(meaning attributed to the stressful event)*. Other individuals may experience a similar type of precipitating event *(loss of a family member)*, but may be able to access and use personal and social resources and support and may have no other presenting challenges, which lessens the extent to which the person perceives the situation as a crisis and enhances her or his ability to cope. Therefore, a crisis is initiated by a combination of the four factors. Based on these factors, Regehr (2011, p. 136) defines 'crisis' as an equation:

> Crisis = the event + the individual's crisis-meeting resources + other concurrent stressors + the individual's perception of the event.

A crisis is initiated by a combination of the four factors listed above, and therefore is seen as subjective. There are a number of events that could serve as a stressful, traumatic or hazardous event to individuals, families and/or communities. Events can be personal or private, which often affect individuals and/or families and could include such events as the loss of a loved one, contemplation of suicide, thoughts of harming oneself or another person, assault or victimization, difficult life transitions (for example, divorce, unemployment or financial, mental or physiological changes). Events could alternatively be public where they affect communities and larger groups of individuals, such as natural disasters (hurricanes, earthquakes, tornadoes, tsunamis, volcanic eruptions, fires, floods and so on), terrorists attacks, shootings or assaults, hostage situations, large-scale motor vehicle, boating, train or aeroplane accidents (Roberts, 2005). The extent to which the individual, family and/or community are able to access their strengths, resources and existing coping mechanisms will determine whether the event is manageable and able to be tackled to the point that the event's effects are diminished or whether the effects of the event are too overwhelming to bear and create a crisis situation.

According to Roberts (2005, p. 13), a person in crisis is often described by the presence of the following characteristics: '(1) perceiving a precipitating event as being meaningful and threatening; (2) appearing unable to modify or lessen the impact of stressful events with traditional coping methods; (3) experiencing increased fear, tension and/or confusion; (4) exhibiting a high level of subjective discomfort; and (5) proceeding rapidly to an active state of crisis – a state of disequilibrium'. Crises are deemed to be time limited, where they last from one day to four to six weeks (Regehr, 2011); after four to six weeks, the individual may experience 'further psychiatric impairment or damage to emotional growth' (Skinner, 2013, p. 428). Crisis intervention is usually implemented at the active or acute state where the individual is experiencing discomfort, often psychologically and/or physiologically based, which can be exhibited through helplessness, confusion, depression, anxiety, anger, impulsivity, low self-esteem, incoherence, fatigue and exhaustion, disorganization, agitation, violence, isolation, social withdrawal, a state of shock, feeling stressed-out or overwhelmed, having difficulty breathing, sleeping, eating, and/or difficulty in communicating (Regehr, 2011; Roberts and Yeager, 2009). According to Golan (1978), crisis intervention is most effective when implemented during this active or acute stage and is the period of time that individuals are most receptive to assistance.

Crisis intervention seeks to intervene in the crisis situation by working with the system (that is, individual, family, community) in order to retrieve established coping mechanisms and resources or develop new coping mechanisms and resources that can be utilized to combat the stressful or hazardous event and prevent further psychological or physiological problems. Crisis intervention can provide an opportunity for personal growth and development by capitalizing on the individual's existing strengths, resources and coping skills and, at the same time, encouraging the development of new strengths, resources and coping skills, all of which can be utilized when faced with a stressful or hazardous event in the future. According to Roberts (2005, p. 5), the 'ultimate goal of crisis intervention is to bolster available coping methods or help individuals re-establish coping and problem-solving abilities while helping them to take concrete steps towards managing their feelings and developing an action plan'.

Basic assumptions of crisis theory

According to crisis theorists (Golan, 1978; Parad and Parad, 1990; Roberts, 2005) there are several basic assumptions to crisis theory and crisis intervention. Each is described below:

1. Systems (that is, individuals, families, communities) encounter stressful and hazardous events throughout the lifespan. These events lead the system to utilize existing strengths, resources and coping mechanism to tackle the event and lessen or alleviate the event's negative consequences.
2. Homeostasis and a steady state are maintained through the use of the system's strengths, resources and coping mechanisms when faced with difficulties, stressful or hazardous events.
3. Systems can encounter a stressful or hazardous event where their existing strengths, resources and coping mechanisms are not effective in lessening or alleviating the event's negative consequences in which case the systems experience disequilibrium where the homeostatic balance is disrupted and, thus, a crisis state ensues.
4. A crisis situation is overcome by intervening in the acute crisis state and building on the system's strengths, resources and coping mechanisms, which can be utilized in tackling the crisis precipitating event as well as serve as tools to be utilized in future stressful or hazardous situations.

Seven-stage crisis intervention model

Roberts's (1991; 2005) crisis intervention model consists of seven stages, which social workers (and other crisis workers) and clients collaboratively progress through in addressing a crisis situation.

As Figure 12.1 depicts, the stages progress from one to another, yet in actuality, several stages overlap or are used in conjunction with one another. For example, stage 1, *Plan and conduct a crisis and biopsychosocial assessment*, will most likely be used in conjunction with stage 2, *Establish rapport and a therapeutic relationship*. Additionally, crisis intervention involves an overlap of assessment and intervention where each influences the other and the worker continually goes back and forth between assessment and intervention techniques (Regehr, 2011).

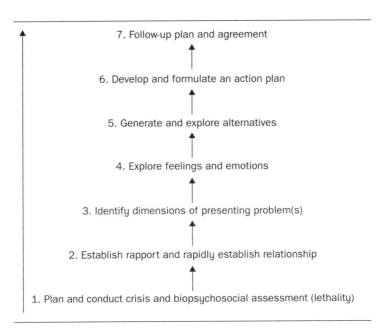

Figure 12.1   Seven-stage crisis intervention model. Adapted from Eaton and Roberts (2009) and Roberts (2005).

Each step as listed by Eaton and Roberts (2009) and Roberts (2005) is discussed in detail below:

1   *Stage 1: plan and conduct a crisis assessment (including lethality measures).* This first stage involves conducting a biopsychosocial assessment with the client where the client's health, both mental and physical, and social supports are explored. The client's health is assessed by exploring medications taken or needed (that is, over-the-counter medications, prescription medications), any medical needs, current use of drugs or alcohol (including names of drugs used, last used and amount used), or withdrawal symptoms from substances. Lethality measures are included where the social worker assesses for any harm or intended harm to the self or others, and any past history of self-harming. If the client expresses suicidal thoughts, the social worker must inquire about the client's suicide plan to determine the extent to which the client has prepared a plan to carry out. If at any point the client appears to be in danger of harming themselves, has been harmed by another or is in need of medical attention, the social worker must contact emergency services and/or the police to ensure the client is safe. The social worker should enquire about the client's social and environmental supports and resources, particularly as the social worker and client could draw upon these supports and resources

when implementing an intervention plan (Eaton and Roberts, 2009; Roberts, 2005). This stage is often conducted in conjunction with stage 2.

2   *Stage 2: rapid establishment of rapport and the therapeutic relationship.* This stage is often conducted in conjunction with stage 1. Social workers may be initiating the first contact with a client without any prior established rapport or relationship and therefore, would not be able to gather information under stage 1 without initiating stage 2. The social worker should quickly establish a rapport with the client in order to gather information and work to resolve the crisis situation. Social workers should utilize the person-centred approach (Rogers, 1957) where they demonstrate unconditional positive regard, genuineness and empathy with the client (see Chapter 7). Eaton and Roberts (2009) stress the importance of the social worker meeting clients where they are while maintaining a calm and in-control appearance. For example, if the client states that she hears the voice of her deceased mother, the social worker should not dispute this statement but, rather, allow the client to continue to discuss her thoughts, feelings and experiences while attentively listening.

3   *Stage 3: presenting problems pertinent to the client and any precipitants to the client's crisis contact.* While continuing to establish a relationship with the client, the social worker should begin to gather information about the crisis situation and any precipitating events. The presenting problems and precipitating events can be identified by establishing answers to the following questions: what led up to the social worker's involvement? What was the 'last straw' for the client? Has the client experienced a similar situation? If so, how did the client cope with that situation or other stressful events? What is different with this situation? (Roberts, 2005). In gathering this information, the social worker must use open-ended questions which allow the client to elaborate on the presenting problems and precipitating events, and fully express her or his experience and story.

4   *Stage 4: deal with feelings and emotions by effectively using active listening skills.* This stage is often used in conjunction with stage 3 whereby the social worker uses open-ended questions and active listening skills when eliciting from the client the presenting problems and precipitating events. As the client is telling her or his story, the social worker should continue to utilize the person-centred techniques of unconditional positive regard, genuineness and empathy, and should acknowledge and validate the client's current feelings and emotions. Active listening by the social worker will include encouraging and acknowledging statements (for example, 'OK', 'un-huh'), and reflective statements, where the social worker reflects back to the client all or aspects of what the client has just said in an attempt to encourage the client to discuss the issue further as well as ensure the social worker is correctly interpreting the client's statements. For example:

Client: I don't know how I can go on like this.
Social worker: You are overwhelmed. Something has to change.

The social worker can reflect back feelings and emotions that are implied in statements in an effort to support the client and encourage her or him to continue in the discussion with the social worker. For example:

Client: I wish I had someone to talk to. There is no one who completely understands what I am going through.

Social worker: You're feeling very alone right now.

This stage is particularly important as clients need to feel that their experiences, feelings and emotions are being acknowledged and supported.

5   *Stage 5: generate and explore alternatives by identifying the strengths of the client as well as previous successful coping mechanisms.* While stage 3 elicits the presenting problems of the client, stage 5 begins to formulate alternatives to the issue and identifies new or previous unused coping mechanisms to deal with the issue. The social worker and client are to work collaboratively to identify alternatives and coping mechanisms that can alleviate the presenting problem or issue. Aspects of solution-focused practice are incorporated into this stage (see Chapter 10), particularly in regard to identifying and building upon the client's existing strengths, resources and coping skills. The social worker can begin this process by asking the client solution-focused questions in an attempt to bring the client's strengths, resources and coping skills to the surface and to remind the client of when things were better for her or him. Such questions could include: (1) exception questions – 'When were there times that you were feeling just a little less depressed than you are now?' 'What was different about those times?'; (2) coping questions – 'How have you managed to get through this experience so far?'; (3) past successes – 'How have you coped with situations like this in the past?' 'How did you manage to get through similar situations to this in the past?' (Greene et al., 2005). In this process, the social worker and client can begin to establish alternative ways of addressing the presenting problems while ensuring the social worker gives attention to the consequences and to the client's thoughts and feelings about each alternative. Although this should be a collaborative process, there may be situations where the social worker could provide several suggestions as options for the client to consider (Roberts, 2005). There will be situations where the client is unable to make decisions regarding alternatives; for example, when a client requires hospitalization due to the current mental health state or is detained in police custody due to threats or plans of harming others.

6   *Stage 6: implement an action plan.* Once alternatives to the presenting problem are identified, the social worker and client can begin to implement the action plan. This is assuming that the client is mentally and physically capable of being involved in such a plan. For example, as mentioned above, if the client requires immediate hospitalization, the social worker will have to implement the crisis intervention plan without the client being a collaborative partner in the process. In this stage, the social worker and client identify the action plan (or steps) that it is agreed will be required in order to address the presenting crisis situation. This could include identifying persons or agencies from which

the client will continue to seek services or identifying coping mechanisms that the client is to implement. The action plan should be documented in a format most appropriate for the client and copies of the plan given to both the social worker and client.

7   *Stage 7: establish a follow-up plan and agreement.* The social worker should follow up with the client after the initial crisis intervention to determine the status of the action plan and to ensure the crisis situation is resolved or being addressed (Eaton and Roberts, 2009). The follow-up session can occur via telephone or through a face-to-face session.

Case example: applying crisis intervention to practice

You are a crisis worker who receives a call from the local school stating that a 14-year-old black British male, Rasheed, has reported to his classmates that he plans to commit suicide later that evening. The school counsellor has spoken with Rasheed who confirmed this allegation and stated he cannot take the bullying from his classmates any longer. Rasheed is currently safe with the school counsellor, but she is fearful that Rasheed might act out his plans if she releases him to go home. Rasheed has asked the school counsellor to not contact his parents as he does not want to upset them. You immediately report to the school and begin to conduct the seven-stage crisis intervention model with Rasheed.

When you arrive at the school, you find Rasheed in the school counsellor's office where he is sitting and staring at the wall. Rasheed does not acknowledge you and moves his chair to where you have to face his back. You first begin by conducting a biopsychosocial assessment, to quickly determine the lethality of the situation and any potential needed medical attention (*stage 1: plan and conduct a crisis assessment including lethality measures*) while simultaneously attempting to establish a therapeutic relationship with Rasheed (*stage 2: rapid establishment of rapport and the therapeutic relationship*). You assess that Rasheed is currently safe and free from harm by being in the room with you and the school counsellor, but need to determine the extent of Rasheed's suicidal ideologies. You ask Rasheed if you can ask him a few questions and he agrees, but only if the school counsellor remains in the room with him. In order to establish a rapport with Rasheed you agree to his request. Rasheed continues to face the wall to talk to you and you meet Rasheed where he is by asking if you can sit next to him without him having to turn around.

You ask Rasheed if he is currently on any medications or has any health problems. Rasheed reports that he has asthma and carries an inhaler, but has not needed to use it today. He does not report any other health problems. Rasheed also denies the use of any substances, such as drugs or alcohol. You begin to discuss the suicidal thoughts by stating, 'You know that the school counsellor has called me to come and talk to you because you stated you would like to harm yourself. Can you tell me more about those thoughts?' Without turning around Rasheed states, 'I'm so tired of being made fun of and being bullied. No one would miss me if I was gone'. You ask Rasheed if he has plans for hurting himself. Rasheed reports that he could find a gun or buy some pills at the pharmacy. You assess that although Rasheed has suicidal thoughts, the actual plans for carrying this out are not fully set or in order as he would have to carry out additional tasks before he could complete the plan (that is, access a gun or purchase medication). You then enquire about Rasheed's social supports and ask about his parents and family. Rasheed informs you that he lives with his mother and father and two younger sisters. He reports that he has not discussed his thoughts of suicide with his parents as they would be too upset and angry with him. Rasheed states that he does have a good relationship with his parents, but they just do not understand what he is going through. You conclude that Rasheed does not need emergency medical attention and proceed to the next stage of the crisis intervention model.

As stated above, you have initiated the second stage in conjunction with the first stage by responding to Rasheed's requests to have the school counsellor present, sit with his back to you, ask for permission to talk to and sit next to him, and listen to Rasheed with empathy and without judgement. Rasheed is progressively providing more information and is beginning to turn his body towards you when speaking. While continuing with establishing a rapport and therapeutic relationship with Rasheed, you proceed to gather from Rasheed the pertinent issues and precipitating events that lead to this crisis situation (*stage 3: presenting problems pertinent to the client and any precipitants to the client's crisis contact*). You begin by asking an open-ended question, 'What happened today that has led to you having thoughts of harming yourself? What was the last straw for you?' Rasheed reports that because he is black in a predominately white school he is continually bullied by his peers. He is often referred to in racist ways and is even physically abused at times, such as being pushed into walls, tripped up in the corridors and having the hot water turned off when he is in the gym shower. He stated that today he was approached by a group of boys in the gym locker room who made remarks about his body and took pictures of him on their phones when he was not looking. The boys then sent the pictures to other kids throughout the school. Rasheed reports feeling humiliated and ashamed that others were able to see his private body parts. He feels that this abuse will only get progressively worse and he does not want to deal with it anymore. While listening to Rasheed report the problem, you actively listen and acknowledge his feelings and emotions (*stage 4: deal with feelings and emotions by effectively using active listening skills*). You reflect back to Rasheed, 'Today was a humiliating experience and you feel this isn't going to end. You must feel angry and hurt'. During this discussion Rasheed had turned himself around to face you. You continue to actively listen to the experiences described by Rasheed and acknowledge his feelings and emotions.

You begin to explore alternatives with Rasheed to his suicidal thoughts (*stage 5: generate and explore alternatives by identifying the strengths of the client as well as previous successful coping mechanisms*). You implement some solution-focused practice questions in order to identify Rasheed's strengths, resources and existing coping mechanisms. You ask Rasheed, 'This must be very difficult for you. How have you been able to cope with this abuse up to now?' Rasheed reports he has tried to ignore the other boys, keep to himself and spend as little time at school as possible. You ask Rasheed, 'When are there times that you feel safe and happier than you do right now?' Rasheed reports that he feels pretty happy at home and when around his family and when playing his videos games. You acknowledge that Rasheed has utilized coping mechanisms in the past, but they are not adequate to deal with the situation that occurred today. You also realize that Rasheed's family is a strong support system for him.

You begin to explore with Rasheed alternatives to committing suicide and address some of the consequences to this action, such as how family members would respond. The school counsellor is invited to participate in this discussion, particularly as the racism at the school is an issue that will require attention in order to protect Rasheed from future harm. The school counsellor reports that she will take this issue immediately to the headteacher to implement a disciplinary plan for the boys who committed the act today as well as strategies for preventing future harm or abuse. The school counsellor will contact the local Race Equality Council to assist in addressing the racial issues at the school. You ask Rasheed's permission to contact his parents to discuss the incident that occurred at school today to which Rasheed agrees. You also want to ensure that his parents are able to watch Rasheed during this time to protect him from harming himself, such as removing medications that could be harmful to him. Rasheed states that he is beginning to feel better by discussing the incident and knowing that something is going to happen to the boys that had humiliated him today. You ask Rasheed if he would like to talk to someone on a regular basis, such as an independent counsellor, to which he agrees. Rasheed asks if he can go home.

You ask to develop an action plan with Rasheed in order to protect him (*stage 6: implement an action plan*). Rasheed agrees and you write the discussed action points on a piece of paper that you both can sign along with the school counsellor. The action plan includes the following:

1 The crisis worker to refer Rasheed to a counsellor to discuss his thoughts and feelings on a regular basis.
2 Rasheed to report any thoughts of self-harm or suicide to either his mother or school counsellor immediately.
3 The crisis worker to discuss the situation with Rasheed's parents and ensure they remove any self-harming objects in the house.
4 The school counsellor and headteacher to take disciplinary action against the teenagers that harmed Rasheed.
5 The school counsellor to contact the local Race Equality Council to assist with the racism within the school.
6 The crisis worker to check with Rasheed the status of the action plan.

Rasheed's parents come to the school to discuss the incident with you and the school counsellor. You, Rasheed and the school counsellor sign the action plan and a copy is made for everyone involved. You follow up with Rasheed and his parents the following day to check how Rasheed is doing and inform them of the referral to the counselling agency (*stage 7: establish a follow-up plan and agreement*).

Strengths and limitations

There are several identified strengths and limitations to utilizing crisis intervention in social work practice. The strengths include the following:

- Crisis intervention, and particularly the Roberts's (1991) model, provides clear steps to follow when addressed with a crisis situation. Although not necessarily easy to implement, the process is clear and practical for social workers to follow.
- Crisis intervention is a brief method that is focused specifically on alleviating a crisis situation, and helping people improve their coping, confidence and problem-solving skills. This method is specifically designed for crisis situations and can be adapted by the social worker to fit various crisis situations and quickly alleviate crisis problems.
- Owing to the brief nature of crisis intervention, this method can be used in conjunction with other theories and methods. For example, a social worker may implement the seven-stage crisis intervention model with a family to alleviate a current crisis and then switch to other theories or methods (that is, cognitive behavioural therapy, task-centred social work) to alleviate additional or underlying problems.

The limitations include the following:

- Crisis intervention seeks to alleviate the presenting problem or crisis and is not always able to address the underlying issues that may be contributing to the presenting problem or crisis, such as discrimination, oppression and/or poverty (Payne, 2005). Although social workers may implement crisis intervention to alleviate a crisis situation, they should be mindful of underlying issues that may be contributing to the presenting problem or crisis, and where possible seek to address these issues through follow-up appointments or through referrals to other resources. Additionally, longer term consequences of crisis situations (e.g. post-traumatic stress disorder [PTSD]) may require longer-term treatment (Regehr, 2011).
- Crisis intervention is difficult to implement with clients who are not receptive to the social worker's involvement. The crisis intervention assessment requires the social worker to gather information from the client or someone who can answer questions on her or his behalf. Without this assessment information, the social worker may have difficulty developing an action plan. The social worker should keep in mind the importance of utilizing counselling and person-centred skills in attempting to establish a relationship with the client in order to gather information (stage 2).
- True collaboration is difficult to practice in all crisis situations. There are some situations where the social worker will have to implement an action plan against the will of the client, such as contacting the police or emergency services to ensure the safety of the client. Such situations can actually be viewed as disempowering (Skinner, 2013). Although social workers should strive to collaborate with clients at all times there are some situations where they will be faced with making such decisions and this should be done in collaboration with a supervisor or colleague.

Ethical and cultural considerations

In conducting crisis intervention effectively, O'Hagan (1991) calls for a sound ethical base. This will include ensuring that the social worker and other systems involved are utilizing anti-discriminatory, anti-oppressive practices and challenging attitudes, behaviours and policies that are discriminating and/or oppressing clients. A sound ethical base also requires the social worker to have the necessary knowledge and training in crisis intervention theories and practices, particularly as they are often dealing with very serious and sometimes life-threatening situations. Social workers should have the adequate resources necessary to carry out this role, such as supervision, support and training. Social workers should also have a sense of self-awareness, particularly as they will be faced with difficult crisis situations that might be emotionally and/or physically tasking. Support and supervision are critical aspects of crisis intervention and social workers should not be left to make critical decisions on their own, but rather should have support and guidance from supervisors or other qualified colleagues.

When incorporating crisis intervention, social workers should be mindful of the role that the client's culture can play in defining and overcoming a crisis. What may appear as a crisis situation to one person or culture may be another's stressful or challenging event. Often the dominant culture will expect people to respond to situations in a particular way and when this does not happen individuals, families and even communities can be viewed as abnormal or experience discrimination and/or oppression. Having the client define the presenting problems and precipitating events to the crisis is critical versus assuming what the client has experienced or is currently experiencing based on the social worker's values, beliefs and culture. Additionally, when exploring alternatives to the crisis situation, the social worker must be mindful that the client may develop alternatives that are different to what would be used in the social worker's culture, or the dominant culture. The client's culture can often be seen as a resource and should therefore be considered when implementing crisis intervention while adhering to the values and principles of the social work profession.

Crisis intervention and anti-oppressive practice

Anti-oppressive practice and empowerment are critical aspects of social work and, thus, should be incorporated into crisis intervention. Crisis intervention stresses the importance of working in partnership with the client in alleviating the presenting crisis situation. The social worker should attempt to establish this collaborative relationship from the beginning of the involvement and should foster this partnership throughout by having the client define the presenting problems and precipitating events, explore alternatives to the crisis situation and develop an action plan. Although the social worker may need to suggest some alternatives to the client's situation, this should be presented as one or several options for the client to consider and determine if they are appropriate for her or his situation. Social workers must keep empowerment and anti-oppressive practices in place in situations where social workers and other professionals (that is, police officers, medical professionals) have to take action to protect the client, such as hospitalization. Social workers can fulfil this need by continuing to practise with unconditional positive regard for the client, expressing empathy and remaining genuine while challenging any attempts to control or oppress the client.

Some theorists and social workers may argue that crisis intervention does not focus on anti-oppressive or anti-discriminatory practice because the nature of the intervention work is to alleviate the presenting crisis situation and not the underlying problems that may be precipitating the event (Payne, 2005). Although the crisis intervention model is set up to be brief and focused on the presenting problem, social workers can incorporate anti-oppressive and anti-discriminatory practices by working collaboratively and assessing for and including any environmental constraints or structural oppression on the action plan. Action can include either referring to another resource or agency or meeting this need by implementing another theory or method in their future work together. For example, in the case example above, the goal for the social worker was to alleviate the crisis situation with Rasheed and ensure he was safe from harm, but the action plan included addressing the underlying problem of racism and bullying that contributed to Rasheed's crisis.

Research on crisis intervention

Crisis intervention is not viewed as a 'curative' method, but is more a brief intervention that works collaboratively with clients to facilitate the process of change. Therefore, evaluations of the effectiveness of crisis intervention may be difficult to establish, particularly as the definition of a crisis will vary from person to person (Dziegielewski and Powers, 2005). Most crisis intervention studies examine how particular difficulties or symptoms, such as depression, suicidal ideations or post-traumatic stress disorder, are reduced as a result of the crisis intervention methods (Everly et al., 2005). Roberts and Everly (2006) conducted a meta-analysis of 36 evaluations of crisis intervention methods that assessed the effectiveness in terms of one of three types of settings: (1) family preservation, which includes in-home intensive family counselling, which can usually last up to three months; (2) group crisis intervention, which usually occurs after a traumatic event and consists of about three sessions; and (3) single-session crisis intervention with either individuals or groups lasting anywhere from 20 minutes to two hours. The meta-analysis revealed that although all three types of crisis intervention demonstrated effectiveness, there were larger effect sizes with family preservation methods than with group or single sessions.

The difficulty in evaluating the effectiveness of crisis intervention methods is the lack of built-in outcome measures (Regehr, 2011). The development and validation of the Crisis State Assessment Scale (CSAS) can assist in determining the effectiveness of crisis intervention methods as experienced by the client. The CSAS assesses the magnitude of the crisis state as perceived by the client by measuring two constructs: (1) perceived psychological trauma; and (2) perceived problems in coping efficacy (Lewis, 2005). Although there are other measurements and scales utilized in crisis intervention, such as the Beck Hopelessness Scale, the Beck Scale for Suicide Ideation, the Linehan Reasons for Living Scale, the Suicide Potential Lethality Scale and the Modified Scale for Suicide Ideation, the focus on suicide does not assess the extent to which individuals perceive a crisis or their ability to overcome the crisis (Roberts and Yeager, 2009). The development and validation of the CSAS can serve as a useful tool to determine the effectiveness of a crisis situation by measuring the individual's perceived level of crisis before and after the intervention.

Summary

Crisis intervention is a brief method which seeks to mobilize clients' strengths, resources and coping mechanisms in an attempt to overcome a crisis situation and improve clients' levels of coping, confidence and problem-solving skills. A crisis occurs when an individual's existing coping mechanisms are not sufficient to deal with a stressful or hazardous situation. There are no specific or predetermined crisis situations but, rather, a crisis situation is one that is perceived by the individual: one person's crisis is another person's challenge. Individuals who experience a crisis usually exhibit symptoms such as withdrawal, depression, agitation, anger, anxiety or possibly psychotic symptoms. The goal of crisis intervention is to assist individuals, families and/or communities in returning to a state of homeostasis where they are able to address challenging, stressful or hazardous events by utilizing their existing and newly identified strengths, resources and coping mechanisms. Roberts (2005) argues that a crisis experience may be traumatic for individuals but this experience can serve as an opportunity for growth and development. This chapter discussed and demonstrated how Roberts's (1991) seven-stage model can be used to assist social workers in working in a crisis situation with clients.

Case study

Caroline is a 19-year-old, white British, single mother of two children, aged 2 years and 4 months. Caroline and her two children live in a two-bedroom flat in a town approximately 30 minutes away from her family and friends. Caroline has minimal contact with the father of her children and he does not support her financially, nor does he visit or assist in caring for the children. Caroline has suffered from depression since she was 16 years old and has received counselling and support through her general practitioner's office, although Caroline has not seen the counsellor since she had her youngest child four months ago. One day, Caroline calls 999 and states that she needs help immediately as she 'can't take it any more'. Caroline is crying and reports that someone needs to come out and help her as she is afraid she is going to hurt her children. Caroline states, 'I can't do it any more. My baby won't stop crying. Someone better come out before I do something stupid!' You are a social worker who is called to report to the house with the police. Describe how you would implement the seven-stage crisis intervention model with Caroline.

Further reading

Regehr, C. (2011) Crisis theory and social work treatment, in F.J. Turner (ed.), *Social Work Treatment: Interlocking Theoretical Approaches*, 5th edn. Oxford: Oxford University Press.
An overview of implementing crisis intervention in social work practice with individuals, groups and communities.

Roberts, A.R. (ed.) (2005) *Crisis Intervention Handbook: Assessment, Treatment, and Research*, 3rd edn. New York: Oxford University Press.
A complete guide to crisis intervention, including an overview of the seven-stage crisis intervention model and guides to implementing crisis intervention with various client groups and in various settings.

Roberts, A.R. and Yeager, K.R. (2009) *Pocket Guide to Crisis Intervention*. New York: Oxford University Press.
A brief overview and guide to implementing crisis intervention.

References

Bott, E. (1976) Hospital and society, *British Journal of Medical Society*, 49(2): 97–140.

Caplan, G. (1961) *A Community Approach to Mental Health*. London: Tavistock.

Caplan, G. (1964) *Principles of Preventive Psychiatry*. New York: Basic Books.

Dziegielewski, S.F. and Powers, G.T. (2005) Designs and procedures for evaluating crisis intervention, in A.R. Roberts (ed.), *Crisis Intervention Handbook: Assessment, Treatment, and Research*, 3rd edn. New York: Oxford University Press.

Eaton, Y.M. and Roberts, A.R. (2009) Frontline crisis intervention, in A.R. Roberts (ed.), *Social Workers' Desk Reference*, 2nd edn. New York: Oxford University Press.

Everly, G.S. Jr, Lating, J.M. and Mitchell, J.T. (2005) Innovations in group crisis intervention, in A.R. Roberts (ed.), *Crisis Intervention Handbook: Assessment, Treatment, and Research*, 3rd edn. New York: Oxford University Press.

Golan, N. (1978) *Treatment in Crisis Situations*. New York: Free Press.

Greene, G.J., Lee, M.Y., Trask, R. and Rheinscheld, J. (2005) How to work with clients' strengths in crisis intervention: a solution-focused approach, in A.R. Roberts (ed.), *Crisis Intervention Handbook: Assessment, Treatment and Research*, 3rd edn. New York: Oxford University Press.

Lewis, S.J. (2005) The Crisis State Assessment Scale: development and psychometrics, in A.R. Roberts (ed.), *Crisis Intervention Handbook: Assessment, Treatment, and Research*, 3rd edn. New York: Oxford University Press.

Lindemann, E. (1944) Symptomatology and management of acute grief, in H.J. Parad (ed.), *Crisis Intervention, Selected Readings*. New York: Family Welfare Association.

O'Hagan, K. (1986) *Crisis Intervention in Social Services*. London: Macmillan.

O'Hagan, K. (1991) Crisis intervention: changing perspectives, in J. Lishman (ed.), *Handbook of Theory for Practice Teachers in Social Work*. London: Kingsley.

Parad, H.J. and Parad, L.G. (1990) *Crisis Intervention Book 2: The Practitioner's Sourcebook for Brief Therapy.* Milwaukee, WI: Family Service America.

Payne, M. (2005) *Modern Social Work Theory,* 3rd edn. Basingstoke: Palgrave Macmillan.

Rapoport, L. (1962) The state of crisis: some theoretical considerations, *Social Service Review,* 36(2): 211–17.

Rapoport, L. (1967) Crisis-oriented short-term casework, *Social Service Review,* 41(1): 31–43.

Regehr, C. (2011) Crisis theory and social work treatment, in F.J. Turner (ed.), *Social Work Treatment: Interlocking Theoretical Approaches,* 5th edn. Oxford: Oxford University Press.

Roberts, A.R. (1991) Conceptualizing crisis theory and the crisis intervention model, in A. Roberts (ed.), *Contemporary Perspectives on Crisis Intervention and Prevention.* Englewood Cliffs, NJ: Prentice Hall.

Roberts, A.R. (ed.) (2005) *Crisis Intervention Handbook: Assessment, Treatment, and Research,* 3rd edn. New York: Oxford University Press.

Roberts, A.R. and Everly, G.S. (2006) A meta-analysis of 36 crisis intervention studies, *Brief Treatment and Crisis Intervention,* 6(1): 10–21.

Roberts, A.R. and Yeager, K.R. (2009) *Pocket Guide to Crisis Intervention.* New York: Oxford University Press.

Rogers, C.R. (1957) The necessary and sufficient conditions of therapeutic personality change, *Journal of Counseling Psychology,* 21(2): 95–103.

Scott, D. (1974) Cultural frontiers in the mental health service, *Schizophrenia Bulletin,* 1(10): 58–73.

Skinner, J. (2013) Crisis theory, in M. Davies (ed.), *The Blackwell Companion to Social Work,* 4th edn. Chichester: John Wiley & Sons.

Thompson, N. (2011) *Crisis Intervention.* Lyme Regis: Russell House Publishing.

Wright, B. (1991) *Sudden Death: Intervention Skills for the Caring Professionals.* London: Churchill Livingstone.

13 Community work

Introduction

All of social work, to some extent, takes place within communities. This may involve a social worker delivering social services to a particular geographical location or to a group of individuals with a common characteristic or interest. Alternatively, it may involve a social worker working directly with community members to assess needs and provide community-based interventions. Regardless of the extent to which communities are engaged, an acknowledgement and consideration of communities are a fundamental aspect of social work practice. This is supported by the International Federation of Social Work's (IFSW) (2012) definition of social work which states that 'utilising theories of human behaviour and social systems, social work intervenes at the points where people interact with their environments'. Environments will inevitably consist of communities where individuals live and interact. Community work is defined as 'a set of approaches focused on understanding individuals as part of a community and on building the capacity of that community to address the social, economic or political challenges facing its members' (Healy, 2012, p. 169).

Communities are an important component when applying systems theory and the ecological perspective to social work practice, which requires social workers to take the focus of assessment and intervention beyond the individual or family to the external environment (i.e. communities) and to consider the ways in which communities are helping or hindering individual growth and development. Likewise, the focus of intervention may be extended beyond the immediate client-system (individual, family, group) into communities or the larger social, economic or political systems. The extent to which social workers participate in community work will vary based on their roles and perspectives. Some social workers may be tasked to work with individuals and families, but may incorporate aspects of community work in their assessment and intervention planning, while other social workers may have communities as their client base with a sole focus of working with communities to meet needs and reach goals. In this sense, community work can be a method that social workers incorporate into their existing role alongside other methods or as their single approach to their practice (Healy, 2012). This chapter reviews the history and application of community work to social work practice.

The origins of community work

Although social work's history is largely focused on individualism, there has been a long tradition of considering communities in social work practice. The origins of social work have been traced back to the Charitable Organization Society (COS) and the Settlement Movement (in the UK and US), which created community-based settlement houses such as Oxford House (founded in 1883), Toynbee Hall (founded in 1885) and Hull House (founded in 1889). Although the COS was more focused on assessing eligibility and on individuals, the settlement houses were focused on creating a community setting that provided social and educational activities for working-class individuals and immigrants.

During the twentieth century, social work and community work began to develop into two different strands of work. Social work took a stronger stance towards individual work, and in the UK, social work began to separate itself from the voluntary sector and move into statutory-run services. This was supported by the Seebohm Report of 1968 that led to the 1970 Local Authority Social Service Act which sought to have the delivery of social services be more reflective of the communities they served. The Act established social work as a profession that delivered statutory responsibilities. At the same time, community work began to develop as a specialist profession, and community workers were employed by statutory and voluntary sector organizations to work with communities to address local needs (Adams, 2010). Unfortunately, the presence of community workers and the role of communities in social services began to decline in the early to mid-1980s, particularly as government became resistant to the idea of community. This is most notably supported by the quote from Margaret Thatcher: 'There is no such thing as society. There are individual men and women, and there are families.' Community work and social work continued to diverge, which was particularly evident in the focus of training: governance, citizenship, community engagement, social capital, democracy and human rights for community workers and anti-discriminatory practice, user empowerment, inter-professional working and individual needs in social work (Teater and Baldwin, 2012).

The 1980s also served as a critical time for the role of community work within social work. The Barclay Committee reviewed social work (Barclay Report, 1982) and proposed community social work where social workers would be placed in communities ('patch-based social work') to work to address needs, provide support to members and build community resources. The focus was more on prevention rather than intervention with the goal of having communities utilize their resources first before becoming dependent on state support. Despite this idea, community social work was never fully implemented. The Griffiths Report (1988) also acknowledged links between local communities and statutory social services, which led to the NHS and Community Care Act 1990; this sought to enable individuals to remain living in communities for as long as possible. Although there appeared to be a community focus, the result of the Act was actually a stronger focus on individualism and marketization versus a focus on community or community work. Despite the push of a 'Big Society' after the Coalition government came into power, social work is still primarily focused on individuals.

Community work, as a separate activity from social work, is still present within the UK and can primarily be found in youth work, housing and planning and regeneration programmes being delivered by paid and unpaid community workers and activists (Mayo, 2009). Community work as a method is beginning to regain a place within social work in the UK, particularly through the radical social work movement, which is arguing for social work to go back to its roots and take a systems and ecological perspective that examines the social, economic and political factors that contribute to social injustice versus focusing solely on individuals (Ferguson and Woodward, 2009).

Community work explained

In order to understand community work, one must first have an understanding of the definition of 'community'. 'Community' is a debated and contested term, with over 90 different definitions in the literature (Cohen, 1985). The *Dictionary of Social Work* defines community as a term 'used to refer to a group of individuals with associated interests and/or common goals; the concept also describes social relationships within groups or territorial boundaries' (Pierson and Thomas, 2010, p. 104). As the definition highlights, community can be viewed as consisting of a geographical area where individuals in close proximity to one another constitute a community, such as a neighbourhood, a village in a rural area, a district or ward of an urban area, or a particular housing block or street. Community can also be viewed as individuals with shared characteristics, interests, culture or experiences despite location, such as individuals from a particular ethnic background, the deaf community, individuals with caring responsibilities, or those with specific religious beliefs. In this sense, community is not geographically determined. Communities of interest could even span across national boundaries, particularly through the aid of virtual resources. Healy (2012) divides the different types of community down even further to geographical communities, communities of association and identity-based communities. Communities of association constitute those individuals who have a common interest or concern and are linked together through formal associations (e.g. British Association of Social Workers), whereas identity-based communities are linked together through a common identity, characteristic or experience (e.g. deaf community) (Healy, 2012). For the purposes of this chapter, the following definition of community will be used: 'a group of people who are socially interdependent, who participate together in discussion and decision making, and who share certain practices that both define the community and are nurtured by it' (Bellah et al., 1985, p. 333). This definition points to community as more than a geographical place; rather, it is place where people interact through a network of relationships where they have a shared identity and a sense of well-being (Teater and Baldwin, 2012).

As there are variations within the definitions of community, there are also variations in what constitutes community work. All social work takes place within communities, but the extent to which the community is consulted, or is the target of intervention, varies greatly. The majority of social work practised today focuses on the individual, and possibly the immediate family, with little focus on the community in which the individual or family lives, and even less active interventions with such communities. Therefore, defining community work within the context of social work is difficult. Adams (2010) equally identifies the problem of defining community work as it could range from delivering services by the local authority to its community members, to holding a community development role where the worker actively engages with community members to develop or enhance a community. Despite such variations in community work, Adams (2010, p. 208) states that all aspects of community work should be 'political in nature' and 'concerned with the supply of resources to meet people's needs'. This is congruent with systems theory and the ecological perspective that very often underpins social work practice.

Twelvetrees (2008, p. 1) defines community work as 'the process of assisting people to improve their own communities by undertaking autonomous collective action'. This is a broad definition in that numerous activities could constitute community work. There are other titles and definitions of work with communities that span from providing education to communities to actively involving a community in assessing their needs. Table 13.1 provides a list of the different types of community work, with a brief description of each.

Table 13.1 Variations of community work

Type of community work	Definition
Community development work	Community members form, identify goals and work together to reach the goals. Goals are often focused on building social and economic capacity/capital (Midgley and Livermore, 2005)
Community profile	'A *comprehensive* description of the *needs* of a population that is defined, or defines itself, as a *community*, and the *resources* that exist within that community, carried out with the *active involvement of the community itself*, for the purpose of developing an *action plan* or other means of improving the quality of life of the community itself' (Hawtin and Percy-Smith, 2007, p. 5)
Community education	Aims to 'recognise and build the knowledge of a community by engaging community members as peer learners and teachers' (Healy, 2006, p. 259)
Community capacity building	'[T]he means by which communities build on their existing knowledge, skills and expertise and develop so as to meet the needs and priorities perceived as necessary by community members' (Adams, 2008, p. 161)
Community planning	Experts work with community members to identify community needs and develop a response to those needs. The expert is tasked with gathering and analysing data and providing solutions to meet the identified needs (Healy, 2012)
Community organizing	'[S]eek to redress the imbalance of social and economic power in society. Community organizers seek to mobilize disadvantaged citizens to recognize their shared oppression and take joint action to achieve a better deal for their communities' (Healy, 2012, p. 172)

Community social work	'[F]ormal social work which, starting from the problems affecting an individual or group and the responsibilities and resources of social services departments and voluntary organisations, seeks to tap into, support, enable and underpin the local networks of formal and informal relationships which constitute our basic definition of community, and also the strengths of a client's communities of interest' (Barclay Report, 1982, p. xvii)
Networking	'[A]n arrangement of relationships between people who are connected by virtue of such bonds as where they live, friendship links, ties as relatives, common occupations or leisure activities' (Adams, 2010, p. 212)

Just as there are typologies of community work, Twelvetrees (2008) described different dimensions of community work that serve as a continuum from one type of community work to another. Community workers are able to look at the dimensions and plot where they are in relation to a specific piece of work. Each of the dimensions is described below (Twelvetrees, 2008, pp. 3–7):

1 *Community development work 'versus' social planning.* Community development on one side of the continuum involves actively engaging community members and facilitating the process of community members identifying and working towards goals. Social planning, on the other end of the continuum, involves the community being bypassed where workers go directly to service providers to develop programmes to meet community needs or achieve community goals.

2 *Self-help/service approaches and influence approaches.* Many communities are full of resources that they can utilize to meet identified needs, which is categorized as self-help or service approaches. Other times, communities may need to draw upon the resources existing outside the community and may need assistance in accessing and receiving such resources, which is referred to as influence approaches.

3 *Generic and specialist community work.* Generic community workers have generic skills that can be applied to work with a variety of community sectors (e.g. employment, housing) and community members (e.g. children, older adults, women). Other community workers may have specialist knowledge and skills to work with a specific community group, such as knowledge of the health needs of particular community groups.

4 *Process and product, expressive and instrumental groups.* Community workers should identify whether the community they are working with are concerned with process goals (e.g. shared experiences and learning), or product goals (e.g. a tangible or material outcome) and should then facilitate the work accordingly. Expressive groups are mainly concerned with process, whereas instrumental groups are mainly concerned with product and need an established leader to reach the product goal.

5 *The facilitating (or enabling) role and the organizing role.* The community worker will need to establish her/his role within the community work. The role

may be one of facilitator, where the worker is more non-directive and moves at the community's pace, versus an organizing role where the worker is more directive and leads the group towards achieving the goal.

6   *Community work in its own right and community work as an attitude or approach.* Community workers may hold positions where community work is their main and only job, whereas other individuals, such as teachers, social workers, police officers or nurses may incorporate aspects of community work into their existing positions and roles.

7   *Unpaid and paid community work.* Some community workers are leaders or facilitators of local communities and are actively involved in moving communities towards goals, yet are not employed or paid as a community worker. Many paid community workers are responsible to their employers and have to adhere to their job description and the policies of their employing agencies, as well as have the necessary skills to be a community worker.

Community work is an important and useful method within social work practice. In particular, social workers are expected to assess and intervene with individuals, families and groups by considering the environment and the surrounding social, political and cultural systems that impact, influence and shape clients. The exact approach that social workers may take in their practice will vary along the dimensions of community work as described above. In implementing aspects of community work, social workers should uphold the two basic assumptions that underpin community work as described by Ife (2002):

1   *Change comes from below.* Community members should be active participants in identifying needs, establishing goals and working to meet the goals. The change that is to take place needs to come from the community members themselves, and not be imposed by outside individuals.

2   *The processes are just as important as the outcomes.* Community members should be actively engaged in the process that leads to the outcome of achieving their defined goals. Equal consideration and attention should be paid to the process and the outcome, particularly as the process can be an opportunity to enhance the knowledge, skills, resources and strengths of the community, which can serve as useful tools as the community grows and develops.

Exercise box 13.1   How can community work fit into your practice?

1   What are the communities that you work with (or should work with) within your placement/practice?
2   How will you – or how could you – engage these communities?
3   What would be the benefits and challenges to engaging the communities? (Consider the communities, the clients, you and your agency.)

Stages and skills of community work

Communities can be engaged in a variety of ways within social work practice. This could range from social workers including communities in the assessment of individuals, communicating with community members to determine the extent to which a social service agency is meeting the community's needs, or social workers undertaking community work through their employment in community-based organizations. Although there are varying degrees to which a social worker can undertake community work, some individuals may find a more staged approach useful in explaining community work. The following details the stages of community work as best described by Healy (2012, pp. 179–99), with additional stages included from the writings of Adams (2010, p. 211) and Mayo (2009, p. 133):

1   *Focus on community practice.* The first stage in community work is for the worker to consider the areas of work where community practice can take place. This assessment of the work and consideration of integrating communities into practice should be examined against relevant theories, such as systems theory and the ecological perspective. Reviewing these theories in light of the work can potentially highlight where communities should be considered during assessment and intervention stages of your practice (Adams, 2010).

2   *Meeting and engaging with community members.* This stage involves meeting with community members to begin to build a relationship and to engage in partnership working. Workers might begin to ask about, and discuss with community members, their experiences, strengths, resources, wishes and goals. The worker must have a useful purpose for engaging the community and be able to relay this purpose of the interaction and relationship to the community members. The worker will need to ensure that a wide range of community members is engaged as often some members of a community may not necessarily identify with the community or may not be aware that the community exists. Including a variety of members will provide a more accurate representation of the whole community. Healy (2012) states that this stage can be broken into two phases:

   (a) *Preplanning* This phase involves the worker gathering knowledge and information about the community and its members prior to the initial meeting, as well as establishing the worker's role and purpose. According to Healy (2012, p. 180), this could be achieved by observing the community, talking with informed community members, reviewing agency documents, and exploring media sources. A preplanning phase can enhance the credibility of the worker and the worker's understanding of the community and their needs (Healy, 2012).

   (b) *Meeting the community* This phase involves the worker meeting community members in order to have a mutual understanding of the worker's role and the community's strengths, resources and needs. This mutual information-sharing phase can involve the worker being present at community forums or meeting places, the worker distributing information about her/his role through leaflets, newsletters, agencies accessed by the community, media and virtual sources, or holding meetings in public places (e.g. parks) in order to meet the community members (Healy, 2012). Healy (2012, p. 182) suggests several strategies for meeting the community. These include: meeting in a neutral place, providing food and refreshments, demonstrating that the worker has knowledge of the community and their strengths and potential needs, informing as many community members as possible about attending (including those from diverse backgrounds), and ensuring resources are available to address any community members' support needs, such as transportation, access and caring needs.

3 *Assessment and sharing ideas.* This stage consists of an assessment, where the community is actively involved in identifying strengths, resources, needs, wishes and potential goals. A community profile could be useful in this stage (see Table 13.1). According to Healy (2012, p. 183), resources are 'those capacities or forms of capital that exist in the community and that contribute to improving the quality of life in the community. These resources can include human and social capital, such as schools and community associations, as well as businesses and physical infrastructure, such as buildings.' A useful tool in identifying community capital and resources is Hart's (1999) community capital triangle (see www.sustainablemeasures.com for a visual depiction and further explanation of the triangle). The triangle's foundation is natural capital, which can consist of natural resources (food, water), ecosystem services (oxygen, water filtration), and the beauty of nature (seashores, mountains). Human and social capital is built upon the natural capital and consists of people (skills, education, abilities) and connections (family, neighbours, government). Finally, the built capital is at the top of the triangle and consists of human-made material, such as buildings, information and infrastructure. As communities are the experts in their strengths and resources, they should be actively engaged in the assessment of their strengths, resources and needs (Healy, 2012).

If you are unable to conduct a full community profile in the assessment stage, due to time and resources, you can rely on other sources of information, such as local and national statistics, or on gathering information directly from community members through surveys, focus groups, community forums or participatory action research (PAR) (see Kindon et al., 2007). Regardless of the methods chosen to gather the information, community members should be involved as and where appropriate in order to ensure the information gathered is shared between the worker and community members and the analyses/ assessment accurately reflects their experiences and desires for a way forward that is owned by the community (Adams, 2010). Despite the ways in which information is gathered to complete the assessment, the assessment and findings of any research should be presented in a way that will 'maximize its accessibility to a range of community members'; it should be written in clear, simple, jargon-free language, have an easy-to-follow structure, a short executive summary, give a summary of the key messages and findings, contain visual images, and use professional printing services, where possible (Healy, 2012, pp. 190–1).

4   *Developing and implementing an action plan.* Once the assessment has been completed with all strengths, resources, needs, wishes and goals identified, the next stage should be the development of an action plan. This could include an identification of goals and the proposed steps to reach those goals, or could include the development of a community project or intervention. The development of the action plan should involve the active participation of the community members. This can be maximized by either holding a public meeting, with as many subgroups of the community as possible attending to ensure all views of the community are heard and considered, and/or holding action meetings with subgroups within the community, to enable the worker to 'better match the facilitation process to specific subgroups' (Healy, 2012, p. 191). Healy (2012) states that the worker may need to incorporate creative approaches to developing the action plan in order to engage as many members as possible. A SWOT analysis may be one way to engage communities; it consists of members detailing the (S)trengths and (W)eaknesses of the community, or the factors within their control, as well as the (O)pportunities and (T)hreats to the community from the external environment (Weil et al., 2010).

   An agreed action plan should consist of short- and long-term goals, with priority given to goals which the community members are most motivated to achieve, and should have agreement and support from as many community members as possible (Healy, 2012). Once the action plan is agreed, the worker should help to implement the action plan either as the established facilitator, or by supporting a community member who takes on the facilitation role. In maximizing the successful implementation of the action plan, Healy (2012) suggests that a broad cross section of the community have information of the plan and are encouraged to participate. Information can be shared to all community members through word of mouth, virtual sources, or through places that community members visit or attend.

5   *Evaluation: reviewing achievements and future aspirations.* Although evaluation of the community work takes place at the end, it needs to be considered from the very beginning. An evaluation can include a focus on the process of community work, which examines how community members were engaged and their experiences; the outcome of the work, which refers to the changes (e.g. knowledge, attitudes, economic, social, physical) within the community; and/or the output of the work, which refers to any resources or materials that were created because of the work (e.g. manuals, DVDs, guides) (Healy, 2012). An evaluation of the work could include quantitative or qualitative research methods, and Healy (2012) suggests the use of both in order to capture numerical data (such as attendance at meetings) as well as experiential data (such as the experiences of members being engaged). The evaluation can be useful for the community, but also for the agency of the community worker and any

potential funding bodies (Healy, 2012). The evaluation may also indicate that further work is needed within the community, which can lead the worker to engage with the community through stages 3 through 5 again (Adams, 2010).

As stages 1 through 5 demonstrate, many resources and skills are required of an individual participating in community work. Initial resources often include a meeting space, time and financial resources. A list of necessary skills for a worker engaged in community work can be found in Table 13.2, which highlights skills for effective community work and gives a brief explanation of each skill's purpose.

Table 13.2   Skills for effective community work

Skills	Purpose
Engagement and partnership working	To begin to build a relationship with the community and gain the community's trust in working together
Assessment	To determine the community's strengths, resources, needs and/or areas for development
Research and evaluation	To gather a picture of the community and its needs, as well as evaluate the work together
Groupwork	To engage community group members. To understand and identify the stages of groupwork and the different roles of community group members
Negotiation	To resolve conflicting and competing views and ensure the voices of all community members are listened to and considered
Communication	Verbal and nonverbal communication skills that can engage and involve a diverse group of community members
Counselling	To resolve conflict and differences between group members. To listen and address sensitive topics and situations. To encourage participation by all community members considering difference and diversity
Organizational	To adhere to timelines and deadlines. To be viewed as reliable, trustworthy and competent within the community and to oneself
Resourcing	To identify ways in which to access resources, such as time, materials and money
Record and report writing	To keep an accurate account of activities. To monitor progress and evaluate the work. To report difficulties and successes to funders

Sources: Healy (2012); Mayo (2009).

Case example: applying community work to practice

You are a social worker working in an older adult services team. You conduct individual assessments to determine whether an older adult would be eligible for social services, which often includes providing in-home support and care to meet basic health and social care needs. Over time, you have noticed that funding has been reduced, and the threshold for services increased, leaving many older adults ineligible for assistance until their needs are critical or substantial. You also have noticed that one particular socially and economically deprived neighbourhood (Highland Court) has a large number of single older adults who are considered socially isolated and excluded. You believe that Highland Court could benefit from community-based preventative programmes to reduce social isolation, which in turn could reduce the number of older adults accessing social services or delaying their need for services *(focus on community practice)*. You bring this to the attention of your team manager who agrees that the development of community-based preventative programmes would be a useful resource, particularly to those older adults who are socially isolated and excluded in Highland Court, but there is little funding to support such programmes. The team manager agrees to give you a half-day a week to develop preventative, community-based programmes in Highland Court, and agrees to provide £300 to fund the initial work.

You begin by identifying the 'community' as individuals over 65 years old who live in Highland Court, including individuals who are socially isolated as well as those who are not. In the *preplanning phase* you conduct research into the effects of social isolation for older adults and gather social and economic data on Highland Court from the latest census data in order to gain a clearer picture of the community. Given the time and resources for the work, you decide that you will engage in an aspect of *community development work* where you will work with community members to identify needs and develop programmes to meet the needs. Although you are taking the lead in terms of identifying needs and developing preventative community-based programmes, you aim to actively engage community members in the work.

You *meet the community* by visiting the local community centre where community members attend a luncheon club, introduce yourself, and discuss what you hope to achieve. Then you ask the members if they would be willing to assist you in identifying the needs of the community and developing a programme to create a stronger sense of community involvement and cohesion, thus reducing social isolation. You discuss with the present members how to best reach those individuals who do not regularly attend the luncheon club in order to gain their views and opinions and to encourage them to be involved. The members are interested in the work and nominate five members to serve as the steering group to assist you in assessing the community for needs, engaging and soliciting the views of those members who are more socially isolated and do not attend the luncheon club, and reporting back to the larger community group to develop ideas for programmes. You arrange to come back to the luncheon club in two weeks to begin the assessment. You agree to make flyers inviting all community members to the meeting, and the steering group agrees to distribute the flyers and to personally encourage the more socially isolated individuals by going door to door. In one week's time, you and the steering group meet at the community centre to discuss progress, and are able to provide tea and coffee for each of the steering group meetings.

Returning to the luncheon club two weeks later you find that many more community members have attended. You begin the *assessment and sharing ideas* stage, where the steering group reports on the progress of informing all the members about the project and any difficulties in reaching 'hard-to-reach' groups. Using flipchart paper, you ask the members to list the strengths and resources of their community. The members are asked to consider natural capital, such as parks, nature and land; human and social capital, such as skills, abilities and specialist knowledge; and built capital, such as centres and meeting spaces. The members are then asked to consider their needs, wishes and goals for their community. You encourage them to think about programmes that can be implemented within the community to encourage participation and community cohesion that could involve using their strengths and resources. At the end of the meeting, you agree to go away and summarize the strengths, resources, needs, wishes and goals to bring to the next meeting in two weeks. The steering group also agrees to visit other members that did not attend the meeting to gather their views and opinions and to report back at the next steering group meeting in one week's time.

Once the assessment is complete and agreed by the members at the next meeting, you begin to *develop and implement an action plan* with the community members. The members have identified goals of more creative programmes within the community, such as singing and gardening. The members have also identified that some members may not be able to attend such programmes and requested a befriending service to visit the members in their own home. Some of the more able-bodied community members express an interest in providing this service. You and the steering group agree to research possible singing, gardening and befriending programmes, as well as the community members developing their own programmes by acting as leaders or providing the befriending service themselves. Over the next few weeks, you and the steering group have identified a community singing club delivered by a local charity that comes to the community centre once a week for one hour. A community member has agreed to lead and facilitate a community garden in the local park with the local government's permission. You have engaged with the local older adults charity to provide befriending services, and many of the community members have agreed to sign up with the charity to provide the befriending service in Highland Court. You agree to end the work with the community, but will check in at the community centre from time to time in your social work role to see how things are progressing. You have also agreed with your team manager to track data on the number of older adults from the Highland Court area that are assessed for services to determine if there has been a decrease in need for social services *(evaluation)*.

You visit the community centre six months after the initiation of the programmes and the members report that the programmes are still running, the number of members participating has increased, and the community is growing stronger by members becoming friends with one another and interacting in other activities.

Strengths and limitations

There are several strengths and limitations to implementing community work in social work practice. The strengths include the following:

- Community work is underpinned by social work values, particularly social justice, empowerment and anti-oppressive practice. Community work seeks to create change through working with local groups to address and challenge social, economic and political structures that are limiting or blocking access to resources and are leading to oppression, poverty, racism and exclusion (Coulshed and Orme, 2012).
- Community work is a way for social workers to employ systems theory and the ecological perspective. It can allow social workers to assess systems beyond individuals and families and plan interventions, where necessary, into these systems.
- Community work enables social workers to assess both individual need and collective need. Working with individuals who are community members can enable individuals to meet their own needs, but also the collective needs of the community. Meeting individual and collective needs can enable the community to build stronger resources and have a greater sense of empowerment to tackle problems that may arise in the future.
- Community work is congruent with social work knowledge and skills. Social workers should possess the necessary skills for community work, such as networking, assessment, negotiating, inter-professional practice, research, groupwork, communication, counselling, information sharing and workload management, which will enhance their ability and effectiveness when engaging and working with communities.

Some of the limitations of community work are as follows:

- Social work is predominately focused on working with individuals. Many social workers adopt a more individualistic approach to their work, causing them to fail to see the importance of community work. Social workers should be reminded of the importance of seeing individuals within their environment and how communities can help or hinder individual growth and development.
- Engaging with communities and participating in community work requires time and resources that are often scarce within social work agencies. Despite the lack of resources, social workers can be creative in their approaches to engaging communities, such as using virtual mediums (e.g. Facebook), using existing data publicly available to assess the potential needs of a community, or holding lunchtime forums in a public park.
- Despite community work being anti-oppressive in nature, some individuals within communities experience oppression and exclusion. Likewise, some groups within communities may compete against one another for access to limited resources. Social workers should be mindful of the various groups within communities and the extent to which they are involved and active, or ignored and marginalized. Social workers should aim to solicit the views and involvement from a cross-section of the community, particularly seeking the voices and experiences of those that are marginalized.

Ethical and cultural considerations

There are ethical and cultural considerations when incorporating community work into social work practice. First, communities constitute a group of individuals who are brought together due to either a geographical location or a common interest, yet there are most likely going to be variations among the group members in terms of cultures, experiences and beliefs. Workers should be mindful of differences between communities and within communities, and should gather as much information about the culture of a community before beginning the work together (pre-planning phase). Any cultural rituals or beliefs should be incorporated into the work together, where appropriate. Second, community work involves workers engaging with communities and working together to identify strengths, resources, needs and goals. In working together, workers will need to ensure that they keep their desires, wishes and beliefs secondary to the community's. This is not to say that workers cannot share their opinions, knowledge or expertise in a particular area, but true community work will aim to have the community's wishes and desires at the forefront with workers facilitating or assisting the community in reaching their goals. There may be times when workers feel tension between their aims for the work and those of the community and, at these times, they should be open and honest with the community about their thoughts and aims and should attempt to reach an agreement about how best to move forward. The work should be stopped if it will involve the worker having to go against the social work profession's values and principles. Third, there may be times when workers are tasked with delivering pieces of work from employing agencies that are not congruent with the community's desires or aims. Again, an open and honest conversation between the worker and community should take place to determine the best course of action for the work together, which might include modifications to the work or that the worker needs to remove her/himself from the project. Finally, if workers are employed to work with the community then any issues of power imbalances between the worker and the community should be made explicit from the beginning of the work, and an agreed plan developed for carrying the work forward, while acknowledging (and attempting to diminish, where possible) the power imbalance.

Community work and anti-oppressive practice

Community work is fundamentally anti-oppressive in nature in that it seeks to challenge the social, economic and political structures that are hindering the community from growing and developing. The role of the worker is to work with communities to meet needs and achieve goals, and this often means encouraging the community to have the power in this process. Although community work aims to be empowering, there are times that the power within the community may be with a select majority of the members who dominate the process and do not represent the views of all the members of the community (Coulshed and Orme, 2012). It is important for workers to identify when this power imbalance might take place, and to encourage the views of all members, particularly those who are segregated, marginalized and oppressed, to be heard and considered. Workers need to be mindful of such situations and need to actively engage and encourage the involvement of all members of the community, which might mean being creative in how some members are engaged and involved. Healy (2012, p. 192) gives several ideas of creative approaches to involving members, such as: holding an 'ideas festival' or 'think tank' in the community, where community members come together and share ideas; using community arts approaches to facilitate community involvement; and/or facilitating field visits to other communities to observe strategies used in those communities. Additionally, an anti-oppressive approach to community work would consider the resources needed for community members to be involved and able to participate, such as transportation, access to childcare, time of day and location of events (Healy, 2012).

Research on community work

Developing the effectiveness of community work depends on the type of methods that are employed and the effectiveness of those methods. Community-based methods or interventions include a wide range of activities with a varying evidence base. Knapp et al. (2012) reviewed the literature to examine the effectiveness and usefulness of three types of community-based methods, or interventions, to determine whether they would be useful for social work and social care. From the review, Knapp et al. (2012) found that *time banks* (see www.timebanking.org) had economic and well-being benefits of individuals gaining employment and skills, an increase in confidence and self-esteem, a reduction in benefit claims and a reduction in social isolation. *Befriending* was found to reduce social isolation and depression, health visits and falls among older people (Knapp et al., 2012). Finally, *community navigators*, who provide emotional, social and practical support to vulnerable individuals, were found to reduce depression associated with financial debt, which can lead to individuals accessing services earlier and more appropriately (Knapp et al., 2012). The authors also found the three community-based services to be economical in that they could yield benefits over and above the cost to the public to run the services.

Other studies that have examined different community-based methods include the individual, social and community benefits of community gardening (Ohmer et al., 2009), service learning projects (Chupp and Joseph, 2010; Stoecker et al., 2010) and the involvement of community members in identifying needs and services (Craig, 2011; Wang, 2006).

Summary

This chapter has examined how community work could be incorporated into social work practice. All of social work, to some extent, takes place within a community, and social workers should have knowledge of how communities can influence and shape individuals and families. The chapter has described how community work can include a wide range of activities, from community education to community-based research, and how workers may take on varying roles, from consulting with communities about community needs to facilitating a community project. Social workers are well equipped to engage with communities in their practice as systems theory and the ecological perspective guide social work practice and encourage social workers to consider individuals and families within their environments. Social workers are also equipped with the necessary skills to engage and work with communities. The chapter has provided a step-by-step approach to community work that social workers can adapt to best fit their practice.

Case study

You are a social worker working in a looked after children's (LAC) team within a child and family social services organization. The organization is located within a mid-size urban area, yet places children in foster homes across the city and in rural areas. You have noticed an increase in gay, lesbian, bisexual, transgendered and questioning (GLBTQ) youth on your team's caseload. You acknowledge this increase at the team meeting, and the team questions whether the services provided by the team are adequately meeting the needs of GLBTQ youth, particularly in rural areas where services are often scarce. The team manager agrees to provide you with some additional time and a small amount of financial resources (£500) to engage with GLBTQ youth to assess their needs (as a community) and to develop any support services in order to address any identified gaps in their needs being met. The manager has requested that you report back to the team in three months time. Describe how you could engage in community work to assess the needs of GLBTQ youth, and how you would include the youth in your assessment and development of new services. Consider the type of community work that would be most useful given the time and resources, as well as the necessary skills, in order for you to complete the piece of work.

Further reading and web resources

Association for Community Organization and Social Administration (ACOSA) – a membership organization and information site for community organizers, activists, non-profit administrators, community builders, policy practitioners, students and educators – http://www.acosa.org/joomla/

Hardcastle, D.A. (2011) *Community Practice: Theories and Skills for Social Workers*, 3rd edn. New York: Oxford University Press.
A complete guide to the theories and skills for social workers who wish to engage in community practice.

Journal of Community Practice – publishes theoretically and empirically based journal articles that address community practice. An overview of the journal can be found at: www.acosa.org/joomla/journalinfo

Teater, B. and Baldwin, M. (2012) *Social Work in the Community: Making a Difference.* Bristol: Policy Press.
Provides an overview of the historical and political context of community work as well as a review of different types of social work in the community.

Twelvetrees, A. (2008) *Community Work*, 4th edn. Basingstoke: Palgrave Macmillan.
Provides an overview of the different types of community work.

References

Adams, R. (2008) *Empowerment, Participation and Social Work*. Basingstoke: Palgrave Macmillan.

Adams, R. (2010) *The Short Guide to Social Work*. Bristol: Policy Press.

Barclay Report (1982) *Social Workers: Their Roles and Tasks*, London: National Institute for Social Work.

Bellah, R.N., Madsen, R.D., Sullivan, W.M., Swidler, A. and Tipton, S.M. (1985) *Habits of the Heart: Individualism and Commitment in American Life*. Berkeley, CA: University of California Press.

Chupp, M.G. and Joseph, M.L. (2010) Getting the most out of service learning: maximizing student, university and community impact, *Journal of Community Practice*, 18(2/3): 190–212.

Cohen, A.P. (1985) *The Symbolic Construction of Community*. New York: Tavistock and Ellis Horwood.

Coulshed, V. and Orme, J. (2012) *Social Work Practice*, 5th edn. Basingstoke: Palgrave Macmillan.

Craig, S.L. (2011) Precarious partnerships: Designing a community needs assessment to develop a system of care for gay, lesbian, bisexual, transgender and questioning (GLBTQ) youths, *Journal of Community Practice*, 19(3): 274–91.

Ferguson, I. and Woodward, R. (2009) *Radical Social Work in Practice: Making a Difference*. Bristol: Policy Press.

Griffiths Report (1988) *Community Care: Agenda for Action.*, London: HMSO.

Hart, M. (1999) *Guide to Sustainable Community Indicators*, 2nd edn. North Andover, MA: Hart Environmental Data.

Hawtin, M. and Percy-Smith, J. (2007) *Community Profiling: A Practical Guide*. Maidenhead: Open University Press.

Healy, K. (2006) Community education, in A. O'Hara and Z. Weber (eds), *Skills for Human Services Practice: Working with Individuals, Communities and Organisations*. Melbourne: Oxford University Press.

Healy, K. (2012) *Social Work Methods and Skills: The Essential Foundations of Practice*. Basingstoke: Palgrave Macmillan.

Ife, J. (2002) *Community Development: Community-based Alternatives in an Age of Globalisation*. French Forest, New South Wales: Longman.

International Federation of Social Work (IFSW) (2012) *Statement of Ethical Principles*. http://ifsw.org/policies/statement-of-ethical-principles/ (accessed 24 June 2013).

Kindon, S., Pain, R. and Kesby, M. (eds) (2007) *Participatory Action Research Approaches and Methods: Connecting People, Participation and Place*. Abingdon: Routledge.

Knapp, M., Bauer, A., Perkins, M. and Snell, T. (2012) Building community capital in social care: is there an economic case?, *Community Development Journal*, 48(2): 313–31.

Mayo, M. (2009) Community work, in R. Adams, L. Dominelli and M. Payne (eds), *Critical Practice in Social Work*, 2nd edn. Basingstoke: Palgrave Macmillan.

Midgley, J. and Livermore, M. (2005) Development theory and community practice, in M. Weil (ed.), *The Handbook of Community Practice*. Thousand Oaks, CA: Sage Publications.

Ohmer, M.L., Meadowcroft, P., Freed, K. and Lewis, E. (2009) Community gardening and community development: individual, social and community benefits of a community conservation program, *Journal of Community Practice*, 17(4): 377–99.

Pierson, J. and Thomas, M. (2010) *Dictionary of Social Work*. Maidenhead: Open University Press.

Stoecker, R., Loving, K., Reddy, M. and Bollig, N. (2010) Can community-based research guide service learning?, *Journal of Community Practice*, 18(2/3): 280–96.

Teater, B. and Baldwin, M. (2012) *Social Work in the Community: Making a Difference.* Bristol: Policy Press.

Twelvetrees, A. (2008) *Community Work*, 4th edn. Basingstoke: Palgrave Macmillan.

Wang, C.C. (2006) Youth participation in photovoice as a strategy for community change, *Journal of Community Practice*, 14(1/2): 147–61.

Weil, M., Gamble, D.N. and MacGuire, E. (2010) *Community Practice Skills Workbook: Local to Global Perspectives*. New York: Columbia University Press.

14 Groupwork

Introduction

Groupwork is a fundamental aspect of social work practice. It can serve as an explicit method employed with a client group, or can be implicitly used when working with groups of individuals, such as family work or community work, or when interacting and working within a social work team. All individuals, to some extent, operate within groups. This could include groups of people such as families, friends, school peers, work colleagues or recreational groups and teams. In this sense, 'groups are central to human experience' (Doel, 2013, p. 376). Groups can serve as a source of support and mutual aid and a place where individuals can grow and develop individually and collectively. Groupwork within social work practice can serve as a useful method to fostering mutual aid among a group of individuals who share a common characteristic, trait or experience. Within groupwork, the group is the primary source of change (International Association for Social Work with Groups (IASWG), 2013a) and the aim is to create an environment where the group can work together to achieve common goals. Groupwork is a flexible method that can range from being highly structured and time limited, to being informal and open ended, and can be combined with a wide range of other social work methods (e.g. motivational interviewing; task-centred social work; solution-focused practice). This chapter will provide an overview of groupwork by discussing the theory and rationale behind it, the types of groupwork, the group processes, and the practicalities of starting and running a group.

The origins of groupwork

Groupwork as a method within social work practice stems from the early work of predominately Christian groups in the late eighteenth and early nineteenth centuries. Group-based activities, such as Sunday schooling, ragged schooling, the YMCA and the boys' and girls' clubs, aimed to bring Christianity to individuals, as well as combat some of the social conditions affecting individuals, groups and communities (Smith, 2004). During the nineteenth century, other mutual aid groups began to develop through meeting houses, working men's clubs, scouting, club work of the Settlement movement, youth work and adult education. Such clubs and activities had a central focus on groups, which contrasted from the Charity Organisation Society's (COS) common focus on the individual. There was an emphasis on working together, learning from one another and working towards common goals. Adult education, in particular, through the work of Basil Yeaxlee and Edward Lindeman, had a specific focus on group processes (Smith, 2004). The focus on groupwork as a method has developed since this time, particularly through psychological and sociological theorists, such as Charles Horton Cooley's 'small group theory', Robert McIuer's 'inter-group relations', George Herbert Mead's 'notion of the social self', and youth workers and community workers, such as Josephine Macalister Brew and Josephine Kelin (Smith, 2004).

Groupwork began to emerge within social work in the 1930s and became prominent as a method in the 1960s. The emergence of social service departments in the UK in the 1970s came with a focus on groupwork as a method with young people, family services and mental health work (Doel, 2013, p. 369). Groupwork was a topic of numerous textbooks and *Groupwork*, a British journal, was started to give specific attention to groupwork practice (Ward, 2009). Since this time, there has been a sharp decrease in the use and availability of groupwork within social work practice (Drumm, 2006), which Ward (2009, p. 116) states was caused by a drive towards specialization of social workers versus generic training, a stronger focus on the law and social workers having legal responsibilities, and the impact of 'new managerialism' with the focus on measurable outcomes not the methods of practice. The result was a social work focus on the individual and individual need versus groups and community or collective need (Teater and Baldwin, 2012). This has resulted in groupwork practice being delivered by other professionals, such as counsellors, occupational therapists (OT) and nurses, or by workers within the voluntary and not-for-profit sectors. Despite this, groupwork is still a method used commonly in social work practice, and the prevalence of groupwork will most likely increase as social workers move into the voluntary sector and become more creative in statutory-run services.

Groupwork explained

In order to apply groupwork to practice, one must first have an understanding of a 'group'. A group has been defined as 'a collection of people who spend some time together, who see themselves as members of a group and who are identified as members by outsiders' (Preston-Shoot, 2007, p. 46). Adams (2010, p. 205) goes further by specifying a minimum number of people to create a group: 'a group is defined as three or more people who interact together and are perceived by themselves and others as sharing experiences'. A common feature across many definitions of a group is the shared characteristic – the trait of experience that ties and binds the individuals together. Groupwork is the practice of bringing individuals together who share a common characteristic, trait or experience, to share their experiences, receive mutual aid and foster individual, but more importantly, collective change.

Social work practice often involves working with groups. This could be a social worker working with a family, within a residential or day centre, with children in residential care, running groups with specific populations (such as individuals who misuse substances), or helping individuals to set up and run a self-help group (Adams, 2010). Each of these examples will require social workers to have an understanding of group processes and dynamics, as well as the necessary skills to prepare a group, engage and work with group members through the beginning, middle and ending phases.

The practice of groupwork is underpinned by groupwork theories that draw on social psychology, such as social modelling and behavioural modification. Groupwork theory holds the assumption that groups create an environment where individuals can collectively influence each other by disclosing their experiences, providing advice and information on successful coping strategies, and providing feedback and advice to others. The group members learn from each other through disclosure and receiving feedback about their own behaviours and advice on new behaviours. Individuals may modify their behaviours based on the feedback they receive from the group. Groups can also serve as a safe place where individuals disclose information about themselves with others who have similar experiences and can learn from the struggles and the successes of each member. Lindsay and Orton (2008, p. 7) define groupwork as 'a method of social work that aims, in an informed way, through purposeful group experiences, to help individuals and groups to meet individual and group need, and to influence and change personal, group, organisational and community problems'.

Adams (2010, p. 206) specifies three main types of groups: *problem-focused*, which includes therapeutic, helping or self-help groups; *development*, which focuses on educational and personal development; and *awareness raising*, which aims to increase the members' knowledge and understanding of a topic or issue. Groups can fall into one of the three types of groups, or a group can fall across the three types. For example, a group that focuses specifically on substance misuse may be considered a problem-focused group, a group that focuses on enhancing self-esteem may be classified as a development group, and a group that focuses on assertiveness training for survivors of domestic violence may include aspects of development and awareness raising. Doel (2006, pp. 23–4) further specifies the types of groups by proposing their seven different functions: consultative, educational, social action, social control, social support, task and therapeutic. Again, the groups may incorporate several types of functions, such as being task oriented while providing a therapeutic aspect. Regardless of the type or function of the group, groupwork can offer the members mutual aid and support, an opportunity to exchange information, learn and test skills, create a sense of belonging, and provide an opportunity to test new ways of thinking, feeling and behaving while receiving feedback from the group members (Coulshed, 1991).

Exercise box 14.1   How do groups help?

In pairs or small groups, think about a group you belong to, and answer the following:

1   What are the benefits of being a member of this group?
2   What are the challenges of being a member of this group?
3   How, and what, do you contribute to the group?

Table 14.1   Principles of a social work group

Principle	
Inclusion and respect all	Each member is encouraged to participate with views respected
Mutual aid	Individuals should acknowledge and respond to their own needs as well as the needs of others. Individuals support and assist one another
Stage management	Groupworkers should acknowledge and pay attention to the stages of group development. Interventions should be implemented at the appropriate stages of development
Use of conflict	Groupworkers should highlight any conflict for the group to acknowledge, explore and resolve
Conscious development, use, and implications of purpose	Groups should continually focus on their purpose, which may develop and change over the course of the group. It is important for the group to have consensus over the group's purpose
Breaking taboos	Groupworkers may need to bring to the surface topics that group members might see as shameful, deviant or abnormal. This might involve saying 'the things people have the hardest time saying, and naming the "pink elephants" in the room' (p. 21)
Value of activity	Groupworkers should select from a variety of activities that best meet the learning styles of the group members
Problem-solving	Groupworkers should allow group members to explore problems and develop solutions to problems. Groupworkers should avoid solving problems for the group

Source: Drumm (2006, pp. 20–2)

Social workers often work with individuals and groups who have had, or are continuing to experience, difficult situations. Groupwork can serve as a useful method of bringing individuals together to share and learn from one other. The group experience can enable individuals to realize they are not alone, and any thoughts and feelings may be similar to the other members. The knowledge and skills learned and developed within the group can then be transferred to client's lives outside the group, in their natural environment (Coulshed and Orme, 2012). Groupwork facilitators (referred to in this chapter as groupworkers) are often then tasked with bringing the common experiences, truth and conflicts (Drumm, 2006) to the surface so members can work on and through difficulties in an effort to resolve problems and achieve goals. Table 14.1 summarizes a list provided by Drumm (2006, pp. 20–2) of the principles necessary for a group to be considered a *social work group*.

Types of groups

Groupwork can take place within many different types of groups. Social workers using groupwork as a method will need to determine the type of group that would be most beneficial to the client group and to the overall purpose of the group. Doel (2013, p. 371) detailed 12 dimensions in which to profile groups, adapted from Doel and Sawdon (1999, pp. 73–4). The dimensions can be used to describe the overall characteristics of a group and can assist in the planning of a group. They are outlined below, and include specific traits that run along a continuum:

1   Group history – A group may be slightly adapted from an *existing group* or may be *created* or planned from scratch.
2   Joining and leaving – A group may be *open* to membership where anyone can join and leave at any time, or *closed*, with membership being confined to a specific group of individuals.
3   Group mix – A group may allow for *difference* among the members, such as a difference in ages or sex, or may specify that the group members have *sameness*, such as females only.
4   Leadership – A group may be led by the group members themselves (*self-help*) or may be led by a groupworker (*practitioner-led*).
5   Duration – A group may run continually with no end date (*open-ended*) versus *time-limited*, where the number of sessions is specified.
6   Extent – The length of each group session may be considered *long*, such as several hours, or *short*, such as 30 minutes.
7   Interval – The group may meet very *seldom*, such as monthly, versus *frequently*, such as three times a week.
8   Size – The size of the group may be *large*, possibly over ten members, or *small*, as little as three members.
9   Focus – The focus of the group may be *outward looking*, such as focusing on community awareness or social justice, versus *inward-looking*, such as focusing on the group processes and development of the immediate group.
10 Choice – Group membership may be *voluntary* where members choose to attend, or *compulsory*, where members have been mandated to attend.
11 Structure – The structure of the group may be *loose*, where no specific agenda is set, versus *tight*, where there is a specific curriculum to follow.
12 Space – The space where the group takes place can be *diffuse*, or the space may be *dense or intimate*.

As Doel (2013) has highlighted, groups can take many different shapes. For example, a smoking cessation group might be a newly created group that is tightly structured by following a treatment manual, practitioner led and time limited, whereas an Alcoholics Anonymous (AA) group might be an existing group that is loosely structured, group led, open to membership, and open ended in terms of duration. The profile of the group will determine the role of the groupworker and the role of the group members. Doel (2013, p. 370) argues that 'experienced groupworkers can work with very different groups because of their understanding of group process and their ability to use this understanding to help groups achieve their purposes, however different these purposes might be'.

Group processes

Social workers utilizing groupwork in their practice should begin with an understanding of group processes. Tuckman's stages of group development (Tuckman, 1965; Tuckman and Jensen, 1977) is a useful model in explaining how a group grows, develops, deals with conflict and reaches goals. The model consists of five stages: forming, storming, norming, performing and adjourning, which run along the beginning, middle and ending phases of a group. The beginning phase includes the forming stage, the middle phase includes the storming, norming and performing stages, and the ending phase includes the adjourning stage. Groups generally progress through each stage in a linear fashion, but can often move back and forth between the stages. For example, a group may move from forming, norming and storming to performing, and then back to the storming stage. The groupworker will need to be mindful of each stage as the group moves through them, particularly as each stage is important in order to have a productive group. For example, a groupworker will not want to quickly move the group through the storming stage, despite being potentially uncomfortable, but rather allow the group to successfully navigate through the stage in order to reach performing. Groupworkers should also be mindful of the group's current stage as this will assist the worker in understanding her/his role and how best to intervene with the group. Each stage is described below, with some key tasks for the groupworker:

1   *Forming.* The group begins in the forming stage where they are learning about the roles and responsibilities of themselves individually, and as a group. This stage often involves the group members getting to know one another, building relationships, and members establishing their identities and determining whether the members and the facilitator can be trusted (Tuckman, 1965). The groupworker should assist the group members in establishing the purpose and goals of the group and assist in creating commonality among the group members and confidence in achieving tasks (Healy, 2012). Several tasks of the groupworker during the forming stage, as proposed by Coulshed and Orme (2012) and Healy (2012), can include the following:
    - Have each member introduce themselves, including the groupworker. Possibly use 'icebreakers' to encourage participation.
    - Develop 'ground rules' that can be revisited throughout the course of the group. This could cover rules such as timekeeping, listening, respecting each other's views and maintaining confidentiality.
    - Agree on the group's purpose, aims and goals. This could also include each member's reasons for joining the group and an exploration of what each member would like to achieve in the group.
    - Encourage the involvement of each member.
2   *Storming.* The storming stage is where the group begins to experience conflict. This might be due to members struggling to establish themselves as the leader or to have power and control. Members may begin to question why they are attending and their role within the group. The group may begin to split into

smaller sub-groups, with members taking sides. This stage is particularly important in the work of the groupworker as the group should be allowed to experience the tensions and conflicts, but should be carefully facilitated in resolving conflict, keeping all members involved and moving towards the performing stage. In some situations, the groupworker's role and position may also be challenged. Several of the groupworker's tasks during the storming stage, as proposed by Coulshed and Orme (2012) and Healy (2012), can include the following:

- Stay calm when faced with the conflict and do not become defensive when challenged.
- Acknowledge and normalize the conflict and help the group to understand its source. This does not involve highlighting isolated or difficult members.
- Facilitate carefully by allowing people to express their concerns while also suggesting strategies for overcoming the conflict.
- Carefully begin to give responsibility to the group.

3 *Norming.* The norming stage is where the group have resolved conflict and are moving into a comfortable, working relationship where agreement and consensus have developed. There is a general commitment among the group, and it has established a suitable working style. Members begin to identify with the group and may establish individual roles. Sometimes the identities and roles of members may not be positive, such as the 'scapegoat' or the 'quiet person' (Healy, 2012). The groupworker may need to facilitate tasks in order to challenge such roles, and encourage a norming stage where all are positively involved. Several tasks of the groupworker during the norming stage, as proposed by Coulshed and Orme (2012) and Healy (2012), can include the following:

- Challenge norms that block the achievement of groups through group activities.
- Observe the group and comment on the observations of process and content, while soliciting the groups' perceptions.
- Take more of a listening versus directing role.

4 *Performing.* The performing role involves the group having a shared vision of the aims and goals, and the group moving forward in achieving such goals. The groupworker may have relaxed her/his role as facilitator and the group may have more control over the direction and working of the group. The tasks of the groupworker during the performing stage, as proposed by Coulshed and Orme (2012) and Healy (2012), can include the following:

- Provide structure and focus for the group to achieve aims and goals while encouraging group members to take more responsibility.
- Provide advice and support when asked for by the group.
- Observe and acknowledge the achievements of the group.

5 *Adjourning.* Adjourning is the final stage where the group has ended and has hopefully achieved the aims and goals. This stage can serve as an opportunity to reflect on the group experience, the achievements and strategies for moving forward. It may be a difficult time for group members who have worked closely

together and formed a bond and group identity and, therefore, the group-worker should be careful in planning the ending phase. The groupworker's tasks during the adjourning stage, as proposed by Coulshed and Orme (2012) and Healy (2012), can include the following:

- Evaluate the group processes and achievements.
- Provide an opportunity to acknowledge and celebrate achievements.
- Give time for the group to express their feelings regarding the ending of the group and feelings of loss.
- Allow time for the group to return to the planning stage if they wish to continue working together towards a different aim or goal.

Planning, running and ending a group

Social workers utilizing groupwork methods will not only need to understand the type of group with which they will work, and group processes, but will also need to give time to the planning of the group. The groupworker's first consideration should be, 'What is the specific need that the group will address?' (Doel, 2013, p. 372). The next focus is to ensure that the type, structure and methods used in the running of the group are congruent with the group's purpose and will most effectively assist in meeting the group's need and achieving its aims. Finally, the groupworker should give considera-tion to the process of ending a group from the beginning to ensure all members are clear on when and how the group will end. Coulshed and Orme (2012, pp. 242–3) provide some initial questions to ask when planning a group, which include the following:

- *Who? And how many?* – The groupworker will need to establish who, and how many, will make up the membership of the group, which should reflect the needs, aims and purpose of the group. This may be a group of individuals the groupworker is already working with, such as individuals with learning difficul-ties at a day centre or looked after children, or the group may be developed for a group of individuals that are new to the worker. When determining the make-up of the group, groupworkers should pay attention to diversity and balance. The size of the group should be 'more than three and less than fourteen' (p. 242).
- *How long?* – The groupworker will need to determine the duration of the group, as well as the length of each group session. Should the group be open ended, where the group has no set end date and group members can join at any time? Or should the group be closed ended, where there is a clear beginning and end to the group and where group membership is often closed to only those that join at the beginning? Again, the decision should be based on the aims and purpose of the group. If a group is structured as open ended, then there should be consideration as to how to manage members leaving the group and new members joining (Doel, 2013) as this could cause disruption in meeting the aims of the group. Doel (2013) recommends that open-ended groups should have regular review points to ensure that the group is on target, despite the changing membership. The length of each session will depend on the needs of

the group members and may need to be shorter for members with needs for regular breaks.

- *Which methods?* – The groupworker will need to determine which methods to use within the groupwork to most effectively reach the group aims. The groupworker will need to consider the needs of the members as well as the skills of the worker. Some groupworkers may choose to use a specific method based on their theoretical approach, such as cognitive behavioural therapy, or psychotherapy, while other groupworkers may utilize methods that are reinforced through the agency. Methods could also include different activities within each session, such as the use of art or music, games or activities.
- *What resources?* – The groupworker will have to consider the resources needed to implement and run the group. This includes practical considerations of finding enough members, an accessible place to meet, equipment needed, as well as financial considerations, such as paying for a room, refreshments, the worker's time, and transportation.

The groupworker will also need to establish their role within the group. Groupworkers will need to determine whether they will be the leader through the duration of the group, whether the leadership will gradually be passed from the groupworker to the group, or whether the group will lead (self-help) with the groupworker merely setting up the group in the beginning and assisting in any practicalities of the group as needed. In many situations (outside of self-help groups), the groupworker is the leader or facilitator who plans the groups, leads the group, monitors and prepares for the group's end. Sharry (2001, p. 5) states that the aim of the facilitator is to 'establish the conditions and trust in the group whereby clients can help one another and then to "get out of the way" to allow them to do it'. This more democratic approach to facilitation provides an opportunity for collaboration between the groupworker and the group members. Healy (2012, p. 149) warns that 'the collaborative approach to group leadership involves a fine balance between having sufficient authority and credibility within the group to facilitate the group's achievement of their goals, while encouraging shared responsibility for processes and outcomes'. Healy (2012, pp. 151–6) states that in order for a groupworker to facilitate an environment for change, she/he must adhere to four main responsibilities: (1) *establishing trust* – the groupworker can facilitate tasks that will assist the group members in establishing trust among the group, such as establishing ground rules, modelling behaviours (e.g. reliability, confidentiality, listening, being respectful), creating a safe environment where group members are listened to and respected and addressing and managing conflict; (2) *building a positive group identity* – the groupworker should highlight the positive aspects of the group by focusing on common strengths versus problems or deficits and creating a shared identity based on the strengths; (3) *promoting group ownership* – the groupworker should encourage the group to take responsibility and ownership of the group as appropriate to the group members skills and capacities; and (4) *creating direction for change* – the groupworker needs to ensure that the group activities are congruent with the group's purpose and moving the group towards their goals. Activities and techniques used within groupwork could include general discussion, role-play, use of letters, graphic techniques (i.e.

artwork; spider diagrams), audio-visual aids, (i.e. computer; photographs), props, (i.e. chairs; tokens; masks) or physical activities (i.e. dance; song; relaxation; games) (Doel, 2013). The groupworker may need to ask the group to occasionally revisit the group's purpose to ensure that the activities and methods employed are useful to the members and are moving in the direction of change.

The groupworker will also need to give consideration to how the groupwork will be documented or recorded and reviewed and evaluated (Doel, 2013). Documenting and reflecting on each group session can be helpful in reviewing the progress of the group, as well as planning for future sessions. Some agencies may have standard forms or ways in which to document each group session, while others may be flexible in allowing the groupworker to decide the best method of recording. Some suggestions for recording can include keeping a register of members and a brief progress note of what happened in the session by noting what went well and what didn't go so well, keeping records and notes on each individual member, or creating a visual record where a diagram is used to note where members sat and what happened within the group (Brown, 1992; Coulshed and Orme, 2012). Regardless of the recording method, the groupworker will need to ensure confidentiality is maintained and that the records are only viewed by those individuals who have permission. Evaluating the group at the end is also important in documenting any changes among the members, verifying whether goals have been achieved and providing input on what to do the same, or differently, in future work with groups.

Finally, the groupworker needs to pay careful attention to the ending of a group, from the beginning stages. The group should be made aware of the planned end of the group and should be given time within the last session to address their thoughts and feelings regarding the ending. The groupworker should highlight the group's accomplishments during this session and allow time for the group to reflect on their work, achievements and plans for the future. The group may wish to end the last session with a mark of celebration.

Case example: applying groupwork to practice

You are a social worker working in a child and family community centre within a socially and economically deprived area. The community has a high rate of teenage pregnancy. Nearly all the teenage mothers who attend the community centre are unemployed and do not have educational qualifications. The mothers often talk to you about how they would like to work, but do not know where to begin to look for a job. The lack of educational qualifications and employment skills is a common characteristic among the mothers, and you identify a common need of skills, education and employment among this specific group (*identifying the specific need of the group*). You ask the mothers if they would be interested in participating in a group that would explore their interests and skills with an aim of moving towards employment. The mothers express an interest, and you begin to develop a group for teenage mothers in the community who would like to further their education and/or gain employment. You are able to raise £350 from a local business to assist in the running of the group.

In developing the group you begin by planning the type and function of the group. Based on the *need of the group* (gaining further education or employment), you decide that the group should be *developmental* and the function should be *task oriented* and *social support*. The group will aim to explore the mothers' interests and skills and develop their educational and employment needs. In achieving this aim, the group will be task oriented in terms of having the mothers participate in activities that move them towards education or employment, but also provide an atmosphere where the mothers can learn from each other, share their common experiences and provide support. You establish that the group will be for no more than ten teenage mothers who live in the community (*who and how many*) and that the membership will be closed in that only those mothers who started in the first session will be able to continue with the group; this is primarily based on the activities of the group that build on each other from one week to the next. The group will be closed ended and meet for one hour, once a week for eight weeks (*how long*), and will follow a structured programme based on task-centred social work that consists of weekly activities and homework tasks (*methods*). The group will take place in a room at the community centre, and you are able to use the funds raised to provide refreshments, and to purchase paper, pens and other craft resources (*resources*). The mothers live in the community and are able to walk or take a bus to the centre for the group; and the group runs alongside a toddler session, which will provide free childcare for the mothers during the group. The group will be *practitioner led* in that you will facilitate each session and direct the group in terms of the group and individual tasks. As this is the first group of its kind at the centre you plan to document each session by recording what went well and what didn't go so well, and you plan to review and evaluate at the end by distributing a confidential questionnaire (*document and review*).

You are also aware of group processes, and when planning the eight weeks you break up the weeks and activities into beginning, middle and ending phases. You start the first session with an 'icebreaker' activity and with introductions, followed by a chance to establish ground rules for the group (*forming*). You ask the group to develop a name in an attempt to establish commonality among the members. The group decides on the 'Blazing Mums'. You also review the purpose of the group and allow them a chance to discuss their individual and collective goals. You acknowledge that the group will run over eight weeks and that you will have a ending party during the eighth week that they can plan closer to the time. You inform the group members that the group will be structured and that each member will have homework activities to complete before coming back to the group the following week. Such activities will include making an assessment of their existing skills, exploring their interests and hobbies, researching educational activities and programmes and assessing what resources they would need in order to attend school and/or gain employment (i.e. childcare arrangements, transportation, clothing). You close the first session with an overview of the next seven sessions.

The group continues to meet over the following seven weeks, and you watch it move through the *storming, norming* and *performing* stages. You are careful to allow the groups to experience such stages while also continuing to facilitate and move the group towards the end goals. The final week (*adjourning*) provides an opportunity for the group to review their progress and celebrate their achievements. The mothers are dedicated to the group, and many complete the activities each week. They report that they were able to assess their skills and needs through the activities, and many had developed action plans to take forward after the group's ending. The mothers also felt a sense of peer support from each other in terms of being a young mum. They all agree that they want to continue to meet to support one another, and you assist them in developing an informal group that will meet on a weekly basis at the mothers' homes on a rotating basis. You end the session with a 'party' where the mothers have cakes and swap handwritten cards. The mothers fill out the confidential questionnaire, which provides positive feedback on the group.

Strengths and limitations

There are several strengths and limitations to implementing groupwork in social work practice. The strengths include the following:

- Groupwork enables members to share their thoughts, feelings and behaviours with others who have similar experiences, which 'can be a way out of the confinement and isolation of dealing with problems alone' (Adams, 2010, p. 204). In this sense groupwork is an empowering method for the members by allowing them the space and opportunity to share their experiences, receive feedback from group members and learn from each other (Adams, 2010). The members can use the space to test out new behaviours or coping skills before implementing them in their natural environment.
- Groupwork can be an anti-oppressive method by encouraging the group to form a group identity, take responsibility for the group and grow and develop individually and collectively.
- Groupwork can serve as a safe place for individuals who might be fearful of receiving help alone. The group provides an environment where individuals can receive support from others with similar experiences, and where members can pool resources and share ideas (Coulshed and Orme, 2012; Lindsay and Orton, 2008).
- Groupwork is a flexible method that is often used in combination with other theories and methods. Groupworkers need to understand the types and structures of groups, as well as the group processes, but may also need to implement other methods when delivering the actual sessions. For example, a groupworker working with adolescents with eating disorders may implement a structured group with sessions based on cognitive behavioural therapy.

The limitations of groupwork include the following:

- Over the years, groupwork has become less prevalent within social work practice. With the focus of social work predominately on individuals and individual need, social workers' ability to implement social work is restricted. This is particularly the case when there is a lack of support within agencies, which is often due to the agency's ethos, or time and financial resources.

- Groupwork is not an appropriate method for every person. Some individuals may find groupwork a scary process and may prefer individual help versus help within a group. This is an individual preference and individual choice should be respected. While groupworkers are to pay attention to individuals, the focus of groupwork is on the group, which means that some individuals may be left out or receive less attention than others.
- Groupwork can be expensive to plan and implement and, therefore, needs the support from the groupworker and the agency.
- Groups can become oppressive. Although forming identities and roles within groups is a normal part of the process, sometimes groups can become stuck in the storming stage where some individuals, pairs or sub-groups take an authoritative role and marginalize or oppress others. Groupworkers should be cognizant to any forms of oppression or marginalization within a group and should bring this to the attention of the group in an effort to resolve the problem and move the group forward.

Ethical and cultural considerations

There are ethical and cultural considerations when incorporating groupwork into social work practice. First, the groupworker needs to provide honest information to group members, which includes potentially difficult topics, such as taboo subjects or the groupworker's thoughts and feelings, as well as confidentiality and the limits to confidentiality (Gumpert and Black, 2006; Northen, 1999). The group should establish confidentiality as a ground rule, but the groupworker should acknowledge that she or he is not able to ensure all members will adhere to the rule. The groupworker should also inform the members at the beginning about any potential limitations or possible negative effects of the group and enable members to proceed only after giving informed consent (Gumpert and Black, 2006). Second, groupworkers should be mindful of each individual's participation and should encourage involvement, while also respecting an individual's right not to participate. Individual members should not be coerced or manipulated into participating, but rather self-determination should be respected and fostered (Gumpert and Black, 2006; Northen, 1999). Third, groupworkers should uphold the principles and values of the social work profession and should ensure that they have the professional competence to plan and run a group (Gumpert and Black, 2006; Northen, 1999). This should include an understanding of the types of groups, group processes and methods used to facilitate and end a group, as well as recording and evaluation. Finally, groupworkers will need to acknowledge the difference and diversity among group members and attempt to facilitate an environment where cultural views and practices can be respected. Groupworkers will need to bring such views to the attention of the group for a discussion while adhering to the principles and values of social work. There may be times when there is a conflict between the views of the group and societal norms. When harmful views are expressed, the groupworker may need to break confidentiality to bring this to the attention of the appropriate outside person. The International Association of Social Work with Groups (IASWG) provides practice standards when utilizing groupwork (see: http://iaswg.org/Practice_Standards).

Groupwork and anti-oppressive practice

Groupwork is fundamentally anti-oppressive in nature as it was built upon the values of social justice, equality and participation (Singh and Salazar, 2010). The aim of groupwork is to bring individuals with similar characteristics, traits and/or experiences together to share information and resources, to receive feedback and support and to learn from one another and achieve individual and collective growth. Such individuals may be marginalized or oppressed within society, and the group can provide an opportunity and safe environment for them to come together to receive mutual aid and support. The skills learned with the group environment could then be transferred into the members' natural environment and can potentially combat the oppression experienced. Groupworkers will need to consider anti-oppressive practice when defining their role within the group by considering whether their role and leadership style will encourage group involvement and achievement of aims and goals, or whether the groupworker will create an environment where the members feel restricted and oppressed. Groupwork should be empowering by encouraging groups to become self-directing and involved whenever possible (Doel, 2013). As noted earlier, self-determination is central to groupwork and the group, as individual members and as a whole, should have their wishes, choices and decisions respected. Just as the individuals may experience oppression outside the group, there are times when individuals within the group become marginalized or oppressed, or labelled as the scapegoat or silent person. Groupworkers should be mindful of such occurrences and should bring this to the attention of the group in order to resolve any conflict and move the group forward. Finally, the groupworker should consider individual and collective needs when planning the group. For example, the venue should be accessible and all activities and group tasks should be presented in a manner suitable for the group members.

Research on groupwork

Groupwork has been utilized in a variety of situations and with diverse client groups. It is often used in conjunction with other methods, such as cognitive behavioural therapy, motivational interviewing or solution-focused practice. The effectiveness of groupwork is often dependent on the methods used and the specific aims of the group. For example, groupwork has been used with persons with intellectual disabilities to enhance autonomy of the members (Carter et al., 2013); a specific treatment programme, 'Skills for Recovery', has been found to be effective in a group environment for veterans with dual diagnosis of serious mental illness and substance misuse (Topor et al., 2013); and a domestic violence intervention curriculum has been found effective when working with immigrant Mexican women (Marrs Funchsel and Hysjullen, 2013). Therefore, the effectiveness of groupwork will depend on the methods employed and the specific aims that are to be achieved, as well as the setting and client group that is participating. A review of the journal, *Social Work with Groups*, provides the current evidence base of groupwork with a variety of clients in different settings. In general, groupwork has been found to be effective for both group members and for the staff that deliver groupwork (O'Conner, 2002). In particular, groupwork as a source of mutual aid has been found to benefit group members in terms of their listening skills and ability to understand others (Steinberg, 2003) as well as their problem-solving skills and ability to deal with conflict (Northen and Kurland, 2001).

Summary

This chapter has explored groupwork as a method that can be used in social work practice to bring individuals with a similar characteristic, trait and/or experience together to foster mutual support and positive growth and development. Although the formal use of groupwork within social work practice has declined over the past few decades, social workers continue to work with groups in their everyday practice – from working with families, to working alongside colleagues, or running structured groups with a specific client group. To be able to effectively work with groups, social workers should have a basic understanding of the different types and structures of groups, as well as the group processes. This understanding will assist social workers in planning groups and in determining their role and the most appropriate methods to employ during group sessions. Groupwork is empowering and anti-oppressive in nature, seeks to encourage the involvement of all members, and encourages the group to be as self directed as possible and appropriate. This chapter has provided an overview of the rationale for groupwork, the types of groups and group processes, and the practicalities in planning, running and ending a group.

Case study

The following case study and discussion questions are from IASWG's (2013b) 'Literature for Practitioners and Educators'.

You are a social worker working in a voluntary organization that provides services to people with HIV/AIDS. You and your colleagues decide you would like to facilitate a group for caregivers who have recently lost their loved ones to the disease, since your agency has never provided any services to individuals once their loved one has died. What type of groupwork service would be appropriate to respond to the potential members' needs? What would be the role of the social worker? How would you structure the group in terms of the number and length of sessions, the use of an agenda, and number of members? What do you anticipate members' thoughts and feelings would be about beginning the group? What would you do to address these?

Further reading and web resources

Groupwork – a British-based journal that focuses on the research and practice of groupwork both within the UK and internationally. An overview of the journal can be found at: http://essential.metapress.com/content/122773

International Association for Social Work with Groups (IASWG) – an association for professionals engaged in groupwork. The website provides additional resources used for practice and education – http://iaswg.org

Social Work with Groups – a journal that publishes research and practice on social work with groups. An overview of the journal can be found at: http://www.tandfonline.com/

Doel, M. (2006) *Using Groupwork*. London: Routledge.
This book provides an overview of groupwork and its application to social work practice.

Gumpert, J. and Black, P.N. (2006) Ethical issues in group work: What are they? How are they managed?, *Social Work with Groups*, 29(4): 61–74.
This article provides an overview of the ethical issues that groupworkers might face and how they can be managed.

Preston-Shoot, M. (2007) *Effective Groupwork*, 2nd edn. Houndmills: Palgrave Macmillan.
This book covers the values, knowledge and skills necessary to work effectively with groups.

References

Adams, R. (2010) *The Short Guide to Social Work*. Bristol: Policy Press.

Brown, A. (1992) *Groupwork*, 3rd edn. London: Ashgate.

Carter, I., Munro., S. and Martin, S. (2013) Exploring autonomy in group work practice with persons with intellectual disabilities, *Social Work with Groups*, 36(2/3): 236–48.

Coulshed, V. (1991) *Social Work Practice: An Introduction*, 2nd edn. Basingstoke: Macmillan.

Coulshed, V. and Orme, J. (2012) *Social Work Practice*, 5th edn. Basingstoke: Macmillan.

Doel, M. (2006) *Using Groupwork*. London: Routledge.

Doel, M. (2013) Groupwork, in M. Davies (ed.), *The Blackwell Companion to Social Work*, 4th edn. Chichester: John Wiley & Sons.

Doel, M. and Sawdon, C. (1999) *The Essential Groupworker: Teaching and Learning Creative Groupwork*. London: Jessica Kingsley.

Drumm, K. (2006) The essential power of groupwork, *Social Work with Groups*, 29(2/3): 17–31.

Gumpert, J. and Black, P.N. (2006) Ethical issues in group work: what are they? How are they managed?, *Social Work with Groups*, 29(4): 61–74.

Healy, K. (2012) *Social Work Methods and Skills: The Essential Foundations of Practice*. Basingstoke: Palgrave Macmillan.

International Association for Social Work with Groups (IASWG) (2013a) *IASWG Practice Standards*. http://iaswg.org/Practice_Standards (accessed 14 August 2013).

International Association for Social Work with Groups (IASWG) (2013b) *Example of Assignments for Social Work with Groups Courses: Beginning with a Group.* http://www.iaswg.org/docs/syllabus/Beginning%20with%20a%20group.pdf   (accessed 19 August 2013).

Lindsay, T. and Orton, S. (2008) *Groupwork Practice in Social Work.* Exeter: Learning Matters.

Marrs Fuchsel, C.L. and Hysjullen, B. (2013) Exploring a domestic violence intervention curriculum for immigrant Mexican women in a group setting: a pilot study, *Social Work with Groups*, 36(4): 304–20.

Northen, H. (1999) Ethical dilemmas in social work with groups, *Social Work with Groups*, 21(1/2): 5–17.

Northen, H. and Kurland, R. (2001) *Social Work with Groups*, 3rd edn. New York: Columbia University Press.

O'Conner, D.L. (2002) Toward empowerment: re-visioning family support groups, *Social Work with Groups*, 25(4): 37–46.

Preston-Shoot, M. (2007) *Effective Groupwork*, 2nd edn. Houndmills: Palgrave Macmillan.

Sharry, J. (2001) *Solution-focused Groupwork.* London: Sage Publications.

Singh, A.A. and Salazar, C.F. (2010) The roots of social justice in group work, *The Journal for Specialists in Group Work*, 35(2): 97–104.

Smith, M.K. (2004) The early development of groupwork. http://www.infed.org/groupwork/early_group_work.htm (accessed 14 August 2013).

Steinberg, D.M. (2003) The magic of mutual aid, *Social Work with Groups*, 25(1/2): 31–9.

Teater, B. and Baldwin, M. (2012) *Social Work in the Community: Making a Difference.* Bristol: Policy Press.

Topor, D.R., Grosso, D., Burt, J. and Falcon, T. (2013) Skills for recovery: a recovery-oriented dual diagnosis group for veterans with serious mental illness and substance abuse, *Social Work with Groups*, 36(2/3): 222–35.

Tuckman, B.W. (1965) Development sequence in small groups, *Psychological Bulletin*, 63(6): 384–99.

Tuckman, B.W. and Jensen, M.A.C. (1977) Stages of small group development revisited, *Group and Organisation Studies*, 2(4): 419–27.

Ward, D. (2009) Groupwork, in R. Adams, L. Dominelli and M. Payne (eds), *Critical Practice in Social Work*, 2nd edn. Basingstoke: Palgrave Macmillan.

Index

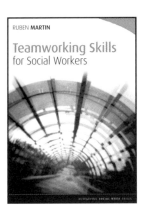

TEAMWORKING SKILLS FOR SOCIAL WORKERS

Ruben Martin

9780335246052 (Paperback)
2013

eBook also available

Social workers are members of teams and need to work in collaboration with colleagues and other professionals in order to practice effectively.
This book explores the dynamics present when people work together, the roles individuals play and the skills necessary for effective teamworking in the context of social work practice.

It provides a practical and applied overview of the different types of teams social workers encounter.

Key features:

- Specific links to the new Professional Capabilities Framework for Social Workers
- Checklists to help the reader rate their capability and plan ways of developing skills for which they score low
- Reflection points

www.openup.co.uk

CONTEMPORARY SOCIAL WORK PRACTICE
A Handbook for Students

Barbra Teater

9780335246038 (Paperback)
February 2014

eBook also available

This exciting new book provides an overview of fifteen different
contemporary social work practice settings, spanning across the statutory,
voluntary, private and third sectors. It serves as the perfect introduction to
the various roles social workers can have and the numerous places they can
work, equipping students with the knowledge, skills and values required to
work in areas ranging from mental health to fostering and adoption, and
from alcohol and drug treatment services to youth offending.

Key features:

- An overview of the setting, including the role of the social worker, how
  service users gain access to the service and key issues, definitions or
  terms specific to the setting
- Legislation and policy guidance related to the specific setting
- The key theories and methods related to the setting

www.openup.co.uk

OPEN UNIVERSITY PRESS
McGraw - Hill Education

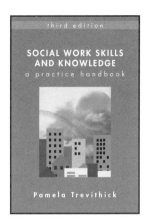

SOCIAL WORK SKILLS AND KNOWLEDGE
A Practice Handbook
Third Edition

Pamela Trevithick

9780335238071 (Paperback)
February 2012

eBook also available

Since its first publication in 2000, this best-selling text has been an invaluable resource for thousands of social workers preparing for life in practice. Written by an influential academic-practitioner, it is widely regarded as the leading book in its field.

Key features:

- 4 new chapters that integrate theory and practice in a Knowledge and Skills Framework
- 80 social work skills and interventions
- 12 appendices describing a range of different social work approaches

www.openup.co.uk

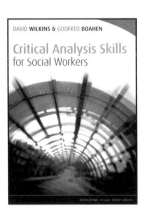

CRITICAL ANALYSIS SKILLS FOR SOCIAL WORKERS

David Wilkins and Godfred Boahen

9780335246496 (Paperback)
2013

eBook also available

Analysis is a critical skill for social workers, yet it is a skill that many practitioners find very difficult. This book will help social workers to improve their analysis skills by offering a very basic, step-by-step model to develop an analytical mindset. It shows how analysis can be woven into the whole process of social work engagement, resulting in better decision making, more efficient ways of working and, ultimately, better outcomes for social work service users.

Key features:

- What analysis is, and why it is such an important skill in practice
- The skills that underpin critical analysis, e.g. time management, planning, critical understanding, logical thinking, research-mindedness, creativity, communication, reflection and hypothesising
- The role of emotion and intuition in critical analysis

www.openup.co.uk